WHITHER THOU GOEST

WHITHER THOU GOEST

THE LIFE AND TIMES OF DAVID TONGE

by

DAVID TONGE

The Memoir Club

First published in 2007 by
The Memoir Club
Stanhope Old Hall
Stanhope
Weardale
County Durham

British Library Cataloguing in
Publication Data.
A catalogue record for this book
is available from the
British Library

ISBN: 978-1-84104-172-8

Typeset by TW Typesetting, Plymouth, Devon
Printed by Biddles Ltd, King's Lynn, Norfolk

Dedication

Whilst I am a lapsed Church of England attendee and not much of a God-Botherer to boot, which in quieter minutes I occasionally regret, I have to turn to the story of Ruth to find a simile for my wife's interpretation of her marriage vows. Said not to her husband but to her mother-in-law, Naomi, Ruth is quoted in part:

'Whither thou goest I will go and where thou lodgest I will lodge.'

Pam has been of the same frame of mind ever since we married and I shall be forever in her debt. I hope this simple tribute repays some of that.

Contents

Part Three: Saudi Arabia, St Helena, Orkney Islands 1981–2002

List of Illustrations

Foreword

by Roy Faiers
(Editor and founder of *This England* magazine)

I suppose it's a sign that you're growing old when, as the years roll by, you start delving into the distant past and try to recall some of the people and events of your earlier life. I began doing just that when enjoying my first taste of David Tonge's new book. It took me right back to my earliest days, for like him I was born in the little-known seaside town of Cleethorpes on the Lincolnshire coast, as were all four of the Tonge children. My family lived only one street away from them and so we shared part of our childhood until the war came along and shattered all our dreams.

David's educational prowess soon became evident, for he gained a scholarship to the local grammar school, whereas his older sister Joan and I had failed the preliminary test and were confined to attending nearby council schools. However, when the war was over I got a job as a junior reporter on the local newspaper *(Grimsby Evening Telegraph)* and Joan joined the paper's editorial department shortly afterwards, being given the role of children's columnist called 'Uncle Peter'.

Meanwhile, David spent his teenage learning years at the elite Matthew Humberstone School – known locally as 'Clee Grammar' – which resulted in him achieving a far higher standard of education than the average Cleethorpes lad. The school became a rock upon which all the privileged pupils could build the rest of their lives, and at a recent re-union of former classmates a breakdown of their lifetime careers showed just how valuable and important the grammar school education had proved to be. There were several doctors, teachers, senior business managers, entrepreneurs, civil engineers, industrial chemists, a master mariner and a British Airways senior captain.

Sadly, Clee Grammar later became one of the growing number of politically-inspired 'comprehensive' schools set up across the country which are now regarded by the Department of Education as being 'sink schools'. Fortunately, David was able to reap the benefit of its earlier success and use it to embark on his extensive career as an environmental health officer – known as a Sanitarian – not only in Britain but all over the world. Throughout his long and highly involved professional life he has spent some 25 years working in such remote places as St Helena Island in the south Atlantic, to where the French dictator Napoleon was exiled, plus the African bush states of Zambia, Malawi and even the Orkney Islands off Scotland.

David is a born story-teller and rich are his accounts of the characters and situations he met and dealt with along the way of his tortuous path . . . including this cryptic description of a Sanitarian's work and its value to society in every part of the world: 'He deals with the Detritus of Humanity'.

Acknowledgements

I know that the family, that 'Dear Octopus', as it was once described, will forgive me for not mentioning them by name. They are all aware of my feelings and I owe them without exception an enormous debt of gratitude for their endless encouragement, love and tolerance of an old man's obsession with his personal 'Itch'.

At the other end of the anonymity scale I must mention, no doubt to their great embarrassment, just two very good friends who pulled me through a bad hiccup when half the book had been lost in the computer. They are mother and daughter Gay Witchell and Barbara Williams, two outstanding people whom I respect and thank enormously.

PART 1

Early Years, 1933–65

CHAPTER 1

The beginning

I HAVE RECENTLY unearthed a copy of the last CV that I ever prepared. It carries a date of 2 August 1990. It was used when I applied for and obtained a post as a District Environmental Health Officer with the Orkney Islands Council, which progressively became over the next 12 years Assistant Director and finally Chief of the Department. It was not a bad way to end a career that had started some 50 years earlier in Cleethorpes, the sister town to Grimsby, then a magnificent, grafting, bustling fishing port of North Eastern Lincolnshire. I make the county obvious because the politicians decided to abolish it and manufacture a 'new' one called 'Humberside', this without so much as a by-your-leave and without the agreements of their equally distrusting and sceptical opposites over the River Humber in Yorkshire. With the future political events concerning the local authorities and the county I had no direct involvement, having departed for pastures new, but I still think of Lincolnshire as such with its three component parts of Lindsey, Kesteven and Holland. I must apologise for not only displaying an old man's tendency to play 'nostalgics' but to digress from the main theme of a wandering life with which to regale/bore/entertain any future generations of the family.

To return then to the beginning.

I was born on 10 February 1933, which as far as I can judge makes me 71 years of age as I start this on 24 July, 2004. My loving parents were Cyril – always known as Dick – and Lily, a member of the Porritt family prior to her marriage. Father told me that he and mother rented No. 50 Hart Street, Cleethorpes, for 5 shillings (25 pence) per week and occupied it on their wedding night. A week long honeymoon followed at the home of his successful older brother, Fred, in Doncaster where he operated a wholesale greengrocery business. Mother and Father finally left Hart Street fifty years later to enter Sheltered Accommodation as tenants of a small and convenient flat next to the church at the end of the road. The lack of travel opportunities was a common feature of life, and holidays with out-of-town relatives were commonplace. Steam trains going clickety-clack over the rails drawing us ever nearer to our cousins who lived all of 27 miles away in Scunthorpe engendered stomach-churning delight for all of us children. Mother had longed to travel when she was engrossed in her geography lessons at school but never succeeded on her own. She lived in other lands through the actions of her children and her grandchildren's lives abroad.

A whole chapter could be devoted to the doings and comings and goings and scandals and minor triumphs and disasters of the time, but this again sidetracks the main purpose of this narrative. Suffice to say that from the earliest days there were many, many relatives of all shapes and sizes and ages, to say nothing of other people's families who lived cheek-by-jowl with each other in those streets of terraced houses with a 16-foot frontage and an outside WC. There were no bathrooms, but one cold water supply tap over the 4-inch deep earthenware sink in the scullery served for all purposes. Off the scullery was the coal-hole, breeding site of the cockroaches, and in the corner was a coal-fired copper boiler always lit early on a Monday morning for wash-day.

Saturday night for us children, my older sister Joan, my younger sister Rita and myself was 'Bath Night' when the tin bath was hauled off the wall in the scullery and placed in front of the fire in the kitchen where the kettle was boiled for each of us in turn to get our weekly scrub. My youngest Sister Betty (known to all and sundry as 'Sally') was born some seven or eight years later during the war.

We were better off than most other streets in the area because we had a plethora of facilities within a short walk of the front door, giving our poor parents some wonderful hours of relief from the usual and very normal squabbles and fights which occurred daily and were covered by the much used expression 'Oh these kids. I'll be glad when they grow up': this when yet another blood stained hero was taped up and sent back out to the fray. Even my normally placid older sister, Joan, 'crowned' a local tearaway with a shovel when he kept throwing snow back onto the path she had just cleared. His mother complained about the boy's head being cut but she hauled him off with a clout when the facts became known.

The facilities within easy reach included the Sidney Sussex Park at the end of the street and at the other end Grimsby Town Football Club, of which I knew nothing until after the war. It was in any case beyond the main road to Grimsby, which we could only cross with parental permission or escort. On the four corners by the main road stood the Ritz Cinema (famous to us youngsters for its 'Two Penny Rush' on a Saturday morning), the Blundell Park Residential Hotel, St Aidan's Church (presided over by the Rev. Tuffin) and the Imperial Hotel, although this 'watering hole' had long since given up its status as a 'Rest and be Thankful' lodging for the passing traveller.

I have not mentioned the most wonderful playground of them all, because the war intervened when I was seven years of age and much of the 'Sands' or 'Foreshore' at Cleethorpes was closed for the duration.

The war years

At an early part of the war probably in late 1939 or early 1940 it was deemed by the Authorities that the East Coast was rather a dangerous place, being too near the Low Countries and having a few 'juicy' ports along the River Humber as well. It was therefore decided to send the children of all parents who desired it and as representative of the future generations to the inland countryside of North Lincolnshire in a large operation known as 'Evacuation'. We were therefore known as 'Evacuees'. Somewhere along the way my sisters and I became separated and I ended up in a village called Laughton some two miles from where they found a home in Blyton.

It was the start for me of two happy years and a totally new experience of playing in fields, in barns and farmyards. There was a much greater sense of being nearer to the seasons, of springtime, muck-spreading, sowing and summer harvesting. The shooting and snaring of rabbits for the pot was commonplace – even 'Gin Traps' were not outlawed in those days. I recall my first ever sight of a pig being killed in the farmyard by the simple expedient of slitting its throat, some spurting blood being retained for the farmer's wife to make black puddings, and the extrusion of waste from the intestines and the scraping and washing of what were then termed 'casings' to make sausages skins; this last to be seen many years later on the island of St Helena. Coupled with all this were the workings of – to me as a small boy – giant horses, the Clydesdales or Percherons – with names which I still remember so well: 'Turpin' and 'Farmer' and 'Ploughman' and many others on the various farms.

I attended the local Church of England Village School, presided over by the Vicar, a small dapper man whose name I do not recall but who took both his religious teaching to the young and his duties to his parishioners equally seriously. I think that most of the villagers were Wesleyan Methodists and I was usually expected to attend the morning and evening services at the local chapel, although for the life of me I cannot remember anything else about it. Oddly enough I was to spend much of my adolescent years within the Methodist community in Cleethorpes and Grimsby, this in spite of being Confirmed as a Member of the Church of England at St Aidan's.

The village schoolroom, with its stove in the corner and its blackboard and easel, and above all the Vicar, stand out in my memory. Probably this is because I received my first 'caning' at his hand. I am not certain that he said a prayer either before or after the punishment, which was normal and the usual practice for misdemeanours. My, or rather our, crime, for others were involved, consisted of stuffing bits of old newspapers down some rabbit holes and setting fire to them in the hope that the animals would then break cover and could be hunted. Nothing happened and we dispersed to our various homes in the late evening only to find out the following morning that the farmer had had his 'rabbitting' intentions ruined by our juvenile antics. Hence a complaint to the school and a caning, with the farmer watching from the doorway to make sure that justice was not only done but seen to be done. The cane was a thin type of the Charlie Chaplin design which when handled by an expert like the Vicar swished down upon the tips of the fingers of (generally) the left hand. As I remember it stung rather than hurt, but was certainly hard enough to be memorable even at this distance in time. The only comment about it at my 'home' was 'Well, you won't be doing that again'. How right the comment was.

I cannot complete this section upon the early days of the war years without some mention of the two elderly people I lived with for just on two years. Whatever the dates I returned home at the age of nine with as broad a Lincolnshire countryside dialect as one could imagine. I was duly held up for some well-meaning and good-natured leg-pulling, as one might expect from my cousins and other members of the community, particularly at school. Yet again I am digressing, as the purpose of this paragraph was to pay a late tribute to Mr and Mrs Edward Briggs who looked after me so well in spite of being in their late sixties. He had been a retired Road Ditcher and Hedger for the County Council when war burst over them. Having been called out of retirement he duly did his bit and returned to the sections of roads where he kept the roadside drains clear and the grass verges cut and the hedges in neat order. Each morning he would set off on his bicycle to whatever part of the highway required his services. So many accoutrements seemed to be attached to his bicycle that I often imagined him falling into a flooded ditch following a tumble off an ice-bound section of road in mid-winter – never to be seen again. What an imagination little boys have!!!

Thinking of hedgerows I enjoyed the egg collecting that all the village boys participated in. Mind you we were strictly enjoined NEVER to take more than one egg from a nest, and should there be only one then it had to be left, and little hatchlings and fledglings were NEVER to be disturbed. All much forgotten and mostly illegal today.

The Briggs lived in a small cottage at the end of a lane winding away from the central part of the village past the farms of Mr Birkett and Mr Redhead, where I had to get a jug of milk every day. The cottage was opposite the blacksmith's forge and agricultural workshop, which was a never-ending source of fascinating delight for all of us youngsters. We loved to watch the noisy bellows which forced the fire to white hot and the heating of the iron bars and horse shoes, the former to be shaped for various repairs to broken articles, the latter to be fitted to conform to the roundness of the hoof with much smoke from the red hot metal and the horn. The filing of the edges and the nailing of the shoe to the foot came shortly after and I never ceased to be amazed at the wonderful patience of the great placid animals as they calmly stood on three legs whilst the job was done.

There was no mains tap water at the cottage, a pump which had to be primed stood in the back yard over the sealed well and for general washing purposes a water butt collected rain water from the roof. There was a small courtyard at the back with outhouses and a no longer used stable. Excrement was disposed of in a privy, sometimes called the 'petty'. This was my first experience of such a thing, but in a long life not to be my last. The 'Petty' (Petit) the 'Small House' or 'Piccaninny Kaya' usually referred to as the 'PK' was a commonly used expression in Central Africa as was the almost onomatopoeic 'Chimboozi' in Chinyanza-speaking areas in Malawi.

'Our' privy stood at the end of the garden path round by the vegetable patch behind the outbuildings In mid-winter when it was freezing cold and the path was muddy and slippery it was quite an experience for a small boy to use it, although in all fairness 'pos' or 'guzundas' were in common use in the bedrooms.

Neither electricity nor gas intruded upon our lives and paraffin lamps and coal fires and ovens were the norm. A small electrical device called an accumulator powered the wireless to which we listened in the evening.

I would have spent most of the quiet evenings with my nose stuck in a book or comic, for I know that I took to reading with great zest and of course in those far off days there were not the distractions that there are today. Whilst I read or played outdoors Mrs Briggs sat in her rocking chair knitting socks, scarves and gloves for the RAF. It always amazed me that she could knit with four needles to make the socks when I had only seen my family knitting with two. The skeins of wool were delivered on a regular basis and one of my chores was to hold them out at arm's length whilst they were wound into manageable balls.

I remember too the lighting of the acetylene gas lamp on Mr Briggs' bicycle before he rode off to his local, which I believe was at the village in Blyton where my sisters were billeted and where

Rita stayed with the Station Master's family. One of the benefits of this was that the station porter and lorry driver, Maurice, used to deliver parcels for the Railway Company, usually on a Saturday morning, within the Laughton area. Hence the lorry would pull up and I would sit on the back holding tightly to whatever handhold was nearest whilst my sisters sat up in front with the driver. I think it was the only time or times that we met, because both of them returned home within a year and for whatever reason I stayed on for a further 12 months, which would make it about 1942 when I left the village and journeyed back to Cleethorpes.

There I had to set about renewing and re-learning the ties and loves with which a family is bound together. First and foremost came the parents and a small baby, my youngest sister, Betty. Mother looked pretty, much as she was to do all her life. A plain but very durable face. She never wore make-up except for Pond's Vanishing Cream. As with so many of her generation brought up in the mean streets around the central market area she was expected, especially as she was the oldest daughter of eleven children, to oversee the family, and it was her duty to the family that she devote her life to them as well as her own. She was on first call for every crisis. I make the point because she was a very intelligent and diligent scholar when she won her place at the age of eleven to the Grammar School at Wintringham. At night her homework having been done she was expected to work in the small fish and chip shop which her parents, Jack and Alice Porritt, rented in Railway Street. Every day being pay-day as the ships were paid off there was much drinking and drunkenness and rowdiness throughout that central area. Sanitary facilities were primitive and the night soil men came around in the wee small hours to empty the latrines. The men led the horse-drawn tank carts with their prominent wheels around the streets and alleyways and finished their work at day-break.

It took courage for a young 11-year-old girl to sally forth in her school uniform carrying her satchel and wearing her 'Boater' down those rough streets to the trams on the main road, pursued by the local louts calling her names because she had broken out of the mould, as it were. Particularly insulting was the cry 'Shit-Cart Wheel Hat', this to be faced day after day until they moved as a family to a slightly better area in Thomas Street. After three years at Grammar School and whilst head of the class she had to leave the school. Her mother had developed heart trouble, which was to plague her for the rest of her life, and Lily as the oldest daughter was duty bound to put aside her personal feelings and look after the family. Isn't the secondary title to the comic opera *The Pirates of Penzance* entitled *The Slave of Duty?* – which could so aptly be applied to my mother. My father once said to me that mother's emotional development stopped when she was 14, and he was probably right. He also admitted that he was sure she had been so indoctrinated that her first care was for the Porritts and their well-being. Since he and mother were 'courting' for seven years and she was thirty by the time they married she had given many years of faithful service to them prior to having her own family. Strangely enough Grandma Porritt outlived her husband and then lived with us in the front room at Hart Street where Mother looked after her until her demise at the age of 72.

I seem to have said very little about my father and this is a singular omission which could be totally misconstrued by the reader. Father was not a 'Big' man in the sense of being domineering but was always around until the war years dis-assembled a very warm and tightknit family. He was employed throughout his life as fish filleter on Grimsby Docks working for a variety of small fish traders operating on the 'pontoon' where the large area of raw fish processing was carried out. The system was essentially simple but this was masked to all visitors – not intentionally – by the noise and bustle and ships and ice underfoot and a massive 'sea' of fish-filled boxes (always measured in 'stones'), prior to their removal to the waiting trains on the opposite side of the dock to the discharging or rather discharged trawlers. Off-loading by the 'lumpers' started promptly at midnight, the auctions for the fish began at 6.30 a.m. The Port Authority Fish Inspectors worked ahead of the auctions, instant decisions being required as to the quality of the fish, since condemnation would destine the product to the fish meal factory at a quarter of the price. Since it took three weeks hard fishing in the extremes of the far north – Spitsbergen, Bear Island and the White Sea and so forth – to finally bring the catch home and on the right tide for the best

Fish Market prices, for it to be condemned tried the patience and temper of the crews substantially. Mind you in the days after the end of the war fishing was easy in the sense that the fishing grounds throughout the Northern Hemisphere had not been fished regularly and systematically for six years, so there was a bonanza and record catches were the result.

Father left school when he was 12 when he was legally entitled to do so. Times were hard and money was needed so in spite of father's intelligence – and he was one of the smartest men I ever knew with regard to general knowledge and particularly with his mental arithmetic, he had to find work. He succeeded in becoming the errand boy for the greengrocers (Dickenson's) on the corner of Harold Street in Grimsby where the family then lived. He then became known in his vegetable delivery role on his bicycle around the area as 'Dickenson's Lad' then 'Dick's Lad' shortened inevitably to 'Dick' as he was then known throughout the rest of his life. He had continued his schooling at Night School for a year or two after he left but by the age of 14 he was employed on the Fish Docks as a barrow boy who, with a long, upright two-wheeled affair, had to go around the various companies where fish had been bought at the auctions and collect and deliver the goods to his employers. There the filleters and packers took over and the young man learned his trade cutting out the fiddly bits that the skilled men did not want to do. 'Cod tongues and cheeks' spring to mind, and many's the time when these sweetest pieces of fish have been enjoyed by the family, not least my daughter who detested fish until her early teens when father brought some home for tea. She was then well and truly hooked, if you'll pardon the pun!

Father's job after processing was to wheel the heavy boxes to the waiting goods trains for transporting via London and the Midlands. As the sales slogan had it at the time, 'GRIMSBY FISH DELIVERED ANYWHERE IN THE BRITISH ISLES IN 24 HOURS'. This was in the 1920s, long before the Second World War, and is difficult to comprehend today.

The boxes were lined with greaseproof paper and the fish packed with ice. Smaller orders even for domestic premises were sent in raffia-type carriers called 'basses', which were packed in exactly the same way. Thirteen long freight trains carried the fish south to

London and elsewhere but two specials commonly known as the 12 O'Clock Fish and the 6 O'Clock Fish left Grimsby bang on time, as I well came to realise when I was a (junior) trainspotter just after the war. By the time of the outbreak of war my father was a fully-fledged fish filleter earning about £3 or £4 per week. As fish landings diminished in 1941 under the Direction of Labour Ordinance, he was despatched to Aberdeen and spent six months there as the fish trade at that port needed his skills. The local workforce was being steadily reduced at the same time as the recruitment into the Scottish Regiments was increasing.

Father's talents were then required elsewhere and at the relatively late age of 38 in 1942 he was drafted into the Royal Navy where he stayed for the next four years. He was always proud of having 'done his bit', but not unduly so, and never ever either wore or displayed his medals, leaving this record of his service years to his only son who was proud to fill the gap at the British Legion's Remembrance Day Parade in Kirkwall in Orkney.

Whilst Father went 'off to the wars' Mother set to in her usual bustling manner, watching over her brood with a parsimonious and eagle eye. Rationing of all things save potatoes and fish obtained until the end of the war, in fact I seem to remember that bread rationing was added to the list after the war had ended, but I could be wrong. Whole chapters could be written and no doubt have been about the fairness/unfairness etc, of the rationing scheme and its vagaries and anomalies. Suffice to say that in our house and with a growing family to feed and clothe and administer we never went short of food and grew up in clothes which were hand-me-downs, although as the only male I had to rely on cousins and friendly neighbours. I remember having to go down the Fish Docks from time to time throughout the war to beg/scrounge/obtain a meal of fish from Dad's former employers, Messrs Drewery and Wilkinson, This when we were no doubt broke or the Navy Pay or Allowance was late or the rations had finally expired in spite of Mother's dexterity with the coupons.

We attended the church services at St Aidan's every Sunday and I was coerced into the choir by the Vicar who simply told me to report for duty on Tuesday, the practice night. I was never a 'chorister' in the real sense, although I have always been able to sing in a warbling sort of baritone, I fancy. My best singing has always been with a pint in my hand at rugby club do's, belting out the coarse and bawdy songs which have their origins not least in the old Music Halls and the Armed Services.

Once being accepted into the choir I became firm friends with two other rascals who declined to take everything too seriously. Their names were Michael Little and George Rands, who lived in the adjoining Coombe Street and Ward Street respectively. We really must have plagued the Vicar's life unmercifully, not least when we passed our hymn sheets in the choir stalls to and fro covered in juvenile jokes and drawings. This would set us going on a massively suppressed giggle, audible throughout the church and especially in the nearby pulpit where the Reverend Tuffin was struggling through his sermon. Inevitably the three of us were separated and forced to sit between the more serious and pious and po-faced members of the community, and especially right under the stern gaze of the adult members on the bench at the rear.

We were available to sing as a choir whenever there was a need, particularly at weddings, which inevitably meant a Saturday afternoon wasted as far as we 'rebellious' three were concerned.

Perhaps I have given the impression that all was a peaceful existence, the social activities being centred on the church, for there was a church hall which was let for various functions where at the end of the war I was taught by my mother to dance. 'Old Time' of course. 'Strict Tempo Ballroom Dancing' came later as did a foray into 'Latin American Formation Team Dancing' at Costello's Dancing School opposite the Gaumont Cinema in Victoria Street in Grimsby. At the Church Hall there was a room set aside for Bible classes and the like which my sisters to their eternal credit occupied on a Sunday afternoon to teach in Sunday school.

The raids

Our relatively peaceful existence was shattered once or twice during the war because of the bombing raids and associated forays. If one looks at a map of the British Isles it can plainly be seen that there is a link between Grimsby and Liverpool, the great port facing the Western Approaches of the Atlantic and a prime target of the Luftwaffe. The 'link' is the line of latitude, so that the most direct route for returning enemy aircraft to the nearest 'friendly' territory is over Lincolnshire. The unfortunate part of this plan is that it flies over the numerous RAF bases in the northern part of the county. They might in a general sense have been bases for bombers but there were fighters around to protect them. Nevertheless a dash for home was the only choice for some of the enemy, flying low to escape the radar. Usually by the time they reached the coast at the mouth of the river, overhead they were being chased by Spitfires or Hurricanes. To lighten their loads and speed up the escape, bombs were dropped at random and not always in the sea. There were also occasional bursts of machine-gun fire for the same reason. One of these chases occurred at about 7.30 a.m. as the town was just stirring.

The warning sirens had gone off in the night but the All-Clear had been sounded some hours earlier, so we were all vulnerable, as the bomb shelters had emptied by then. On this specific occasion I remember the increasing noise of the approaching planes and the terrific 'BANG' as a bomb went off nearby, followed quickly by the rattle of the machine guns. There was a further rattle as a stream of empty cartridge cases spewed down the adjoining passage between the houses and into the garden. We had only a broken window but the bomb had demolished a house about a quarter of a mile away in Campden Crescent where I believe some lives were lost.

This was the only near-miss encounter that I remember of this period but there were many nights of being crowded in the confines of the Anderson Shelter dug into the bottom of the garden, as the sirens had dictated. When after many such disturbed nights and the raids being directed with awful ferocity against the midland cities and towns, Mother decreed that a good night's sleep was as important to everyone and she would keep a watchful 'ear' open for anything untoward happening. I like to think that with her sturdy and practical outlook, she could out-think Adolf Hitler and his bombers anytime. The reasoning would probably be that first the Lutwaffe would have to find Grimsby, then Cleethorpes, then Hart Street, then No. 50, and having done so would find that we were visiting relatives in Scunthorpe! I think 'fatalism' comes into it somewhere.

Naturally we couldn't escape the nightly cacophony of the anti-aircraft guns (Ack-Ack as they were called), and one night when coming home I had walked to within a short distance of the house when the sirens sounded.

This was unusual as it can only have been early evening, say 8 or 9 p.m., although it was pitch dark. At the end of the road as I passed by the Ritz Cinema the searchlights with staggering intensity and reach came on with startling effect. After wandering around for what must have been a few moments one of them fastened on to what appeared to be a silver bird, which the remaining lights quickly homed onto. Then all hell broke loose. The noise of the Ack-Ack's and the exploding shells high in the sky were fascinating and I, along with hundreds of others as the Ritz emptied of its patrons, stood transfixed by the free show. Suddenly the lights went off and the guns stopped. We were left with the speculation that it was either 'One of Ours' which had wandered off course with faulty recognition signals, or it had been 'One of Theirs' in which case it had probably found a cold and silent grave in the dark and muddy waters of the Humber Estuary. We never did find out.

It finally happened. The war reached us with vivid intensity with a high-explosive raid in what must have been the middle of 1943. I can remember Ron Newby, the son of one of our neighbours, calling out to Mother as he banged on the front door that the raid looked serious as flares were being dropped. These I could see from my back-bedroom window, and Ron wanted to know whether Mother needed help to get to the shelter. We had all made it as far as the kitchen when the first bombs went off. The startling noise drove us under the table as the only 'shelter' available, the only one left standing on the kitchen floor being the toddler, my youngest sister Betty.

As the noise receded so we made a dash down the garden path to the shelter and there saw the night sky lit up with flares and explosions and searchlights, The noise was deafening at times, the guns driving out the noise of the bombers which were concentrating their efforts on the Docks some two miles away.

When dawn broke and the' All Clear' sounded we could look out to see that nothing had changed very much in our street. The main road to Grimsby was a different matter, and several houses had been demolished. The search and rescue teams were already hard at work, with fire appliances and ambulances standing by. It must have been difficult for them to get to the scene as the main road was blocked with debris. All this I could see as I made my way to Barcroft Street School, it being opened like all others wherever possible on the 'Business as Normal' precept. Once there we youngsters left nothing to the imagination as we told and re-told our experiences of the preceding night.

It must have been the best part of a year before a different kind of raid took place, I say 'different' because of the nature of the missiles used, Whilst the first one used bombs filled with a high explosive substance, the one about to descend upon us was designed purely to terrorise the local population and bring the town and docks to a standstill. The bombs used were new to the Disposal Squads so they posed a much greater threat than normal devices which exploded on impact.

These were about the size of a large tin can with a central spindle around which the two side 'flaps' turned to prime and arm the device. Because of the visual effect created by the spinning and extended 'flaps' they quickly became known as 'Butterfly Bombs'. Again because of their construction they were liable to hook on to any projection, whether it was a garden wall, a branch, a roof rafter, a telephone or power line – the list was endless They contained some quarter of a pound of explosive and when fully armed would explode at the slightest touch. Along with the 'Butterfly Bombs' were dropped thousands of incendiaries which in retrospect were there as diversions.

They certainly were as far as our street was concerned. In our immediate vicinity several houses were affected and even next door suffered a blaze in the roof dealt with by the occupier, Harry Treacher, by the simple expedient of using a stirrup pump and tackling it speedily from the loft hatch whilst buckets of water were passed to him. It was a good job as he was later to remark that the incendiary was not tight against the roof timbers, which would have meant more than his own house could have been burned down. One must remember that these were close-knit terraced properties and the Fire Services would have been stretched to the limit following the raids.

As was typical of Hart Street the rain of incendiaries and Anti-Personnel (Butterfly) Bombs was totally indiscriminate and being scattered over such a wide area of the two towns, Grimsby and Cleethorpes, created considerable alarm and confusion. A television programme broadcast many years after the event filled in the background. The bombs were the first attempt by the Germans to 'terrorise' a whole district and bring it to a standstill. If it worked in North Lincolnshire then a similar raid upon a large city anywhere in the British Isles could have devastating results. A security clampdown resulted whilst the work of the Bomb Disposal Squads became paramount.

When dawn broke and the All-Clear was sounded teams of Air Raid Wardens and Police moved up and down the streets and back alleys and passages shouting 'Don't touch anything, don't touch anything', at the same time making notes of the sites and disposition of every unexploded device. Some were lying in the road and obvious but others were dangerously located in garden sheds and attics, both difficult to get at and to deal with. I believe that a medal was won that night by one of the Disposal Squad who picked up a bomb of which the vanes had only partially opened causing the priming spindle to malfunction. He guessed what had happened and taking his life in his hands, literally, wound the vanes back down and clamped them to the bomb casing by the very simple expedient of tying them together with string.

Where the devices were lying in the open, a simple sandbag wall was placed around them until there was time for the Bomb Disposal Units to detonate them.

The park at the end of the street was ultimately closed to all and sundry for several weeks whilst its several acres were gone over with a fine tooth comb. The adjoining Recreation Ground, basically a large field for footballers, became a dumping ground for all the rubble and waste timbers and so on from the bombed out houses in the Town. It would have been impossible to guard and police the mounds of building waste, although the park keeper did his best. It became a veritable treasure trove for all the lads. 'Dens' were built everywhere and we burrowed and built as industriously as any bunch of beavers, but to what effect I cannot now remember.

'Park View' was the nearby street which overlooked the northern edge of the Park. After the raid and before the Wardens could get their message across some youngsters came out of the houses, all of them being friends and acquaintances, and one of them picked up what looked like a tin can from the footpath. As they clustered around it the bomb exploded killing, I think, four of them. One of the group escaped because he had taken one look at the strange object and had turned to flee believing it to be dangerous. The two or three yards he made with his back turned saved his life although he received some serious wounds from the shrapnel. I think his name was Barry Smith and I am fairly sure that he was a member of the church choir. The Vicar took the young members to visit Barry in hospital and his story was a fascinating but tragic one.

The most tragic and sorrowful part for the choir was to attend the funeral service for the young victims. I can still remember, although now somewhat vaguely, the packed church and above all the four coffins on their trestles across the nave of St Aidan's Church, the stones of which could rarely, if ever, have witnessed so sad a scene.

It would be as well to end this part of the story by relating a somewhat amusing incident which could well have ended in yet another tragedy. The Milne family lived in Coombe Street and had several sons, the most notable at the time being 'Fatty' and 'Ginger' who were noted by the local constabulary for their lively escapades. One of them found an anti-aircraft shell somewhere in the district and instead of informing the authorities decided to take the unexploded and dangerous device to the local Wardens' Post at the end of the street. There the lad proudly displayed his prized find and the alarmed Warden could only 'suggest' that he place it gently in the WC and close the door. The crestfallen boy was then told bluntly what he could do with any future shells he might find and the Bomb Disposal Squad was informed. It was decided that the safest way of dealing with it was to blow up the shell *in situ*, which was done. In the process the Wardens' Post was demolished which, as was said at the time, was a pity since it had only been built and occupied for the previous four weeks.

It would perhaps not be thought inappropriate to mention at this time of the raids on Grimsby the effect of the sight of RAF Bombers – principally Avro-Lancasters – forming up and flying out over the estuary to the Wash and thence Germany. To this day I can still remember the sound of those mighty Merlin engines. The noise was unique. The aircraft came from what seemed dozens of bases of which Scampton, home of 617 Squadron, the Dam Busters, was the most famous. Oddly enough and many years later I met a lonely looking Scotsman in the bar of the Savoy Hotel whilst on holiday in Madeira. We began a conversation which when I mentioned that I hailed from Grimsby and Cleethorpes seemed to inject his whole being with a 'born again' rush of adrenalin. It transpired that he was the 'Archivist' of the Squadrons based at Killingholme RAF Station (now Humberside Airport) whence he had been flying Lancasters during the war. At that stage he was in his early twenties and it would have been, as one can well imagine, a very responsible as well as socially glamorous but very dangerous job.

It was apparent that his memories formed the highlight of his life and affected him for the rest of it. He told me, for instance, that the Squadron bus would leave the base for such social activities as were on offer in the two towns. It contained the crews entitled to a night out as they endeavoured and desperately hoped to complete their mandatory 30 operational sorties. The first stop he told me was 'The P & M' in the Old Market Place in Grimsby and then the nearby 'Mucky Duck', before going across the road to a hotel for a Dover sole meal. When I identified the hostelries as 'The Pestle and Mortar', 'The Black Swan' and 'The Ship Hotel' he knew I was a genuine 'Lincolnshire Yellowbelly' and a Cleethorpes 'Meggy' to boot. I could easily identify with him the other spots visited, notably the 'Café Dansant' and the 'Winter Gardens' at the far end of the seafront at Cleethorpes. The old boy, Jimmy Jones was his name, could have reminisced for years about that time in his life. He had developed a successful business flying freight around the world from his home in Scotland and the RAF Historical Society seemed to absorb most of his spare time.

This chance meeting encapsulated the feelings engendered by the war in just one individual. I tried to relate his experiences to anything that was relevant within my own small world at the time but it was impossible. Nevertheless I could associate myself with the comings and goings of numerous relatives, apart from my father, who were dressed in uniform. One of my uncles, Mother's brother Tom, was a Sergeant, I think in REME, whilst his wife, Doris, was of a similar rank in the ATS. One of the oddest careers was that of Uncle Chris (Porritt) who was an engineer in the railway workshops in Bolton. Being a member of the Territorial Army he was immediately called up at the outbreak of the war. Sent to France he arrived back in England via Dunkirk, whereupon his unit, with no home leave, was despatched to the Middle East. He finished the war there having been transferred to the RAF in the meantime, almost one feels as an after-thought. He was away for four and a half years in total but the marriage survived.

On the basis that what goes around comes around my Uncle Sid (Porritt) being a Territorial Army Member (Terrier) was called up at the beginning of the war from his home in Scunthorpe, where my maternal grandparents Jack and Alice Porritt ran the Theodore Road Working Men's Club. Sid, being unfit for active service, drove a vehicle for the RASC delivering rations to the many Army and POW camps for the whole of the war throughout 'Bloody Orkney' as the old song has it, little knowing that his nephew would serve there for the final 12 years of his career in local government.

I have already mentioned the fact that Father was recalled from Aberdeen where he had to serve in the Home Guard over and above his job on the Fish Docks, only to be called upon to serve in the Royal Navy as it turned out for four years from 1942 until 1946. His Navy Service Number was PJX 394244 and he was held at the rank of 'Able Seaman' after his initial training. This I can well remember as I posted a letter from my mother to him at least twice a week on my way to school. He was posted to a supply ship, the *Mull of Kintyre*, which as its name suggests necessitated a trip to Scotland, Glasgow to be exact. The trouble was that the ship was attached to the Pacific Fleet and lay at anchorage in the harbour at Vancouver Island, Canada. This would have followed various naval base postings in the UK and would probably have been in early 1945.

The next leg of his journey was undertaken aboard the majestic pre-war liner the *Queen Elizabeth*, which had been adapted and converted into an extraordinary personnel carrier. With every last space on board occupied it was said that she could carry a full Division of Troops, say 15,000 personnel, and was still too fast for either convoys or U–Boats. Be that as it may she lay in the Clyde waiting for her next voyage to begin and Father duly boarded her. The fact that it had taken a war for Father to see at first hand let alone board and sail in one of Britain's great nautical triumphs was not lost on him. Dad was a great believer in the history and traditions of the British Empire. He was a firmly right-wing monarchist of the labouring classes. The military and naval heroes of the land were as real to him as if they were still living. He knew the history of England's kings and queens and just once in his life did he fall from his firmly held conservative beliefs. Being sick and tired of the war in which he and his family had been involved and separated for years at a time he voted for the Labour, i.e. Socialist, Party in the 1945 Election. His worst fears were realised when the 'Red Flag' was sung in the House of Commons and he never made the same mistake again.

The weather was good and the Atlantic was crossed in six days. The great liner sailed up Long Island Sound and the Hudson River and docked at her usual berth in New York Harbour. Sightseeing took up most of the next 48 hours whilst the transit crew waited for trains to carry them on the next stage of their journey to Vancouver. As anyone who has studied a map can easily see the journey by rail from New York to Vancouver has to be one of the great scenic thrills of a lifetime, and so it proved with Father. Whatever route was taken, and I cannot remember what was said at the time, I seem to remember that Banff and Calgary with its acclaimed 'Stampede' were mentioned, although I am sure he never saw it. What was spoken about time and again was the vastness of the American continent and the beauty and magnificence of the 'Rockies'. Coming as he did from the rich, agricultural but flat lands of Lincolnshire it was not surprising that the sights and sounds of that four or five days' journey coast to coast was both a highlight of his life and a lasting memory.

Sailing south-west from Vancouver they made landfall with the Hawaiian Islands before sailing on to Darwin in Australia. Half way across the ocean VE Day was declared, but the war against the Japanese continued until the atomic bombs were used, after which Japan surrendered. Sailing from Darwin the *Mull of Kintyre* followed the cruiser *Sheffield* through the Malacca Straits and into Singapore Harbour. The world has been littered with strange coincidences for centuries and as a family we have had our fair share over the years, but none as odd as when the mail from home finally caught up with Father in Singapore. Remember he had been away for many months and had sailed halfway round the world, so that letters from home were infrequent. On this occasion the letter from Mother brought the news that her youngest sister, Mary, had become engaged to a Chief Petty Officer in the Royal Navy serving in the cruiser *Sheffield* called Mick Fitzpatrick. Being berthed only a cable length away Father duly boarded the ship and introduced himself via the Officer of the Watch to Mother's future brother-in-law, for Mick and Mary were married shortly after the war. Two further months were taken up with the voyage and sojourn in a 'Rest/Transit Camp' in Trincomalee in Ceylon (now Sri-Lanka). Eventually a troopship collected them and the home voyage was undertaken via the Indian Ocean, the Red Sea, the Suez Canal, Mediterranean, the cold Atlantic and back to a grey and weary England, having been away for 18 months in total. Whereupon he got his 'clogs' out and his working clothes, put his uniformed life to one side, oiled his bicycle and set off for the Fish Market to earn a living to support his growing family as a fish filleter, which he did until his retirement.

This ends Father's war during which he sailed the world and crossed the American Continent. He was discharged from the Royal Navy as he had started it as an 'Able Seaman' with a 'Good Conduct' rating. He had endured no privations such as Mother had with her constant concerns over rationing and air raids and bombs and shells, and bringing up a young family. On the other hand Father was nothing if not a family man and being apart was a torment in itself. Because he tended to be older than most of his shipmates he made, as far as I can remember, no close friends, but his pride and faith in the Senior Service was to stay with him for the rest of his life. During his naval service he neither heard nor saw a weapon fired in anger. The only discharge that comes to mind is when he was put onto the infamous Gunnery Course at Whale Island when he was 42 years of age and the average age seems to have been about 20. Whilst he was never in the thick of battle he 'did his bit' and the Government recognised his varied service career by sending him his decorations. They included the Home Defence Medal, the General Service Medal, The Atlantic Star and the Pacific Star with a Bar added for the Burma Campaign. The expression used at the time was that Father had a 'good war'. Indeed generally speaking the family survived intact and only one member, Mother's youngest brother, Arthur, was unfortunate to go into the 'Bag' in France and spend the next six years as a POW.

Totally out of both chronological order and placement within the story I must briefly mention one calamitous event which occurred in the Spring of 1953, known as the East Coast Floods. They occurred when the 'Neap' Tides backed up by hurricane force winds from the north-east blasted the North Sea into thousands of towns and villages, houses and homes, land and businesses, from the River Humber in Lincolnshire to Canvey Island in Essex. Hart Street and No. 50 were no exception. More damage was caused in one night across that part of the British Isles than occurred during the whole of the war from the Luftwaffe offensive.

The postwar years

The immediate concern for the family apart from the struggle to return to normality in the years from the end of the war, covering roughly 1944 to 1947, was to consider the options available for the further education of the older children. One must remember that there was a 'Scholarship' Examination taken at the age of eleven which was the fore-runner of the 11-plus and which selected those children thought to be capable of further academic education. All three of us failed, in spite of being fairly 'bright' in the Junior Schools which we attended. Betty the youngest was some little way behind in age so the years of her secondary schooling and later training as a hairdresser (where she was known as 'Sally') are a trifle obscure so I cannot put forward an accurate picture of the time and for this I must apologise. I do however remember the difficulties of cramped living conditions in the small terraced house with three bedrooms and a 'Front Room' occupied by Grandma Porritt. My poor parents with four teenage space seekers and their friends plus the added family burdens of their own must have wondered at times just how to cope. The fact that they came from large families living in similar accommodation probably helped.

In the event Joan attended the Secondary Modern School at Reynolds Street until she left as she was entitled to do at the age of 14, when the process of securing a job other than 'something' in an office or some such had to be a distinct possibility, given the nature of the times. Joan's problem was that she thought totally in classical terms and was definitely neither scientifically nor mathematically inclined. At all 'written' subjects she was good but with the English language she was intellectually gifted. Thus when Mother saw in the *Evening Telegraph* an advertisement of a vacancy there for a 16-year-old 'copy boy', as one could do in those days, she immediately saw this as a vital opportunity for Joan to apply.

The trouble was that Joan was two years short of the requisite age. Under Mother's tutelage Joan composed a most persuasive letter to the newspaper persuading them that they were quite mistaken in their belief that a 16-year-old boy could do the work when what was really required was an industrious and highly intelligent 14-year-old girl. Whatever arguments she used bore fruit and she duly started work for the *Telegraph*. Seven years later she was a first-rate journalist, writing the whole of the Women's Page, in the meantime and through Night School she took her O and A Levels in English Language and Literature. She also became highly proficient as a typist and short-hand writer, which two skills have stood her in good stead throughout her life.

Rita was educationally re-assessed when she was 13 after 2 years at the same Secondary School as Joan. Being thought of as a 'late developer' she then made it into Grammar School where she stayed to take her senior examinations before getting a place at Furzedown Teacher Training College in Tooting, West London.

In 1944 when I was eligible for the Scholarship Examination Father was still serving in the Royal Navy. I failed – probably miserably – but Mother realised that there was a different way to skin this particular cat. It was still possible to go to a Fee-Paying Grammar School such as Clee Grammar School (Matthew Humberston Foundation School as was) if one could pass the Common Entrance Examination. The fees were risible by modern standards – about £4 per term – but when the average wage was somewhere around that it was a substantial amount that had to be found every 13 weeks. The key to it was that the money could be reclaimed via Father and the Royal Navy. All I had to do was pass the examination and interview held by the very stern looking and be-gowned Headmaster, Lt Col S.F. Thomas. As usual I was carted along by my indomitable mother, gleaming I have no doubt from head to shining boots. The joint effort succeeded and I joined the Grammar School in September 1944.

Nothing of note springs to mind in the following five years. I played all normal sports and ambled along intellectually in about tenth place in the 'A' stream of the class. I can remember that I always responded to slightly 'odd' teachers, who to my mind were characters. 'Sam' Osborne was one such. He took the 'B' stream Mathematics Class to which I was demoted following my disastrous showing in the end of year examinations at the age of 14. I scored a total of 40 marks out of a possible 300, so my demise was not unduly unexpected. 'Sam' was a tall, bony man with a booming voice, an un-erring eye with a piece of chalk and a gift for writing pithy comments upon badly executed work in between studying the 'Racing Post' at his desk.

The word 'Abysmal' appeared upon one of my pieces alongside the figure 3. Funny how these minor episodes stick in one's mind, as also does the memory of his stained, torn and tattered gown with its green sheen, the original black having long since given up the ghost. Incidentally all teachers wore gowns throughout the teaching day and were resplendent with their distinctive and varied 'hoods' in addition on Speech Day.

As with Mathematics so with 'French'. I remember so well the cool, clear and to my mind the 'cold' teaching methods of excellent members of staff led by the austere Col Thomas and Deputy Head, 'Syd' Boot. In all honesty I came to know 'Syd' and his wife (whose name escapes me) when I joined school parties on hiking holidays in North Wales and Yorkshire and Derbyshire which were led by the couple and were most enjoyable. As a 16-year-old I used to do quite a bit of cycling and walking as a hobby, even with a friend, Jack Ives, managing a 'hike' of 34 miles in one day through the North Lincolnshire Wolds. In my late teens I obtained a tandem bicycle and travelled all the way past Nottingham to stay a weekend in Ilkeston at some relative or other's home.

One thing I should perhaps mention is that I fancied myself as an athlete when I took part to represent the County in the Long Jump when the English Schools Championships were held that year in Purley in Surrey. I was really selected as a Reserve because I had not won the 'Champion' title, but as there was only half an inch between us – eighteen feet eleven inches as against eighteen feet ten and a half inches – I was also selected for the team. On the day I failed miserably with a jump of barely eighteen feet.

I left that year (1949), having obtained 6 Subject Credits in the School Certificate Final Examination but with two failures – Chemistry and Physics, and since Father was in no position to support a growing lad at school with an indifferent academic career behind him I looked for a job. I should point out that no financial assistance was available prior to entering University, always assuming that one was offered a place. So to work.

Local government

'Sit on your arse for 40 years and hang your hat on a pension' was one person's embittered and critical comment on the life-time prospect of working in Local Government. Conservative in the extreme, staid but not boring, committee orientated but staffed by genuine well-educated people who lived in the main within the Borough and were consequently rate payers. They had therefore a very real interest in keeping expenses under control, and as the Councillors were unpaid a very watchful eye was kept upon the Rates.

When I succeeded in obtaining a Junior Clerk's post in the Borough Engineer and Surveyor's Department my parents were pleased. Father was adamant that I was going nowhere near the Fish Docks in any capacity but said that experiences during the

1930s depression years convinced him that Security was the aim in life. With this at my young age it was difficult to disagree, although like all youths with parental advice, I had reservations.

Cleethorpes Borough Council was not a bad place to work and was within easy cycling distance of home. In some ways I was fortunate because I earned an extra £20 per annum on top of my £130 per annum salary. To obtain this I had to cycle/travel along the sea front for a half-mile or so to the Weather Station where every day at 9 a.m. and 5 p.m. I took the readings of the instruments. Some were easy, such as the wet and dry bulb thermometer, the temperature and relative humidity gauges, but some required physical effort, e.g. going up a free-standing 10 ft wooden ladder onto the roof of the swimming pool office. There was mounted the Sunshine Recorder. If it was mid-winter and the ladder had blown down in an on-going gale it was quite a job to resurrect it, and on a couple of occasions I found myself stranded at the top and having to shin down a rainwater pipe to the ground. It was a job that could not be avoided as the climax was to go back to the office and compose and send a telegram to the Meteorological Office in London giving the recorded figures for the day. Some were not recorded but estimated, i.e. cloud formations and types.

There was one student post in the drawing office, which was fully occupied for the foreseeable future, and trainee posts were difficult to come by as all returning servicemen were given priority. The thought of having a clearly defined career aim and associated structured training programme came to dominate my thoughts in the year I spent in that office, because quite plainly looming in the next 12 months would be two years of National Service. I had not the slightest desire to follow that, at the age of 20 or 21, trying to obtain a post with no qualifications whatsoever.

It was therefore with some relief that a post became vacant as a 'Pupil Sanitary Inspector' in the Public Health Department of the Borough Council. I succeeded in the transfer over and for the next four years my National Service was deferred until such time as training was completed. A brief word on the training. Basically three nights a week at Night School – 6.30 to 9.30 – for up to three years taking Building Construction, Building Maths and Building Science as subjects. In addition in the third and fourth years a Day-Release Public Health Course at Nottingham Technical College. Leave home at 6.30 a.m. for the 6.58 a.m. train to Nottingham. Course runs from 10 a.m. to 4 p.m. but there is no train until 7 p.m. Home at 9.30 p.m. The following day being Saturday and there being a five and a half day week in operation it was back to work in the morning.

The reader must be wondering whether there is a comic side to this training travail. A sardonic and rueful grin is the answer as I recall the tangible rewards. I have mentioned already the watchful eyes upon the level and control of expenditure. It was never so obvious as it applied in the 'Pupillage' System in the Health Department. There were anything up to three of us at any one time, all in the pipeline of seniority. The newest recruit became in essence the Clerk for the Medical Officer of Health under whose 'General Direction' we all worked, although the real Boss was Herbert Brant, Chief Sanitary Inspector and Cleansing Superintendent. The catch was really that in return for our training we would act as the non-existent clerical staff. We learned how to prepare reports for committees and enquiries, for housing and refuse collection and disposal and infectious disease and bugs and insects and rats and mice and staff to the umpteenth degree of what a Public Health Department stands for, or at least did in those days. As a reward the remuneration consisted of £80 p.a. rising to £220 p.a. after four years. Having succeeded in my Finals, at the age of 22 I was called upon to complete my National Service. The pay? £1 per week! After two years service I found myself earning £4 per week, exactly the same as before I joined the Royal Army Medical Corps.

As a 'greenhorn' Pupil and being in all respects an innocent abroad I can recount one memorable incident, often quoted in the Department, which occurred just after I joined it. I was alone in the office apart from the Chief when there was a knock on the Enquiry Window. This I opened, to be confronted by a scruffy looking individual who from his dress I took to be a fisherman from one of the local boats. He said 'I've got bloody crabs. What are you going to do about it?' I asked him to wait and went and politely told Mr Brant that there was a man selling shellfish and that I was uncertain what to do. He came through to the main office with a puzzled look and then discovered to his great amusement that the man sought assistance with an infestation of *Pediculus Humanis Corporis* – body lice to the layman. A call to those great Salvationists at the Army Hostel Headquarters in Grimsby, where a complete outfit of clean and decent second-hand clothing was provided, a trip to the Cleansing Station in Cleethorpes with advice and treatment given by the Medical Officer of Health, and the man went on his way rejoicing as it were. I should perhaps mention that such facilities were still available following the war when lice were a constant problem. In mitigation I always claimed that the local fishing industry distorted my judgement, but privately I knew that I had no idea that 'crabs' equated with 'lice'.

From being an 'innocent' to the qualified article took four years, the third year of which was spent in the Cleansing Department Office where one learned a great deal about life and where I was obliged to draw up timesheets, working schedules, pay and tax and 'subs' and refuse collection and disposal and incinerators and gross and tare weights and workshops and rat catchers and cullet and whatever else demanded attention.

Two memorable comments stick in the mind. 'Where there is muck, there is money', and the more pithy and ruder one 'It may be shit to you but it is my bread and butter'. Both of these have their merits and both could be demonstrated in the Cleansing Department.

I was even there when my sister Joan came from the *Grimsby Evening Telegraph* to report upon the installation and operation of a new 'Electrolethaller' as the device was known. It was for the electrocution and disposal of unwanted, old, injured or senile dogs and cats. Two shillings and sixpence (twelve and a half pence) for dogs and one shilling (five pence) for cats.

It was about this time that Joan was helping to organise the North Lincolnshire Press Ball. My great friend at the time, Geoff Holmes, and I were coerced into providing the escorts for four local Beauty Queens at the Winter Gardens. Apart from the dancing, which we both enjoyed, plus the free tickets, we won between us three of the first four prizes in the raffle. On the other hand we were a bit miffed when taxis were provided for the girls home and Geoff and I had to walk!!

Geoff and I were reasonable local club footballers – he better than me – and avid followers of Grimsby Town FC. Changing facilities were sparse on the local playing fields and we rode our bikes after the game to the Public Bath House near to the Grimsby General Hospital where for sixpence one could enjoy the luxury of a steaming hot bath with soap and towel provided. A cup of tea followed at Geoff's home, whereafter we parted until Geoff came on the bus to Cleethorpes for our Saturday night forays along the Promenade.

Geoff and I became friends because we were friends with two local sisters, Eileen and Maureen Dennison. Geoff's relationship had become serious enough to warrant an engagement. As he returned after his National Service the relationship withered and he and Maureen parted company.

The youth club at the Beaconthorpe Methodist Church was run by one Alan Hughes, who induced two of us (Ray Wenham being the other), to try smoking a pipe, which I believe turned the pair of us green. This apart we played a lot of table tennis there with our friends, even inventing a form of three-a-side, which did neither the table, the net or the floor much good, but stimulated great gales of laughter, so it must have had its uses.

Geoff by virtue of living at the far end of Grimsby took no further interest in Beaconthorpe once his engagement was over. About four months later I split from Eileen, or was it vice versa, and as fate would have it met Geoff again on the football field when we renewed our friendship. The pair of us eyed the nurses, after our disappointments, at the Grimsby General Hospital, the one I frequently squired around being a rather wild girl called Rosemary whose father was the Deputy Head of a large Secondary School. I think my parents were rather pleased that this relationship sank without trace once I departed for National Service.

A colleague in the Department was Don Keighly who lived in the little village of Marshchapel. I went to the Methodist Chapel there on one occasion to hear his grandfather, a lay preacher, conduct the Harvest Thanksgiving Service. It was a tiny circular building and the early evening sun shone through the windows and onto the central area. The choir and packed congregation sang their hearts out as only Methodists can. Was it not Charles Wesley who posed the question 'Why should the devil have all the best tunes?' He little knew what he was sowing.

The sermon given by the gnarled old gentleman in his best Lincolnshire dialect was outstanding, talking as he did of the sower going forth to sow and the fruits to be harvested from the good soil. A very moving evening.

I suppose it is sufficient to say that the year spent in the Cleansing Department was a great learning experience, none more so than when the Boss took me on one side and explained that I should not be so abrupt on the telephone as I was a 'Public Servant'. He explained that I was such because since they paid my salary they were entitled to due respect, however tiresome that might appear.

One other thing I learned to do was to drive, using a 1932 Albion Tipper long since past its prime around the Department Yard at lunchtime when Mr Brant was not around. It had the accelerator between the clutch and the brake with no synchro-mesh and a gate change with double-de-clutching being the norm for gear changing. It was so worn out that it was only used for transporting 'clinker' from the combustion chamber of the incin-erator to the controlled tip. Daylight could be seen as the road raced past beneath the floor pedals. Strange that having passed the Driving Test at 18 years of age and driven throughout my life in a dozen different countries, in road and weather conditions of all kinds and in many different vehicles, I can still remember clearly at the age of 71 both that old truck and the driver, Eric Appleton, who first taught me. My Finals at age 21 were taken in London and I remember little of the papers but I do remember being with fellow students from Nottingham Tech. College. We decided to have a night off prior to the exams taking place. My sister Rita, being at Furzedown Teacher Training College in Tooting, duly joined us and we sat in the stalls, I think, to see the 'in' farce at the Whitehall Theatre – *Dry Rot* starring Brian Rix.

National Service

For me National Service was in an overall context enjoyable. For sure there were the awful boredoms of weekend duties in the

Guardroom which seemed to drag interminably, but there was a sense of belonging and many good friends and acquaintances to remember and admire. Indeed only recently have I met with an old friend, Mike Jacob, who served with me in Northern Ireland some 40 years ago. Elsewhere I have written of strange coincidences but to have three people playing together at the same UK golf club who were good friends in different parts of the world is surely remarkable. Keith Girling was the family dentist and fellow hockey player in Ruislip (1965), Mike Clarke was an accountant and golfer in Malawi (1975) and Mike Jacob is mentioned above. We meet for lunch once a year.

The basic training having been completed at the RAMC Depot at Crookham in Hampshire, I was posted for Specialist Training to the Army School of Health at Mytchett in Surrey. This consisted of lectures in Infectious Disease Control – Smallpox, Typhoid, Malaria, Cholera and so on, water purification, particularly under emergency and battlefield conditions, but there was also a particular emphasis upon nuclear explosions and their aftermath. One should remember that the first atomic bombs had only been dropped on Japan some 10 years earlier in 1945. The Russian, American and British Governments were embroiled in experiments with further developments of such weapons up to and including the extreme cobalt bomb, which terminated with the advent of the nuclear deterrent philosophy.

At the end of this phase of training and instruction I was accepted as an NCO Instructor at the School of Health, which was the start of a new phase of Army life. I seem to remember that the commissioned staff were all medical officers and the NCO instructors had a variety of civilian qualifications as well as being somewhat older than the average 18-year-old in the line regiments, if you will pardon an old-fashioned expression for the much maligned infantry.

Time passed agreeably enough with stints in charge of the library and displays for training courses but with plenty of time for sporting pursuits in the rugby (not much good) and cricket (probably even worse) fields. But it was the social side of such activities which were much the more enjoyable. I have always enjoyed a good party, particularly as the host, and would be an extremely rich man if I had not discovered such a talent.

Meanwhile in the real world in London my sister Rita, having completed her Teacher Training Course, had applied for and had been accepted as a Probationary Teacher by the London Education Authority. Unbeknown to her a fellow student at the Training College had done the same. The school they were both appointed to was situated in the East End of London, the toughest dockland area in the land. The district was Plaistow (West Ham and Millwall Supporters to the last) and it was witnessing although not realised at the time the steady decline of the sprawling London Docks as a giant industrial centre. The school was called Faraday Secondary School and was one of the toughest and most down-to-earth schools imaginable. The other Probationary Teacher was Pamela Lineton from Shrewsbury, who was destined two years later to become my wife. Both of them are agreed that the only real teaching they learned was in that tough school, survival, it would seem, being the name of the game. Suffice to say that time has mellowed their memories but not their fond recollections of the characters, good or bad, who abounded.

Eventually the girls set up home together with one other friend, Margaret Flint, at a top-floor flat in Primrose Hill Road in Hampstead, a far cry from Docklands.

This duly became a much used weekend retreat for myself and a few other close friends from the Army School of Health, notably Mike Jacob from St Austell, Neil Sharp from Stirling and Peter Richardson from Scarborough. The 'girls' were always welcoming, particularly when they were broke at the end of the month. We were paid weekly so the first salary was spent on food, the second on alcohol, the third on travel and the fourth on cheap tickets to the theatre or cinema. Remember beer was still only a shilling a pint (one pound bought 20) and the last performance at many theatres, sitting on benches in 'the gods' was not expensive.

The Army then decided that Mike and I could be spared for three months while we went on secondment as recorders on a Combat Ration Trial involving two companies of the Northumberland Fusiliers. The trial was to take place in Northern Ireland. The basic plan was to issue one company with the old ration packs and one with the proposed new one. Putting both companies through the same training programme and measuring the energy output of each was an essential part of the job. The first month was for training and familiarisation, the second for the actual trial and the third for analysis of the data and records. All in all an interesting variant of Army life, although we were lucky in that there was no IRA activity in the training area.

We returned to the Army School of Health whereupon I found myself posted to a Field Hygiene Section in preparation for the invasion of Egypt and the aborted Suez operation with the French in 1956. All in all from start to finish the event took about four months to complete. We flew out via Nice and Cyprus to Port Said and after withdrawal came home on a troopship through the Med and landed in England in the New Year. By then I only had a couple of months to do, so I was held at the School as cover for staff on leave. Being of little worth to the Army in what little time was left to serve I had plenty of time to look at the future, which apart from any professional considerations involved marriage to Pamela.

The years 1957–65

In the year prior to my departure from the Army I had come to know and love Pam. I had also been introduced to her family on several occasions. She was the oldest of seven children with four brothers (David, Barry, Greg and Glyn) and two attractive sisters (Pat and Pauline). Her father was Jim, always known to his intimates as 'Jockey', and her mother, the sweet-natured Ethel. The latter was the lynch-pin of the whole family, Jim being a somewhat weaker establishment figure. He was employed as a Press Operator on permanent night-shift at Sankeys, the Sanitary Ware Company, in Wellington. Mother (Ethel) was also a (Permanent) Night Shift Ward Assistant at the local hospital. I do not think that it was any joy to them to work throughout the night week on and week off, but sheer necessity. Bringing up such a large family was a financial burden apart from anything else and the night shifts paid higher wages.

Having no brothers of my own I quietly adopted the four belonging to the Linetons. One thing that struck me as I visited their semi-detached council house in Berwick Avenue was how on earth did I warrant a bedroom to myself and where did all the rest of the family rest their weary heads. Mind you the comings and goings throughout the day and night took some figuring out and in any case we were young and it really mattered little. It was an era when everyone seemed to smoke cigarettes so that at times Mother must have despaired, house proud as she was, to come home in the morning sunshine to enter a smoke-infested lounge with full ashtrays and hearth littered with burnt out fag ends. The modern housewife would die!

Before I forget: the house had a separate BATHROOM, although there was an outside WC to make me feel at home!

The social life of the District centred upon the four public houses on nearby Coton Hill – The Woodman, The Bird in Hand, The London Apprentice and The Royal Oak, of which the latter was the most popular.

For me there was a fascination about the town, dominated as it is by the always changing River Severn. It also possessed a plethora (to an outsider such as I was) of extraordinary street and passage names. The 'Pig Trough' was one as was 'Dog Pole' and 'Bear Steps' 'Gullet Passage' 'Grope Lane' and so on. For someone hailing from Grimsby with its never ending 'Streets' it was a revelation. Ever since I first arrived at the railway station and enquired the way to Berwick Avenue and walked by the river and up the hill to the house, I have felt at home and at ease. Not that it seemed to register upon the first person who answered the door to No. 8. It happened to be a 9-year-old Pauline who promptly giggled and slammed the door when I enquired after my beloved. Such was my first meeting with a member of the family other than Pamela.

It would be very much to be regretted if I forgot to mention that as part of this lovely and ancient town the part that the Quarry and the 'Dingle' play in its undoubted success through the years. This great park is the site for visiting fairgrounds and circuses but above all else it hosts the superlative Annual Flower Show, than which no finer exhibition exists

Having left the Army in March 1957, Pam and I were married six weeks later on 27 April. The marriage took place at St Saviour's Church in Hampstead in London. It was really a very small affair, the reception taking place in the same Primrose Hill flat that the three girls occupied. 'Small' weddings were commonplace even in those days and no great fuss was made of family travelling on early morning trains to the event and departing on the midnight one for home. The beer and sherry ran out just before opening time at the 'Washington Lion', the pub over the road, but by that time Pam and I were long gone to our hotel in Southampton Row en route the following day to Paris for our honeymoon.

I particularly mentioned 'small' weddings to emphasise our modest financial resources, and a word about the overlapping needs of both of us would not be amiss at this point. We were both qualified in our respective professions: Pam with a post in London, me with a post in Cleethorpes, which, as it had been held open for me whilst in the Army, I felt honour bound to return to. This would have meant separation yet again which after the Irish and Suez ventures of the previous year would have been wearisome.

We therefore decided to marry and move up to Cleethorpes and stay with my parents until I could get myself (professionally) sorted out. Whilst I had my basic qualifications I still needed further training in meat and foods and atmospheric pollution. Pam therefore resigned her job in the East End. Her popularity was such that her 'girls' made her petticoat for the wedding dress and a party of them appeared at the Church!!

In the midst of all this planning and so on my sister Joan had left the journalistic profession and had started a new career in the Foreign Service. Her first overseas posting was to the UK Delegation to NATO, one of the senior diplomats being Donald Maitland whose brother Lt Col Douglas Maitland was the Senior Instructor at the Army School of Health when I was there.

Joan being established in Paris and installed in a wonderful old world apartment in the shadow of Notre Dame it was the obvious aiming point for a modest honeymoon, lasting just a week, as we had to get back to being gainfully employed as soon as possible. Father's wedding present of £10 following a winning bet on 'Sundew' in the Grand National that year bought a lot of beer in England but soon went in Paris where they charged what we thought were exorbitant prices for coffee – although the wines were cheap.

The Paris trip was a success, apart from one incident which has always provided both family and friends with joyous amusement. In the middle of the week I succumbed to a dose of tonsillitis. Never before and only once since have I had such a wretched time of it. After flying home I had to collect a van and load it with all our worldly goods before driving north out of London up the Great North Road and thence via Peterborough, Spalding, Boston and Louth to Cleethorpes.

In short order came Pam's appointment as the Mistress of Class 3C Girls at Harold Street Secondary School over the border in Grimsby. As its title suggests this was not an academic class and most of them would be destined for the fish factories and docks in whatever position they found most lucrative. The relieving part of the day's work for Pam came with her walk through the park at the end of Hart Street. I say 'relieving' because she felt she had survived another day whilst I waited patiently for another post which would give me access to a Meat and Other Foods Training Course. These had to be undertaken at a specified college with access to a large abattoir under the control of the veterinary services. The nearest one to Grimsby was in Birmingham and quite obviously I needed a post within striking distance of the city so that I could attend the twice weekly evening classes and practical instruction on Saturday afternoon. A post was obtained with the Bromsgrove Urban District Council some 15 miles south-west following the line of the A38 Bristol Road.

Before this could happen I had to return to work but my tonsillitis grew steadily worse and in total I was absent for about a month. At the height of this my dear old grandmother, then in her eighth decade, took Pamela on one side and told her to stop being so demanding in bed as she was sure this was contributing to the problem!! Eventually I was fit enough to return to the office and saw out my notice prior to departure for the Midlands and our first married home.

During this time at home I enjoyed my father's company on several occasions over a beer or two and was fascinated to learn that he had a couple of convictions for being a 'bookie's runner'. In those days there was a huge market for off-course betting on the horses but there was one snag. Cash betting was only allowed on the racecourses. This provision of the legal system discriminated against the working classes who could not afford to open credit facilities with the bookmaking fraternity. The local bookies therefore operated a system whereby they sat in shady 'dives' – the back room of a club being a favourite. A string of ready cash bets came to them from a variety of sources e.g. milkmen, local postmen, road foremen and so on. Father's connection with the industry started when he met Lily, her father being a minor bookie who had by then graduated from the fish and chip shop to stewardship of a local club near the Old Market Place in Grimsby. Being a very bright mathematician in working out the bets at the returned odds and with the winnings calculated, please remember, under the Duo-Decimal System (12 pence to 1 shilling), Father's talents were rapidly sought after.

It was the ideal occupation for a supplementary income after the fish market had closed down, to sit in the back room at the Club and work out the book for his future father-in-law. Because of his skills it was something that he enjoyed doing, but it came to an end when the Club was raided by the local constabulary. Betting slips were taken as evidence and father was fined £5. Two years later the same thing happened. A £15 fine was imposed with the warning that if he came before the Magistrates again he could expect a custodial sentence. The fines were all paid by Grandad Porritt, the main culprit, according to the law as it stood at the time. Being on reasonably affable terms with the local police, Father was warned of an imminent raid as he approached the Club some months later and thus escaped the intended gaol sentence. The Club was closed down for a time, after which the war supervened and it then re-opened under different management. The new steward was Uncle Bob Porritt who was unfit for service in the armed forces. He and his wife Eva ran it throughout the war, after which Father became yet again the 'Clerk' in residence in the back room, calculating the winnings and balancing the 'Book' until licensed betting shops were allowed.

I suppose that in these days of total aural and visual subjugation to the televisual mantra that 'anything' goes I remember that whilst mild cussing was tolerated in small doses in the home but by adults only, the fouler forms were left, as Father said, 'on the Docks'. He once told some astonished 'youngsters' off for using such language in the bar in the Conservative Club, the only trouble being that the men were forty-something market traders!! On reading this I hope the reader does not get the impression that Dad was a narrow-minded old cuss. Far from it. He was a proud ex-matelot who had seen life around the world and it changed his basic moral standards very little. This, after the war, in a changing world where duties and responsibilities came to be pushed to one side. It would have been particularly difficult when he returned to his testosterone-strewn teenaged brood, and as for my implacable mother the mind can only wonder at her fortitude as once again 'The Slave of Duty' springs to mind.

There are times in the modern world when the phrase 'Care in the Community' is used as a palliative for inaction rather than a call to render help for some small section of society. The soporific cushion of a badly functioning committee quite often dominates the agenda. It's an excuse for doing nothing whilst sounding good to the press and politicians. It is also a phrase which belittles the massive unsung care provided by friends and neighbours at all levels of society throughout the land for years past. People just did what was expected of them without recourse to any committee or in response to any 'Care in the Community' energising slogan.

One 'skill', if that is the right word, that Mother possessed was the washing and laying out of dead bodies. She, together with her friend and neighbour Millie Newby, did this on many occasions throughout the war and after. Whilst many deaths were peaceful, where open mouths could be tied and pennies placed to keep eye-lids closed, it was not always easy for the body to be cleansed and laid out with all orifices stopped and fluids removed. A cup of tea at home for the pair of them followed the event with a quiet discussion about the deceased.

These were without exception kept at their homes after being suitably dressed and laid in their coffins by the undertakers. I do not recall 'Chapels of Rest' being available at the Funeral Director's premises but if they did then one can only surmise that their use would have entailed an extra expense for the relatives. One must remember that in those far off days funerals were much more marked by solemnity and reverence by neighbours as well as relatives. Coffins were left open for viewing by all, curtains were drawn in the street until after the funeral, men doffed their hats and everyone stood silently as the funeral cortege passed by, nobody would dream of overtaking the slowly moving vehicles, all in the name of respect.

Once the relatives returned from the graveside it was 'party time', or at least 'high teas' were served to the mourners and helpers. The invitations extended to the pall bearers, who had probably had a 'tot' prior to proceedings commencing (no drink-driving laws were in being) and the Vicar. As the afternoon extended into the evening so the initially jolly gathering fell to maudlin reminiscences of the deceased. 'Wouldn't our Jack/Bill/ Joe/Rosie???? have enjoyed this?' . . . which led then to usually amusing anecdotes. The family archives were opened, often to the astonishment of some participants. 'I never heard that before. Did that really happen? Well I never!' were often heard expressions. With eyes like 'organ stops' we young teenagers sat enthralled.

Grandmother Tonge died on Christmas Day in the year after the war ended. Her home prior to her marriage and life in Grimsby had been the Swineshead Village area near to Boston in South Lincolnshire when she had been Maud Gilding. I remember her brothers coming to the funeral, all ruddy-cheeked, healthy looking farmers, one of whom was missing. His name may have been David and he was aged 82 and having some problem in travelling, but according to his side of the family, it hadn't stopped him having a 'fancy woman'. There was a silence, followed by one of my aunts saying 'You shouldn't say things like that in front of the children'. Although I had not immediately understood the impli- cations for the family, I had experienced and seen enough encounters in the back passages of my home area during the war to know 'what was what', in Max Miller's parlance.

Mother's fondness for trotting out a constant stream of sage sayings and aphorisms was mind numbing – at least when one has heard them all several times over. Amongst her favourites were 'Keep on keeping on' and 'Better to have been a "has been" than a "never-wasser".' She was also prone to singing verses of the old music hall songs and some that she had heard on the radio, which was still an infant medium in the 1930s. Among her many fine attributes as a housewife was the fact that she arose and prepared a cooked breakfast for my father every day before he ventured forth on his bicycle in whatever weather to cycle the couple of miles to his work. A hot meal was always waiting for him when he returned some 10 hours later. Occasionally when fish landings were small he would return with his mid-day cheese sandwiches still intact. Rich pickings for small children prior to the war.

One of my outstanding memories of my mother was the ability and dexterity which she displayed in cooking delicious pies and stews and bread and puddings in an old cottage range coal-fired oven. It was not until my wife and I lived in Africa many years later and failed miserably to cook with a wood-burning stove that we realised the full extent of her culinary skills.

Once installed in Bromsgrove, a first-floor 2-bedroom council flat being the accommodation provided, we set about providing ourselves with a modicum of furniture and household goods, but neither of us developed any warmth of feeling for our first marital home. There was no soundproofing for a start and miserable neighbours downstairs were a bit of a pain, but at least we were on our own and could start to live a little.

The post I held, apart from a totally council-cowed Chief, Harry Holden, was of interest for two reasons. One was that my semi-rural District was full of professional interest stretching from Bromsgrove to the Lickey Hills, taking in Barnt Green and Rubery on the outskirts of the City of Birmingham at Longbridge Motor Manufacturing Works. The second was that I was able to get on with both the theoretical studies at night school at Birmingham Technical College twice a week and on Saturday the practical work at the abattoir near to the old Bull Ring in the city centre. As you will appreciate it meant a lot of toing and froing in and out along the A38, and this was added to by Pam obtaining a position at the Dame Elizabeth Cadbury School in Selly Oak, a round-trip of some 30 miles, although mostly done by bus.

A left-over in the area from an earlier age was the situation of four small slaughterhouses behind the respective butchers' shops. Each butcher selected and bought the animals he wanted at the local weekly cattle market, transported them 'home' and killed them the next day. Pigs, sheep and cattle on different days in different establishments in different parts of the district meant that the other District Officer, Jack Burford, and I were kept pretty busy on meat inspection duties, in which I, although only partly qualified, was fully expected to participate.

I had mixed feelings at the time but I came to realise over the succeeding months that to carry out a total examination of a carcass with some indication of a pathological condition with the butcher standing over you and ready to query every move was an 'on-job' training experience not easily gained in the larger abattoir-dominated cities and towns The conditions might range from fluke infested livers to generalised tuberculosis, but each bit of condemned meat meant a financial loss to the butcher, so he was always prepared to argue the toss.

I mentioned earlier that I had very little in common with the 'Boss', Harry Holden, and his excruciating fear of the Council and Councillors. I once had a run-in with him over the fact that I was reading an article in a magazine and he proceeded to dress me down because he thought that a member of the public or (horror of horrors) a councillor might suddenly appear and see me. The fact that the magazine was *Municipal Engineer* bought by and provided for its officials by the Council and that the article was about sub-standard housing and its demolition seemed to have escaped him.

The other occasion that I remember well was when Jack and I were taken out for a drink on Christmas Eve by the same Harry Holden. He insisted that we drive out of the District and into the Rural Council area to some hidden hostelry whereupon he bought us half-a-pint each and then drove us back to work! This in spite of there being two public houses next door to the offices, namely 'The Golden Cross' and 'The Shoulder of Mutton', both of which were crammed to the doors with architects, housing managers, surveyors and engineers – all of them employees of the Council.

One item of note was that the post I occupied was such that it warranted the use of a car, which in those days was a luxury which Pam and I enjoyed to the utmost. We were not only enabled to make long distance trips to Shrewsbury and Cleethorpes but also occasionally to London. It meant that we explored the highways and by-ways of that beautiful county, Worcestershire, with its wealth of villages and off-beat public houses. The Bell at

Bellbroughton, The Chateau Impney at Droitwich, The Mug House in the village churchyard at Claines where the Vicar came for a pint after evening service still dressed in his cassock and surplice.

One particular place that I remember stays in the mind because it was the start of a lifelong friendship with Reg and Kath Scanlon. He was the manager of a local grocery store – either the Maypole or Home and Colonial – who had twice won a marketing competition for his company, earning 10-day holidays in Scandinavia as a reward. It so happened that his very busy shop was right in the centre of the High Street and I inspected the suspect and damaged foods from time to time prior to issuing Condemnation Certificates. On this particular occasion I was there in the rear store when Reg approached me with a special request. It being his wife's birthday at the weekend he would be delighted if Pam and I would join them for dinner at the Fox Lydiate Hotel on the Redditch Road on the following Saturday night. I thanked him for his invitation and he then said that there was only one condition, this being that we would have to use my car as he didn't possess one! Whether it was the car or the company he craved we never did find out. Suffice to say that we had a splendid meal followed, as usual with Reg, by a 'supper' (Irish) at his home at the back of The Shoulder of Mutton. Subsequently, Reg, who was a good businessman, left the grocery business and bought a small bakehouse and shop at Water Orton near Coalshill, reverting to his original trade as a baker. Some years later he returned to his native Ireland where the family farm was redeveloped under his management into a small stud establishment. It has the lovely name of 'Cool Bawn' and is in Kilkenny in Eire. Its prosperous development enabled Reg, ably supported and assisted by Kath, to pursue his hobby of carriage driving. In this he was good enough to win the outright championship at the Royal Dublin driving a Victorian Phaeton harnessed to two matching 'Connemaras'. One other incident should be recounted involving Reg and Kath, but it occurred some time later when we lived in Eastcote working for Ruislip-Northwood UDC.

At the time one could purchase unsold tickets for sporting events from the usual ticket agencies in Central London. I thus managed to get three four-shilling tickets for the forthcoming rugby match between England and Ireland. The tickets at the stated price were the cheapest available and they were for the North Terrace, Twickenham, which was not then an all-seat stadium as it is today. Pam came with us, she being six months pregnant with Victoria. All went well until just before half-time when with the score 5–0 in Ireland's favour she fainted, the dense crowd being just too much for her. The first aid guys were wonderful and with me tagging on behind she was lifted over and into the East Stand where we obtained seats for the whole of the rest of the match. England won the match 8–5 in the very last minute, Pam at that point standing on her seat screaming her head off. Obviously indicative of a very sportingly conscious family. I do not think that Reg ever forgave her!

The time spent in Bromsgrove had climaxed on 1 November 1958, with the birth of our son, Simon Jonathan, in the General Hospital there. There was strict governance of visitors and the times of visitation. I remember having to request the Ward Sister to display our son to my mother-in-law, Ethel, who had travelled by early morning train on her day off to see her first grandchild. She was not allowed to hold the baby and it was held up within the glass-walled nursery unit, be-swaddled and fast asleep. At least in those days nosocomial infections were kept ruthlessly to a minimum. Florence Nightingale's dictum that 'a hospital should do the sick no harm' seems to have been largely forgotten in the present world of 'Super Bugs'. The writing was surely on the wall when twenty years later our daughter, Victoria, in labour with her son Nicholas in the Central Middlesex Hospital, was forced to 'swat' cockroaches crawling on her bedside locker.

At this point I feel a comparison can be made with the events and actions taken to combat an outbreak of septicaemia in the 'Burns Unit' at the Mt Vernon Hospital in Northwood in Middlesex. The Hospital was on my allotted District when I was employed by Ruislip–Northwood District Council.

The causative organism was 'Staphylococcus Aureus,' the ancestor of the aforementioned 'Super Bug', as dangerous then as it is considered to be nowadays. This was especially so in a 'Burns Unit' where the wounds are so open to infection.

At the request of the Hospital Authorities and after due consideration by all of the responsible officers it was decided to close the ward entirely and move the patients out of harm's way while an effort was made to sterilise the ward. This was the problem that I and our 'General Factotum' Albert Cox were faced with. Albert was a very valued employee within the Department being, as he was, responsible for all disinfections, disinfestations (apart from rodents) and domestic drain clearances. He was also the Mortuary Attendant liable to be called upon at any time of the day or night to wash and layout the bodies of those who were victims of sudden death. Just two incidents will bear witness to his valued and under-rated services to the community.

The Station Master at West Ruislip Station crossed over the Main Line between platforms one misty night and never heard the approaching West Country Express on its final non-stop run into Paddington Station. The remains of his body were transported to the Mortuary at Northwood where in the middle of the night Albert proceeded to do his best to make them presentable. Not something to dwell upon.

The other occasion occurred as the result of a dreadful road accident when a mother and some children died when their car was demolished by a drunken hit-and-run driver. Albert did not have enough permanent 'slabs' in the small mortuary for the four bodies but knew that one small child 'belonged' to the mother. He managed to put them together instead of rigging up a trestle table in the corner of the room.

I mentioned his 'value' to the community. Priceless to my mind, but unappreciated in local authority terms. He was for instance paid one shilling per incident 'danger money' for dealing with wasps' nests. A stipulation was made that this payment could only be made if the nest was 'inside', the inference being that Albert had a chance of legging it down the road should he enrage the 4,000 or so creatures before the insecticide took effect. In my innocence I once had the temerity to question his claim for a shilling for dealing with a nest at the site of a rolled up piece of old lino propped against the side of a garden shed. He was a good friend and treated me kindly for my impertinence by calmly stating that the wasps had been seen 'Inside' the rolled up lino.

We agreed that the best way to tackle the Mt Vernon problem was to spray, nay, drench everything in sight within the ward, working from the far end and sealing all doors and windows behind us as we went. We used a neat formalin/formaldehyde standard commercial preparation with 4-Oaks Pressure Sprays. Since face masks and breathing apparatus were not even thought about let alone supplied, protective clothing was limited to overalls and gloves. Under these conditions we dashed in and out holding our breath wherever possible and with streaming eyes we steadily fought our way through the ward. Every item of bedding, equipment, tables, chairs, desks, drawers, lockers, lamp shades, loo seats, wc pans and so on until the final sealing strips were in place. Notices were placed in position stating that the ward was to be left untouched for 21 days, when we would return to unseal it. The Laboratory Technicians then took samples of the air and swabs for analysis. It worked successfully and all the results indicated a 'sterile' environment. The Ward was re-opened and the patients suffering from burns were returned without fear of further septic problems arising.

One thing that recurs in these narratives and retrospections is the thought that I have given the impression that it was a somewhat callous age of actions rather than a considered, compassionate and 'caring' world which is supposed to be the norm today.

This seems to me to be stretching things too far. There is no longer the freedom to act which one used to have. All public officials now look over their collective shoulders in case they ignore the health and safety implications, the compensation culture of society at large, the political correctness of their words and actions and so on. It stifles objectivity and resolution of problems with which in the 'old days' one was expected to cope.

The disease of 'Anthrax' is a case in point. Known for many years as 'Woolsorters Disease' it was brought under control as an imported infection by the simple expedient of passing all animal hides through the cleansing stations established at the major ports, particularly Liverpool. It was a disease which was respected rather than feared, in a public health sense, being very rare as a human infection in 99% of the population, and even then it was confined to people employed in certain trades. Admittedly it could be found in animals in all parts of the country, usually because of what were known as 'Anthrax Fields'. These were agricultural holdings where animals had died unexpectedly and suddenly overnight later were confirmed as Anthrax.

The usual symptom with which all farmers in those days seemed familiar was dark red blood trickling and congealing in small quantities from the orifices, whereupon the Ministry of Agriculture veterinary officers would be contacted. Blood slides would be taken for analysis and the provisional diagnosis made. If positive the problem of disposal of the carcass would be handed back to the owner in conjunction with the local authority District Sanitary Inspector, this to prevent any harm coming to the general public. The causative organism lived quite 'happily' in the bloodstream but once the blood was exposed to the air it transformed itself into a spore-forming organism which then became a dangerous airborne infection.

The problem of the disposal primarily became one of containment because there was no way in which the carcass could be opened and chopped up into smaller parts for easier handling because of the blood release. There were therefore only two ways in which disposal could be carried out. One was to bury the body *in situ* in a 6 ft-deep pit of quick lime. Since the anthrax bacillus could remain dormant for up to 15 years this could and did result from time to time in the so-called 'Anthrax Fields' spawning a further case many years after the original had been forgotten. The second way was to incinerate it.

This always created problems for the burning took place in the open and could last for many hours, depending upon the fuel feeding the fire, since a body will not combust naturally. In discussions someone came up with the idea that the local TA might be willing to become involved, as they had 'Flame Throwers' but no practice targets! The suggestion proved fruitful and the Army duly created the inferno necessary reducing the carcass to fine and harmless ash in the process. Because of the speed no neighbours complained of the smoke and smell. Primed as people are by television and the press this could not happen today. Compensation would be sought immediately any sniff of the fumes produced a reaction in the claimant ranging from asthma to peptic ulcers and from dried eyeballs to over production of earwax. In addition of course there is the (minimal) threat of a terrorist involvement to frighten people even further.

Two other hostelries that I remember with some affection near Bromsgrove were The Bell at Belbroughton with its lovely ingle-nook fireplace where the fires in midwinter were heart-warming affairs and The Chateau Impney where two Great Danes complemented the scene, stretched out as they were on the hearth. A third one was The Stewpony Hotel and Roadhouse at Kinver near Stourbridge. Pam's brother, who was recovering from a nasty bout of pneumonia and convalescing in Bromsgrove, came with us to the hotel for dining and dancing when I celebrated success in the Meat and Other Foods Examination taken in Liverpool the previous month.

Armed with enough qualifications and accompanied by a wife and 9-month old son I moved down to a new job in the Greater London Area as a District Public Health Inspector, as by then the ancient title of 'Sanitary Inspector' had been changed, although it was retained in Scotland for many years afterwards. The original was 'Inspector of Nuisances' dating from the 1834 Public Health Act, changed in the 1857 Act to 'Sanitary Inspector'.

You see what I mean about being an 'ancient title'. The employing authority was Ruislip–Northwood Urban District Council. With a population of 65,000 it lay on the western edge of London suburbia in the County of Middlesex. It was July 1959 and we were destined to stay there until 1965 when the Local Authority landscape was altered for ever. The London Boroughs were created – 'Big' being thought beautiful by the Government of the day – and Ruislip–Northwood UDC was amalgamated with Hayes and Harlington UDC, Yiewsley and West Drayton UDC, and Uxbridge Borough Council to form the new London Borough of Hillingdon.

When I joined R–NUDC I was allocated the Northwood end of the district, a comparatively wealthy area with a large number of beautiful Victorian villas and modern equivalents. The district also contained rows of council houses and terraced properties in other parts. Like the district the duties, while very similar throughout, demanded differing types of management.

A blocked drain from a council house with effluent spilling out onto the pavement triggered one urgent reaction and a plaintive complaint from the Secretary of the Northwood Golf Club that his members were complaining that their balls were covered in oil after being deposited in the stream crossing the course met with quite another. In this particular event it took four days of back tracking through the storm water system, with some manholes up to 20 ft in depth, before it could be ascertained that the problem was caused by a leak from the cracked feed pipe of a 1,000 gallon tank serving the oil-fired central heating system of one of the aforesaid Victorian villas.

The hundreds of properties throughout the urban district meant that drainage and its problems took up a great deal of time, the other chief problem areas being rodent control and food safety. I have already mentioned Albert Cox and his undoubted service to the community, but it won't be a bad thing to do so again. To be called upon at any time of the day or night to attend to his mortuary duties was one difficult task which could be compounded by an arduous and difficult blocked drainage system. In this respect the bane of his life was the newly-invented disposable nappy being flushed down the WC. Young mothers seemed to interpret the title as being 'dissolvable nappies' and this patently was not the case and they produced an endless stream of difficult-to-remove obstacles in the drains and sewers. One memorable such was the total blockage of a vertical soil vent pipe some 40 ft high and serving about six flats. Normally but with some difficulty one could 'pull' the items through from the manhole at the base, rather like extracting a cork from a bottle, obviously using the proper tools. In the case I remember there was a severe frost and ice and icicles covered all the pipes, which were frozen solid, as were the contents. The solution? Cut the whole pipe and remove it with solid contents to the tip. Replace unit. Two days work.

In 1961 the Rivers Pollution Prevention Act came into being and the Inspectors of the Thames Conservancy Board were given powers to enforce it. This entailed pinpointing sources of pollution throughout the catchment area and securing the assistance of the local authority in resolving such problems.

One can well imagine the vastness of the undertaking as the river is one of the longest in the British Isles. For Ruislip–

Northwood UDC the problems were relatively simple as most of the suburban building work had been carried out in the 1920s and 30s. In other words relatively modern drainage with few Victorian sewers to contend with. The majority of problems entailed cross-connections where foul water drains had been connected to storm water ones. The result would be an intermittent discharge into the nearest stream which, ultimately poured into the Thames tributaries. Multiply this by many thousands and one gets some idea of pollution levels of the main river, particularly in its lower reaches through the London Docks which were still in existence and very busy. Our most intractable problem resulted in me crawling through a 4 ft storm water sewer to identify a foul connection some distance away from the manhole in the road.

We departed for Africa in September 1965. That same year a trial 'fish' was held in the Pool of London (Docklands) where only eels had been caught since the Nineteenth Century, so polluted was the river at that point. Many anglers with rod and line sat upon the quaysides at the invitation of the Conservancy Board to see whether it was possible to catch fish. At the end of the experiment a total of 150 had been caught, the largest weighing just four ounces. This might not seem a great event to many people BUT please remember that these were the first ones to be caught in over a century. It made our small contribution from the urban area seem wholly worthwhile.

What made the whole of the six years that we spent in Ruislip really worthwhile was for Pam to give birth to two lovely children, our daughter Victoria and our youngest son Matthew on 30 June, 1960 and 23 May, 1963, respectively. We felt that it was a particularly good place for families to develop in those days with both medical care and education well taken care of. Good friends and colleagues there were aplenty, and although the immediate 'Boss' Eric Jenkins was a somewhat weak character, the Department functioned well enough. I even found the time to complete a further part of my professional qualifications, namely the Diploma in Atmospheric Pollution which I undertook at Tottenham Technical College. As the crow flies it is miles away from Ruislip across North London and it really is a tiresome journey, especially two or three times a week throughout the winter months. The course was developed following the appalling effects of the dreadful 'Smogs' of 1952, which lasted 10 days (when 4,000 people died), and 1954. The Clean Air Act of 1956 gave the local authorities power to create 'Smokeless Zones' within their areas in which only smokeless fuels could be burned. The first of these was the City of London. It is difficult at this distance in time for people to realise just how 'black' the major cities and many towns were. Centuries of industrial emissions from railways, factories, mills, power stations and so on resulted in layer upon layer of congealed soot which in many instances destroyed the stone fabric of ancient and beautiful buildings. The main culprits in this, believe it or not, were the millions of houses burning soft bituminous coal as well as all kinds of household rubbish. One can see even today the thousands of chimneys protruding from old terraced properties, tenements and lofty town houses in all the districts of the British Isles. It was not for nothing that London gained its nickname of 'The Smoke' and Edinburgh 'Auld Reekie', of which a picture taken in the late forties shows one chimney protruding above a pall of smoke which successfully blots out the entire city!

It has taken years to 'recover' the lost cities, and what splendours have been revealed. Most notably in the heart of London where proudly stand the cleaned and restored Houses of Parliament whose beautiful buildings were, when I first worked there, was a totally black hulk.

After six relatively pleasant years it became time to move on, not initially through personal choice but because of the staffing implications of the new Borough.

To explain. When the London Boroughs were formed there was a 'No Redundancy' Agreement with the Unions concerned. On a professional level it meant that all senior staff retained their status and their posts, albeit under a different name. It became a situation whereby the four Chiefs and four Deputies of the Public Health Departments of the respective Authorities were appointed to posts of at least similar ranks, thereby blocking the way to promotion for the District Inspectors for, as I saw it, at least five years before the oldest of them retired. Hence my search for another post.

PART 2

The African Years – 1965–80

CHAPTER 2

Zambia 1965–74

WHILST THERE WERE plenty of jobs advertised none caught my imagination as one seen in January of 1965. A newly created Ministry of Overseas Development had a greatly enhanced role and budget to assist in the emergence of former colonies into the rarefied air of 'Freedom and Independence', the political rallying cries of the day. Since the 'Wind of Change' speech to the South African Parliament in Capetown in 1960 by the then British Prime Minister, Harold MacMillan, there had been a release of liberal feeling within Britain for the UK Government to grant the independence sought by so many countries. As a result of this, in 1965 'Zambia' came into being after the break up of the Federation of Rhodesia and Nyasaland, or the Central African Federation, as it was more commonly known.

Its constituent parts of the Rhodesias and Nyasaland became the independent countries of Zambia (Northern Rhodesia) and Malawi (Nyasaland), but the Self-Governing Colony of Southern Rhodesia remained just that, which from years of retrospection and observation was a sad mistake to make. The massive influx of international aid into countries which had neither the qualified staff nor the infrastructure to absorb it together with newly empowered politicians' scramble for the lucrative jobs on offer laid the foundations for the 'Rape of the Fair Country', as one author had it.

Be that as it may in 1964 there was a post available in Zambia on a 3-year contract basis and I was offered it; so in September 1965 myself, my wife and three young children – Simon (aged 7) Victoria (aged 5) and Matthew (aged 2) left England for pastures new to take part in the exciting developments taking place in Zambia. Brain-washed politically as I now consider we were, we went out with the feeling that the downtrodden majority population, i.e. black, had been badly treated by the Colonial oppressors, i.e. white settlers, and that we would take part in a great resurgence of political advancement, ably assisted by numerous International Aid Programmes and Western 'know how' and techniques.

The reality was somewhat different. It is difficult to disagree with the crude comments so often expressed that if an African cannot 'eat it, drink it or stuff it he'll fucking break it'. In political terms, although I am no politician, one can think of calm, peaceful, well-run countries under the control of dedicated officials of the Colonial Services which when once given independence rapidly degenerated into a hot-bed of large scale looting of the National Treasuries and where the weaker sections and tribes of the countries concerned went to the wall. Ghana (Kwame Nkrumah), Uganda (Milton Obote and Idi Amin), Tanzania (Julius Nyerere), Congo (Tsombe), Angola, Mozambique and as I write, Zimbabwe, have all gone the same way, including the one with which I am most familiar, Zambia, and where I completed three 3-year contracts. The President was Kenneth Kaunda. Under his political control and 'Humanist' philosophies the downward spiral was set into motion. In those nine years I witnessed not only the economic ruin of the country but also the constant bleat that it was not 'Independence' that was at fault but 'Colonialism' itself. Therefore it required ever more international and United Nations Aid led by the former colonial power, Great Britain, or as it was rapidly shortened to 'the UK'.

The best analogy that I can make is to relate a conversation that I had with a Senior Health Assistant, Lefan Kamfwa, in my final posting in the little town of Kawambwa in the northern part of the Luapula Province. Prior to Independence there had been a European Sports and Social Club in the centre which adjoined the Government Offices (Boma). To call it by its grand sounding title is one thing. The reality was somewhat different. A 9-hole golf course had been laid out, a couple of tennis courts likewise and a one-room clubhouse with bar and loos had been built. All of this had been steadily created over the years by the European community which had diminished rapidly as the Zambianisation programme took effect. The club closed, the newly created Rural Council Offices were built over part of the golf course, which untended reverted to its roots as part of the 'Bush'.

The European dominated clubs became subsidiary targets for the 'Zambianisation' programme. Even the churches were not immune and certainly the powerful parts of Government, i.e. the Police and Army, were rapidly reorganised regardless of the qualifications and experience of the promoted. For instance the Commissioner of Police was a large and imposing African of the Bemba-speaking majority plus a card-carrying UNIP member. He had been held at the rank of Sergeant in Colonial days but this was rapidly glossed over and was considered a failure of the old system and not because of any defect in his character or mental capacity to do the job.

A new District Governor in Kawambwa determined that the near derelict clubhouse and overgrown golf course should be reinstated and approached Lefan Kamfwa to undertake the task. He refused point-blank, which was astonishing in that the Governor was the top UNIP party man and political boss to boot. He was annoyed that his wishes could be so thwarted but took no serious action against Lefan, although he was not of local stock but hailed from the Eastern Province where he had been serving in the little town of Petauke in 1964.

Lefan confided to me that he had taken the action he had because of events at the Petauke Club once the Africans gained control. He freely admitted that Africans did not know anything about 'European Clubs' and his experience of being a committee member had soured him for life. He explained that all his fellow members thought that once elected they would be members for free and that any profits made from the bar were the entitlements of the committee. In other words if these amounted to a case of beer then the committee were entitled to drink the same. 'How long did the Club last?' I asked. 'Six months,' he said, and because of the missing assets there was a police investigation but the Club remained closed probably for ever. This was a tragic end for all concerned, not least the founder (European) members of some 50 years earlier.

Abercorn, Kasama and the Northern Province

The little town lay some 30 miles from the southern tip of Lake Tanganyika and its port of Mpulungu. It was called Abercorn, originally Fort Abercorn, but within five years it would be renamed 'Mbala' by the new Zambian Government. I always knew it as Abercorn – still do for that matter. The area I was supposed to administer in a preventive health sense – 'prevention' being better than 'cure' – was about the size of half of Europe and was composed of three districts of the Northern Province, namely Mporokoso, Abercorn and Isoka. Quite clearly a combined 'District' of that size needed an army of similarly qualified officers by European standards. In that vast area the population was sparse, which told against such schemes, and the result was that there were but two of us, the other being Nick MacPhail in (Provincial) Headquarters, Kasama. He it was who had greeted Pam and me on the dusty airfield there as we disembarked from the Central African Airways DC3 (Dakota). On the one-hour stopover he told us the news that he had only received advance notice of our arrival that morning! A somewhat disconcerting start to our African venture. However he also assured us that by great good fortune the telephone line to the North, i.e. Abercorn, had been re-opened, allowing him to communicate with the Mother Superior (Marie Therese), the Matron, who administered the hospital with her team of White Sisters. She was as much in the dark about our arrival as MacPhail had been, but having had the benefit of a few hours' notice one could only hope that some sort of arrangement would have been put in hand to accommodate us.

In the event we lived for the first 10 days in Abercorn in The Grasshopper Inn where the proprietor, Anne Parton, was a wonderful help and solace to us. Nothing was too much trouble and we were even privileged to be introduced to her fabulous and famous Grey Parrot, which had the most extraordinary range of language, both sacred and profane, ever heard.

The Grasshopper Inn had originally been the Rest House for the visiting staff of the Red Locust Control Service, of which the town was headquarters. Ground spraying for the pre-flight forms of the locusts (hoppers) occupied three months of the year in the breeding area of the Rukwa Valley in Tanganyika (now Tanzania). A change in policy meant that aerial spraying using light planes and helicopters was the preferred option, being much more efficient and cheaper. Hence there was no longer a need for large teams of sprayers, mainly University students on vacation employment, to be used. It was much regretted by the local traders but in a social sense was no doubt to be welcomed. The other 'watering holes', apart from those dispensing the native beer 'Chibuku' in the African townships, were The Abercorn Arms and the Club. These took the brunt of the onslaught by numerous 'three-month thirsty', no doubt, virile, young men. The phrase 'Lock up your daughters' springs to mind. The Grasshopper Inn had been bought or was leased by the Partons once it became surplus to requirements by the Locust Organisation.

Anne's husband, Peter, had left the Locust Control Service at about the same time and had taken over a local garage. Peter was a marvellously skilled and dedicated mechanical engineer who had built himself a 'sea-going' boat to cope with such conditions on the nearest inland sea, Lake Tanganyika. Capable of carrying a dozen passengers, its main purpose was to provide a 'water taxi' service between Mpulungu and the Game Lodges at Kasaba Bay. In this respect I was lucky enough to travel there on the boat just once, which was a splendid day out.

The quickest way from Abercorn was to fly there by un-scheduled and private flights. Shortly after our arrival Pam and I were lucky enough to be invited to do exactly this on a privately owned Cessna. Our lasting memories of the afternoon visit, apart from the pleasure of first-time flying in such a small four-seater aircraft was (a) the buzzing of the 'Bush' airstrip to clear the antelopes off it prior to landing and (b) sitting under a wonderfully large, shady and thatched rondavel built with a dwarf wall surrounding it. We were having tea and biscuits with the owners, some six of us in total, when from the edge of the encampment and very silently came an African elephant! Our first ever WILD ONE! I make the point 'silently' because when one comprehends its size, and truly in close-up they are very large indeed, they can come and go with such silent and graceful movement that one tends to doubt one's visual senses.

Our hosts assured us that the animal could get no further than the dwarf wall and was merely seeking some food, preferably a variety of fruit. We were to learn that they are very partial to the nuts of the Marula Tree when in season but which have the unfortunate effect of fermenting in their capacious stomachs, thus causing a mild case of intoxication with its attendant hangovers.

This one having raised its trunk and explored every possibility of a free meal, simply raised it one more time, snorted, one felt in disgust, flapped its huge ears at us and . . . vanished. One moment it was there pivoting delicately on its padded feet and then it had gone, slipping silently down the alleyway between the guests' rondavels. No wonder they were enjoined not to venture forth without checking thoroughly that there were no animals lurking around.

Whilst my wife and I had already fallen for Africa within a month of arriving, this one afternoon clinched it for us. From then on we were committed, and simply 'felt' for this huge and magnificent continent with all its attendant joys and sorrows. In retrospect I suppose it was something akin to the marriage vows – for better for worse, for richer for poorer, in sickness and in health and so on. Certainly we have never wavered in our affection, and prayed for it to recover what should be its proud and rightful status in the world. Unscrupulous politicians, the stifling international politicising and bureaucracy, coupled with the indifference of the Western World and rapaciousness of the Third has crippled it and our hopes for its future are 'such stuff as dreams are made of'. Someone once said to us – probably an old Settler – that there was nothing wrong with Central Africa that 30 million Europeans would not cure. In the light of the post-independence political feeding frenzy it would be difficult to disagree with such sentiments.

One huge factor was the international influence wielded by the United States, to which 'Colonialism' was a word associated with Satanism and the Mongol Hordes. This conveniently overlooks the treatment accorded the American Indians, or is this too cynical a view?

I had been briefed by the Chief EHO in the Ministry of Health in Lusaka as to my duties and responsibilities in Zambia, the post having been sponsored as part of the post-independence aid programme agreed by the respective Governments. 'Brief' is as near as one can get to the instructions I received:

Fly north via Ndola and Kasama to Abercorn where you will be met and housed by the hospital authorities. Last year there were 2,000 cases of smallpox in the Northern, Eastern and Luapula Provinces and whilst at the moment it seems to be under control there is a large-scale vaccination programme in place which will take precedence over all other commitments. It is being funded by the World Health Organisation through the medical services but you will organise and spearhead the work of the vaccination teams in your designated districts. By the way, there was a civil insurrection last year prior to Independence and fighting took place between various political parties, particularly the ANC and UNIP. There is therefore a Refugee Camp outside Abercorn, but people are steadily being re-settled back in their homes. I believe that there are only some two to five thousand left, so there shouldn't be any further trouble. Off you go then and I will see you at the end of your contract in 3 years' time.

I was to find that I had no office, no clerical staff and no transport. A rude awakening to the realities of health service priorities.

One confusing thing which as a newcomer from Europe was an obvious pitfall was the business of what constitutes 'Black' and 'White' in an African context. For instance, the 'White Sisters' were called that because of the 'White' robes that they wore and not because they were of European origin. Similarly the 'White Fathers' who ran many of the mission schools, churches and mission agricultural stations were called that because of their dress and not because of the colour of their skins. Another word which caused confusion to us was 'Coloured' a polite euphemism for 'Black' in the liberal-orientated society of 1960s England. This was before the world decided that 'Black is Beautiful'. This political scenario had been sparked by Harold MacMillan's 'Wind of Change' speech to the South African Parliament, heralding a policy of de-colonisation throughout the Commonwealth. We were quickly disabused of our views, since unbeknown to us there was a large section of the population throughout Central Africa, but particularly in South Africa, whence the problem originated, called 'Coloureds'. This arose because of the mixed breeding between the original seafarers and settlers and the native population. Over the centuries, since Jan van Reebeck founded Capetown in 1652, a sizeable community had developed, steadily spreading to the north following the railways and the mining developments, from its origins and roots on the southern coast of the continent

Another difficulty which we never got to grips with was the complexity of the African languages. Suffice to say that in 15 years in Africa both in Zambia and Malawi, neither my wife nor myself learned anything other than a smattering of any one of them. One might well say 'What a waste' and you would be quite correct in your views. It is indeed a sincere and lasting regret, but one could claim certain mitigating circumstances apart from the obvious ones of family, social and sporting commitments. For instance we were always on three-year contract terms and not permanent settlers. The postings I had (nine different ones in nine years) in Zambia, the complexities of the languages themselves, the lack of teachers, the fact that in Zambia alone there were seven major languages and 86 dialects. At the University of Malawi all teaching was in English which the students had to study to degree level. Dr Hastings Banda was the President there and his view was that whilst the local languages would suffice within the country English was the only one which would be recognised internationally, hence the policy.

In the days when there was a separate Colonial Office in London many were the young men recruited to serve the Colonies overseas where they became 'Cadet' District Officers for a period of probation before being thought of as mature enough to administer a District of their own. This would have entailed a knowledge of the language and there were bars upon the promotion ladder until both written and oral language examinations had been passed. In addition to this one must never forget the part played by the dedication of the missionaries and their mission stations as well as the much derided 'White Settlers', without whom the countries that I knew would never have been developed at all! They and their children learned originally out of sheer necessity and their descendants learned as children will from their parents and the house servants as well as the village children.

In the 1960s there was a quite famous (for its time) Sunday night television interview show hosted by John Freeman. Sir Roy Welensky, President of the Central African Federation (Northern and Southern Rhodesia and Nyasaland), was in London for political negotiations which would ultimately entail massive changes for both the countries involved and their inhabitants. Sir Roy had come from humble beginnings in Broken Hill where he and his father had been employed on the railways. From there he had made his way into the political arena via the Trade Unions.

His reply to a question by John Freeman stunned both the interviewer and the watching nation as to its implied appeal to common sense after all the political rhetoric and hot air spoken at Lancaster House during the previous week.

The question was 'Sir Roy, do you understand the African mind?' His reply was 'Considering I swam bare-arsed with the local children in the Mlobezi River as a youngster then Yes I do.' Swear words were never used on the BBC or come to that in society. but the times were against Sir Roy and merely confirmed what everybody had been indoctrinated with, that 'White Settlers' were a coarse ill-educated land-grabbing lot who were not capable of running a pig farm let alone a national and independent government. On the other hand that obviously well-educated and groomed (token) African, smoothly and charmingly stating the case for 'Freedom', was being deprived of his national inheritance. It only remained for Sir Ian MacLeod, the Colonial Secretary and International bridge player, to enter the fray and run political rings around Sir Roy and his advisers for the Federation to be broken up.

One tended when touring to rely upon the skills of the African staff for interpretation purposes and inevitably the long-suffering driver bore the brunt of this. The gods were kind to me when Simon Chiwaya was seconded from the hospital pool of such personnel and worked with me throughout the year I spent in the Northern Province both in Abercorn and Kasama. The battered Land Rover I was 'grudgingly' allocated may have been temperamental, spending more time in the Government Workshops than it was ever on the road, but Simon did a marvellous job in coaxing it over the dirt roads, which became mudbaths in the rains and quagmires over the worst low-lying 'dambo' areas. In the dry seasons the roads were badly rutted and potholed with thick dust problems being presented by the flying wheels of the vehicles. This was of particular concern when overtaking a large truck and trailer churning the dust with anything up to 22-wheels!

For much of our Zambian sojourn Simon's younger brother, Peter, became our much loved and respected house servant. Both brothers were Bemba speaking and hailed from the Luapula province near to Samfya on Lake Bangwelu and could interpret most dialects into passable English for their 'Bwana', a term much derided in a modern context but which simply meant 'White Man' in its original form and became the equivalent in African terms of 'Sir' in English.

To overcome many of the difficulties of communication, particularly on the mines where safety was of paramount importance, a 'man-made' language was developed. All the employees could learn it and understand each other no matter what their native language. Somewhat akin to 'Esperanto' it was called 'Chilapalapa' or 'Kitchen Kaffir'. Even so, difficulties still arose over either interpretation or whatever it was thought had been said. Two incidents spring to mind.

The first concerned two recent recruits to the country employed in the Copper Refinery in Ndola who came from the north of England. A bar in the city centre was a Saturday night 'watering hole'. One of them called for more drinks from the Barman, addressing him as 'Gaffer', the noted English term for a 'boss'. The Barman thought he said 'Kaffir' . . . Near riot, police involvement, deportations threatened, etc. etc. 'Kaffir' is another word much departed from its original Arabic of 'Unbeliever'.

The other incident concerned the elderly, straight-laced and very religious lady visiting her son, my boss, the Provincial Medical Officer, Harry Bwanausi. In the local mission church on the Sunday morning in the little town of Solwezi, near to the Congolese Border, a collection was made during the service. Each time the girl carrying out the task said to each parishioner 'Thank You' in the local language. To the old lady it sounded very much like a very rude and coarse word of a sexual nature in her own South African dialect. Grossly offended and believing that her son was living amongst a tribe of barbarians she decamped the following day and high-tailed it back home

Some years later when I lived in Malawi I remember that I was lecturing to some students at the Polytechnic about sewers and drainage systems. I answered a question with extremely careless colloquial, not to say Cockney rhyming slang. I said in answer (the question doesn't matter) 'Well in that case you must use your loaf!' As soon as I said it I realised what I had done and the damage caused. The looks on their faces said it all – 'He's got a baker stuffed in the manhole somewhere. How did we miss it?' One must remember that the students came mainly from latrine dominated territory in the villages and main drainage systems were always a mystery. It was impossible to explain away but I dug a hole in trying. Such misunderstandings highlight particularly the problems faced by newcomers to the country but could also inflict themselves upon the local people when a ripple effect could involve many who were not party to the original act.

The main road to the east from Abercorn wended its way to the Nakonde – Mwenso International Border Post with Tanzania, a grand title for such a dusty place where gathered many waiting, often for many days, for battered, travel-girt and diesel-stinking buses. The road then divided and whilst the eastward bound one travelled on to Arusha and beyond the Zambian part swung at right angles to the south on the way down the border to Isoka. It is patently obvious that with such a long international border bestrewn with small villages and inhabited by many thousands of people, a thorough and complete Smallpox Vaccination Programme would be undertaken with immense difficulty, in any case without any hiccup occurring which might disturb the local inhabitants.

There were half-a-dozen teams of native vaccinators working in the area of the Nakonde-Mwenso Border Crossing led by a Sanitary Orderly called John Banda. They all had bicycles and endeavoured to vaccinate all inhabitants and travellers as they slowly wended their way along the border. Since they had to cover all schools and buses and trucks and villages and bush tracks crossing the border you will appreciate that these up-market labourers very often became careless and bored and 'tired' – particularly as pay-day neared. The work could in no instance proceed unless there was the support of the local Chief and his village Headmen plus the UNIP Councillor for the District. There was therefore an on-going need for these 'permissions' to be in place prior to the approach of the team doing the work. Something went wrong when the team led by Banda came to a small village where there were only women and children present, the men being away in the fields or so it was said. I always thought that they were probably away on a beer-drink!

When the team of strangers suddenly appeared there was a rush of the villagers into the nearby 'Bush' and in the chaos one of the women dropped a basket of finger millet, a poor substitute of the staple diet of maize (mealie) and probably the equivalent of cassava. The basket was collected by John Banda and taken back to his main tented camp some miles away.

Two days later the law caught up with Banda and he was locked up in the jail at the Police Station at Nakonde charged with stealing the millet. Being a hundred miles away in Abercorn I was unaware of the problem until a week later when a message arrived stating that the case would be heard at the Local Native Court presided over by the (ranking) Chieftainess Waitwika. Since word of the theft had spread and had lost nothing in the telling, all vaccinators were now regarded as thieves and vagabonds. In short the work had come to a standstill. My presence was therefore thought to be necessary when the case was to be heard.

One further complication was that the case would be heard in the local language of 'Namwanga' which even my driver, Simon, found very difficult being, as was most of the staff, Bemba-speaking. Because of the added problem we travelled on the day of the case to Mwenso Hospital, ten miles from Nakonde, and picked up the elderly and respected Principal Medical Assistant, who had lived all his life in the area.

The 'Court' was held, not in a formal court building, but at Chieftainess Waitwika's village. She sat under a large and very shady tree where, once she had been told of who and what I was and of my interest in the case, she asked me in her excellent English to join her. I was glad to do so because it was extremely hot and I had been only three months in the country and was barely acclimatised.

It was obvious at the outset who was in charge. The command-ing presence of the lady was daunting to all and sundry. She stood no nonsense from anyone, even the UNIP Councillor who thought he could make an entrance into the case but was told to sit on the ground along with everyone else. She was quite a remarkable being. Her presence came about because when the Colonial International Borders were being drawn up the line cut through the Paramount Chief's Authority. He had no option but

1. The author in 1935

COUNTY BOROUGH OF GRIMSBY.

EDUCATION COMMITTEE.

This is to Certify that LILY PORRITT was awarded a BURSARY IN 1917. VALUE THREE POUNDS AND FREE TUITION, tenable for One Year at the Municipal College, Wintringham Secondary School, in accordance with the terms and conditions of the Scheme of Scholarships for the above County Borough.

(Signed)

Chairman of the Education Committee.

Clerk of the Education Committee.

2. Mother was 14 when she was awarded this bursary. The same year she left the school to look after the family

3. *Grimsby in prosperous times*

4. The author aged 9 years

5. Unloading the catch at Grimsby Docks

6. *The Tonge Family in 1943: Lily and Dick; Betty, David (author), Joan and Rita*

7. *RAMC Depot, Crookham 1955. The author is 3rd from left, back row*

8. Wedding of David and Pam, London 1957

9. Simon and Victoria with their friends the Taylor children in our front garden at Abercorn. Frangipani bushes at the rear

10. The White Sisters, Abercorn. Sister Benedicta 2nd from right

11. Peter Chiweya, our much-loved house servant

12. The Theatre in Lusaka

to put a subordinate Chief in the Northern Rhodesian (Zambian) part. This would normally have been one of his sons but he believed that the only person he could trust was his daughter and the custom had carried on, the present Chieftainess being the granddaughter of the original. The Paramount Chief stayed in Tanzania.

The case hinged upon whatever mitigating circumstances John Banda could produce. The facts themselves were not in dispute and fortunately the goods concerned were still in existence and produced as evidence to the Court. Banda claimed that he had taken the millet as he believed that the woman accompanied by her friends and relatives would come to his camp and he would then be able to vaccinate them all. This was accepted by the Court since the millet had not been used. As Banda had spent a couple of weeks inside it was considered that this was sufficient punishment but a recommendation was made that he should be moved to a different District if the work was to continue. The Chieftainess decreed that if this was done she would send her messengers out essentially to tell the local population that 'Vaccination is Good for You'. With that we adjourned to her large, thatched veranda for refreshments. There she plied me with questions about London, which she longed to visit, and in anticipation of which she possessed a large tourist poster dominated by a red London bus. Her only reservation was that she had heard that it was very cold and wet. I tried to explain the 'Four Season' scenario as against the 'Two' (Wet and Dry) persisting in Zambia. Whether she understood completely is doubtful but I certainly made her laugh when I mimed all the clothes I would normally wear in a severe winter in England. We strolled around her plentiful garden from which she picked a bag of crossed orange/lemon fruit for my wife. She was very kind and certainly was a most memorable character.

Whilst this was an eventful experience my next trip along the same road was to prove even more character forming as the modern idiom has it. It started as a Pay Run destined to terminate in Isoka some 120 miles distant, necessitating leaving at daybreak, or as the locals had it 'Sparrow Fart'. The first part went well. There is after all nothing like an African sunrise. We arrived at a camp some twenty miles short of Mwenso, itself ten miles away from the border at Nakonde. There we found that the team needed to move down the road towards Abercorn. As we only had the Land Rover it was obvious that we could barely move the tents and baggage and that the bulk of the personnel would have to cycle to the new camp during the day. We arranged the pick-up for about 5 p.m. which was our ETA on the return journey.

Isoka was reached in mid-afternoon where the Asian doctor insisted on displaying his 'star' patient, a poor creature who was dying of rabies. A distressing experience as the man displayed the classic symptoms including, as the Doctor demonstrated, his hydrophobia or fear of water. In spite of the diversion we made good return time on the main road and reached the camp just as the sun was starting to fade. To my annoyance there was still one tent standing. I was informed that a vaccinator called 'Joseph' had gone for a rest and was still sleeping. Upon entering I shook the man only to get no response. Further examination revealed the man to be dead, although from what cause I never discovered. The only thing to be done was to take the body to the nearest hospital which was at Mwenso, so back up the road we journeyed with the body in the back. Once there the Principal Medical Assistant advised us to leave 'Joseph' in the mortuary and the business of informing his family would be undertaken by them the following morning, it now being entirely dark at about 8 p.m. So far so good and back down the road we went.

Upon arrival at the village to collect the goods and chattels of the team we found a crowd of villagers being stirred up by the local UNIP Councillor who was apparently miffed by not being included in the consultation prior to the body being taken to Mwenso Hospital. According to him I was displaying all the characteristics of 'Colonialism', 'Racialism', and was 'Anti-Zambian' into the bargain. To argue against the tirade with one's back pressed hard against the side of the Land Rover with a baying mob in one's face was a new experience and one not to be repeated. I could not see Simon in the dark but there was a sudden and urgent tug on my leg from somewhere down by the wheel-housing and an urgent plea from him that we would have to go back to the hospital. The correct thing for us to have done was to seek out

'Joseph's' village and take the body there immediately. This error we must now correct. At the hospital we were told that to arrive in the middle of the night with a dead body would be dangerous and that we must first take it to the police station at Nakonde. So back up the road we went.

Once there, it being now approaching midnight, the Inspector told me that the only way to deal with this was for me as a European to stay behind while a joint team of his staff and mine in two vehicles located Joseph's village, which fortunately was nearby, and informed his relatives of his death. It took about an hour before the vehicles arrived back. The body had been transferred to the police Land Rover and was to be transported to a burial site. As far as I remember I was introduced to a 'senior' relative whereupon I was told that it was customary for his employer to contribute to funeral expenses. Relieved of £2, Simon and I were free to go. 'Free' in the sense of being able to leave Nakonde for the 100-mile drive to Abercorn but not so 'free' in the responsibility we still had of moving the team fortunately nearer to our destination. It was still with a degree of apprehension that we approached the village, but all was quiet, the 'boys' patiently waiting by the remnants of the the dying campfire. Loaded to the eyeballs with tents and poles and bedding and equipment and with staff hanging on to the sides, we again set off at a steady ten miles per hour to the new campsite. What marvellous all-purpose vehicles those old 4-cylinder Land Rovers were. So rugged, durable, adaptable, and what was even more important in the African Bush – so easy to maintain.

Once back on the road I was to find one more hazard had to be faced before we finally got home at daybreak. There were rabbits on the road, and Simon by means of his skillful driving managed to hit eight of them, each time necessitating a stop to throw the body in the back. He was delighted to obtain so much free 'Nyama', but it was difficult for me to share his joy with so much delay being involved, but with no traffic on that road at such a late/early hour it was safe enough.

It did bring home to me the views expressed by older and wiser local inhabitants to start long journeys early and finish the day's work early, roughly between the hours of 6 a.m. and 4 p.m. This would leave about two hours of daylight for personal chores like seeking a bed for the night, whether it be a Government Rest House, a hotel, a night spent with friends or under canvas at some spot in the Bush.

Two instances should be enough to convince anyone that not a word of this advice is wrong. The first occasion that I can recall occurred on the long uphill portion of the road from the airport to the city, which apart from the last three miles was largely unlit. It 'climaxed' at the top of the escarpment that runs through the forest where the locals were allowed to hew timber to sell in the townships as either logs, firewood or charcoal. The transporting wagons were usually grossly overweight, bald of tyres, under-powered, ill-lit and covered on top with a load of hitchhikers, chickens, goats and a motley assortment of hired woodchoppers. To cap it all the tree trunks and long saplings protruded beyond the back end of the track, thus lying in wait like some medieval pike or lance ready to impale any vehicle unfortunate enough to be travelling on that section of winding road, particularly at night.

The man had just greeted his wife after her long flight from Europe. Suitcases were loaded into the back of the Peugeot and they set off on the last dozen miles home. Speeding at 65 mph with headlights full on the car came round the last bend before the street lights appeared. The lorry was travelling up the last of the incline at about 10 mph. The resultant crash killed the woman outright as one of the overhanging timbers speared her through the shattered windscreen. The man was badly shocked but being free of serious injury and as he came to his senses realised that the car was hooked up to the forest of protruding logs and tree trunks. It was being dragged along with its front wheels airborne and with the rear ones barely scraping along the tarmac.

With some difficulty he opened the driver's door sufficiently to escape and managed to stagger along the length of the towing truck to the African driver and his mates who were totally unaware of the tragedy at the rear. They were sufficiently alarmed by the white, bloodstained apparition screaming, shouting and banging at the door to bring the top heavy machine to a halt.

The second occasion was somewhat more pleasant in outcome but again the dangers of travelling by night become obvious. I had occasion to travel about a couple of hundred miles south in Central Africa. The distance was no problem but instead of getting away in early afternoon I was delayed in the office so could not set off with the family until about 4.30 p.m. We had made good progress until I drove out of the hills, crossed the Zambezi and climbed the escarpment on the far side of the river at about 7 p.m. after darkness had descended. Driving up the last of the hills I saw at the extreme limits of the headlights what looked to be a solid wall.

My immediate reaction was to brake and come to a standstill as I thought that a truck had overturned. Before I could get out of the car I realised that there was movement close to my side window. It turned out to be a herd of elephants crossing the road. It is disconcerting to say the least to find oneself in the midst of twenty or thirty of these huge beasts in broad daylight, but to come across them in the night is not to be recommended. It is sufficient to record that after all of 15 minutes trembling plus a further five for normality and heartbeats to stabilise we set off again upon the remainder of our journey.

Hospitals and the smallpox vaccination programme

It occurs to me that I have neither mentioned nor paid any kind of tribute to those hard working, dedicated and courageous missionaries commonly referred to as 'White Sisters' or 'White Fathers'. Defenceless and vulnerable, they were always prime targets for gangs of terrorists where shelter, food and medical supplies could be found at gunpoint. The atrocities carried out on these people throughout Central Africa and elsewhere are too well documented to need repeating, but one or two personal reminiscences will perhaps be found interesting.

It was just prior to Christmas and the rains had broken. The Doctors Taylor, John and Winifred from South Africa, newcomers like ourselves, we were entertaining to dinner. There had been a violent thunderstorm, which had passed, but the rain following it was torrential. A Land Rover came up the drive from the road and there came a knock on the door. There had been an accident and John was urgently required at the Hospital. Off he went and two hours later he had not returned. Winifred sensed that he might be needing help so I drove with her down the flooded road as the rain still streamed down. I should perhaps explain that there existed in those days in Abercorn both the main 50-bed hospital and a small converted bungalow which served for the few Europeans requiring hospital admittance, that was but rarely staffed. The differences in habits, food, lifestyles and so on were such that the only sensible and practical way was to separate the two peoples, even though the sicknesses and the treatments might be the same.

When we arrived at the main hospital we found that a car had skidded off the road and into a ditch, the driver suffering facial injuries, a broken arm and arterial bleeding from a cut on his head. He had somehow extricated himself from the car and was found by another motorist some quarter of a mile from the crash, totally exhausted and bemused at the height of the storm, going one knows not where but dangerously near to a fatal collapse.

The driver of the 'rescue' vehicle was a young schoolteacher who had been in the town but a day or two and had not the remotest idea as to the whereabouts of the hospital, his only points of contact being the school (five miles away), the Boma (closed), and the shops (closed), so that the Club (nearby and open) became the only choice. There he found one or two 'barflies' enjoying themselves, but all very anxious to help once they knew the seriousness of the situation. At the hospital the medical staff, realising the danger the patient was in, also discovered that his blood-group, whilst not exactly rare, was sufficiently uncommon to warrant a frantic search through the lists of local donors as no such type was found in the hospital. John's presence had been required at the outset.

The call at the Club and the phone calls to locate blood supplies had spread the word through the 'European' elements that an emergency was underway, the patient being a well-known local. The difficulties were greatly enhanced by the fact that Christmas was nigh and party time was the order of the night. The required donors were either out of town on holiday, at dinner elsewhere or were enjoying a party somewhere. As the word spread, non-donors began to arrive at the hospital with helpful suggestions as to the quality of their blood and reminiscences as to when it had been found to be the right sort some ten years' previously when

(You remember, Sister!) Fred fell out of the tree, or some other rich tale.

As the rain still continued to fall, so the outside veranda became a gathering point of the many good-hearted but semi-sozzled souls determined to do their bit to save the patient's life. The harassed medical staff, headed by John, who had been doing the necessary repair work in the Operating Theatre. The White Sisters were doing their level best to cope with the noisy and frequently raucous crowd on the veranda in addition to their normal duties.

Eventually the two or three pints of the right kind of blood were located and the patient's life was saved by the transfusion, but it had been a 'close run affair'. The problem then was to move the patient to the European Hospital.

The only vehicles available at the Hospital were Land Rovers, all of which had many miles behind them. The one true ambulance, also very 'weary', was back in the workshops for the umpteenth time, so we had to look elsewhere. The only vehicle which could manage it and was available in the car park belonged to a local trader, Arthur Landry, and was a large American Shooting Brake – a Dodge or Pontiac I think. Whatever the case there was just enough room for the patient and stretcher to fit into it.

The stretcher was carried from the Theatre, down the main corridor to the large outside veranda where Arthur's vehicle was backed-up to the steps. The noisy and vociferous crowd pressed on all sides and the patient added to the cacophony by declaiming in his semi-conscious state over and over again 'I want to piss, I want to piss . . .' although the necessity for this we never did discover. The duty nurse was, I believe, Sister Benedicta, although I seem to recall that Sister Romana was also around. As the patient reached the top of the steps, Sister Benedicta's quiet Irish reserve broke.

'Oh for God's sake, bloody piss!' she screamed. There was instant silence. It was as if the Angel of the North had turned into a Vampire Bat!! A subdued and nervous whispering took over from the previously loud declamations offered up by the crowd which now quietly began to disperse as Arthur gently drove the car away. The good Lord only knows how many Hail Marys Sister Benedicta

suffered as a penance but it can safely be said that the Mother
Superior, Marie Therese, was not best pleased, so I suppose that
Benedicta spent some portion of the following week on kitchen
fatigues.

One intriguing sight occurred when I first saw that Hospital. It
was the fact that it was surrounded by barbed wire. As was
explained later, it was there to keep the smallpox patients in rather
than the other way round, as they had a habit when they once felt
somewhat better to stroll off to the market and shops, spreading
cast off and dangerously infective scabs from their bodies as they
went. Did you know that the original 'Great Pox' was reckoned
to be venereal disease, probably syphilis, and that 'Small Pox' was
thought to be the lesser of the two?

The large (African) Hospital where all essential work was carried
out also contained within its grounds a 'shelter' for accompanying
relatives of the patient, so that the external appearance of the
premises always appeared to have a local market attached to it! One
aspect that impressed itself upon my mind was the constant
movement and turmoil within the wards. I once accompanied John
Taylor on a visit to the Children's Ward at night. I was astonished
to see that the sick children were lying in their cots or beds with
their mothers squeezed in beside them. The sight of the large adult
feet and legs protruding from the ends of the cots was to say the
least memorable, as was also that of a mother drinking the
supplementary reconstituted milk from the bottle intended for her
desperately malnourished baby. The Sister on Duty explained that
the general belief amongst the villagers was that the baby could
only absorb benefit from its mother's milk. Therefore the way to
feed the child was for the mother to drink the milk and it could
then be expressed through the breast to her baby. The way to
counter this was either for the desperately overworked nursing staff
to supervise and teach each mother or to give the bottles of milk
to each baby individually, a very time consuming task.

In addition to the above labours of dedicated work at the
hospital the sisters ran the out-station clinics of the district which
added immeasurably to the work-load and put stress upon the
creaking transport service, to say nothing of the medical stores and
clerical staff.

The first case of smallpox that I ever saw was that of a three-year-old boy who also had Malaria and was destined to die within a couple of days. It was at Mwenso Hospital on the Border where the physician-in-charge was Dr Hope Trante, who was 80 years of age and whose service there dated from well prior to the Second World War. She lived at Nakonde and had a pet monkey named 'Audrey' whose various afflictions including diabetes and a hysterectomy were treated by the Doctor as if the animal was human. Dr Trante also paid for everything in the normal way as for a private patient! She was a lovely person to have met.

Smallpox was a dreadful scourge of mankind, as Pam well knew by having her first vaccination at the age of 25. As front-line 'troops', the Medical Officer in London required all the staff and our families to be given booster doses, little suspecting that my wife would be receiving her first ever vaccination. I had never even given it a single thought, so as an EHO the failure was as much my fault as that of her father who did not believe in vaccinations of any kind. Her arm five days later had to be seen to be believed, it was so red and swollen and painful to the touch. She got over it but has never forgotten the incident. In mitigation I suppose I could say that it would have been a unique chat-up line when we first met. 'Hallo, Pam. Have you been vaccinated?' Her possible – and probable – answer would bear some research!

The vaccination programme and search for cases and contacts dominated the work certainly for the first two of the three 3-year contracts that I completed in Zambia. Although I had intended only to 'do' one, the work and lifestyle and endlessly fascinating continent of Africa suited me and my wife to the extent that the original three became nine (1965–1974). A similar thing happened when I moved over the Border to Malawi, just, as we thought, for two years. This became six (1974–1980). The most extreme of these was the next when I went to work for the American companies in the Middle East, namely Saudi Arabia, 'just for three months', as I thought. This ultimately became five and a half years in the Abdibdibah Desert up near the Kuwaiti Border, from approximately 1980 to 1986.

To return to Zambia. Six months after arrival I was transferred to Kasama because Nick MacPhail's services were required at the

School of Hygiene in Lusaka. We left Abercorn with mixed feelings as we were settling into the society happily and had no desire to move home yet again.

The work overall continued pretty much as one might have guessed. Enormous districts and distances by any standards, small numbers of supervising staff with some sort of training and qualification, minimal transport allocations, getting in retrospect the cast off and clapped out vehicles no one else wanted, but in Kasama I did obtain two things. First a designated office and clerk; second, a charming and sympathetic Provincial Medical Officer, Derek Braithwaite, who was a fine physician but somewhat backward when it came to administrative detail, who as a result carried on a running war with Ministry Headquarters in Lusaka. He was a batchelor who possessed not only a large ten-seater Land Rover in which many a seriously ill patient was transported out of the Bush to be treated at the hospital in Kasama. He also possessed a Cessna 182 four-seat aircraft for which he received a mileage allowance equivalent to driving a large Mercedes.

Kasama was centrally situated so that one could oversee the work in a general sense, but one still got caught up in much of the detail which seemed to plague the teams of vaccinators. Even when newly qualified Health Assistants arrived, there was always difficulty in settling them, vulnerable as they were to 'bullying' by the more senior medical staff at the clinics to which they were attached. Quite often they would get into trouble on their own account, usually through drunken behaviour in the bars where we tried to operate some degree of identification, treatment and isolation of the 'Bar Girls' infected with VD. We endeavoured to get them to go for regular checks at the clinic but it was an impossible task to keep them away from 'business'. Perhaps I should have used a phrase such as 'withdrawal of services' rather than 'isolation'.

Generally the staff did their collective best, although individually there were some problems. One such incomer to the staff, a shiny new product of the School of Hygiene, arrived and was given his posting and district. Within a couple of months the whole of the work in that area and elsewhere had come to a complete halt. Why? The man had run off with the junior wife of the local Chief, who was threatening to castrate or at least maim any of the associated staff let alone the miscreant, for whom the old Zulu habit of impaling victims on an anthill would have been a kindness.

Months later when the Health Assistant had long since been dismissed and forgotten, he arrived in my office seeking reinstatement. Having paid a fine in the local court he was allowed back into the district under sufferance, but I still had to see the Chief (was 'Kashili' his name?) for his approval of the arrangement. I found him at a table in his local beer hall with an array of bottles in front of him. Since he neither asked me to participate nor even to sit down and talk, an unheard of discourtesy, I figured that he was still rather disgruntled. An hour spent with him and his senior headman plus a gift of half-a-dozen bottles of Castle Lager seemed to assuage his feelings, and we parted on fairly amicable terms. To European eyes this may have seemed an unnecessary price to pay, but the Chief took the view that we were also to blame in posting the man to the district in the first place, a view difficult to argue against. On the other hand, as the legal age of consent was the apparent age of 12 years or 85 lbs in weight, and there were hundreds of young girls in this category throughout the villages, it is difficult to figure out why the young man had to tangle horns with the Chief in the first place. Because of staff shortages I was forced to accept him back into the fold, but made sure that his posting was at the far end of the province and out of the ambit of the offended Chief.

The Africa House

The above was the title of a book by Christina Lamb published in 1999 and concerned the life and times of Sir Stuart Gore-Browne. The title referred to the house that he built as the centrepiece of the estate that he carved out of the Bush at Lake Shiwa Ngandu (The Lake of the Crocodiles), lying roughly between Chinsali and Mpika. After his death in 1967 the estate was taken over and run by his son-in-law, Major Peter Harvey. He, together with his wife, was murdered by bandits some years later when the great house and estate began its slow decline. As I write I believe that the family is trying to resurrect and restore it all, but in these difficult times for Africa I can only visualise some of the daunting problems that must be faced.

When there is so much to relate about my life why, you might well ask, do I spend so much time writing about what turned out to be my only visit to Shiwa and a one-night stopover to boot. I suppose that the best way is to put the experience into a simple narrative form and the reader can judge whether I was correct in my belief, that I witnessed a part of the history of Northern Rhodesia/Zambia that was granted to few Europeans at that time.

My original trip was from Kasama to Isoka, but I was asked to divert to Shiwa for some reason or whatever and duly arrived at the hospital there at about 4 p.m. It being inadvisable to start a journey to Isoka at that time I was taken to the Estate Management Office and introduced to Sir Stuart, who even then at the age of 85 was an imposing figure. He and I had a stroll around the vegetable garden and I was then taken to my 'quarters' for the night's lodgings. These consisted of self contained bedrooms and bathrooms built around a courtyard, rather reminiscent of cloisters in a cathedral setting. Shiwa House I have always thought of as a cross or hybrid of a French Chateau and an English Country Mansion, although perhaps Scottish overtones might be added to the canvas. Whatever the case it was certainly an impressive 'pile', being the more so because of where it was so unexpectedly situated in the middle of the Zambian Bush. As I recall there was a terrace where at 6 a.m. and 6 p.m. a large native drum was sounded to signal the beginning and end of the working day, or was it for sunrise and sunset. I had been given instructions as to how to find the library if I was of a mind to join Sir Stuart in a 'Sundowner' before dinner, which would be served later in the family dining room.

The library was a most imposing room, highlighted by the marble fireplace, with comfortable and cosy armchairs around it, the walls being covered by bookshelves and thousands of books. Somewhere nearby there was a glass case containing personal memorabilia and family heirlooms, the one particular item I remember amongst all the medals and decorations being an Invitation Card to the Funeral Service of the Duke of Wellington in St Paul's Cathedral.

When I arrived there was no sign of my host but an immaculately dressed servant showed me the drinks table set out with gleaming crystal glasses, water jug and bottles of a variety of drinks − alcoholic and otherwise. Having poured me a lager the servant departed, and left alone I prowled this wonderful room and had buried my nose and was quite engrossed in a particular book when Sir Stuart arrived. The book was inscribed by Jo Grimond, the then leader of the Liberal Party in Britain, and was the first volume of *The Life of Winston Churchill* by Lady Violet Bonham Carter who was, as far as I remember, related to Joe − probably his mother-in-law.

Sir Stuart was dressed for dinner. By that I mean that he was wearing a dinner jacket and black tie, which put me in the shade somewhat. When I apologised for my simple safari suit he was charm itself. 'My dear boy,' I recall him saying, 'you are on tour and have a job to do so don't worry yourself about it,' and we then fell to talking about his early days in the country and what brought him there in the first place.

Apparently he had been a serving officer bored with his lot in peacetime Edwardian England. Thus when volunteers were required to go to Central Africa and join a survey team to map the borders of Northern Rhodesia he gladly added his name to the list. The work took three years, the highlight being negotiations with the Belgian Government to include 'their' Katanga Province into 'our' colony. If one looks at a map one can see that the Province inserts itself into just such an area, being called for ever more the 'Congo Pedicle'. Whilst according to Sir Stuart verbal agreement was reached upon the proposed change it was never acted upon. By the end of the Great War (1918), copper having been found in vast quantities, there was no way in which the Belgian authorities would ever relinquish economic, industrial or political control of Katanga until 1960 when the Belgian Government hastily and in a panic withdrew control and handed it to the African Nationalists. The resultant bloody carnage as the various gangs headed by Tshombe, Lubumba and then Tsche Tsche Seko, fought for control brought the whole country to a standstill, let alone the Katanga Province.

The European Residents were left to fend for themselves and many were massacred, including the defenceless missionaries, before political control was re-established in 1965. With copper production at a low point the price of it upon the world commodities market was very high, thus swelling the Zambian Government 'coffers' considerably at the time of Independence in 1964.

Sir Stuart saw Lake Shiwa Ngandu when engaged upon the work of the Survey Team. He thought it extremely beautiful and unspoilt – which it was – and resolved to return and build a house and estate carved out of the African Bush which would be worthy of a wealthy European Baronet, which he was. The war intervened and delayed his grand design somewhat, so it was not until the mid 1920s that he was able to pursue his dream.

Some perilous business ventures into 'new' African agricultural crops and the gradual switch into what one supposed to have been basically mixed farming followed over many years before the Estate prospered. During that time the village grew as the workforce increased. Any number of houses were built to accommodate the workers, as was a clinic-cum-hospital to serve the area, in addition to a school to educate the children. All of these were built from the raw materials to hand, mainly local timbers and sun-dried bricks and paid for from funds provided by Sir Stuart and the Estate.

When we had finished our drinks in the library Sir Stuart led the way to the small 'family' dining room where we were fed a very simple meal, a mince of some kind as I recall, probably curry, by three indoor servants immaculately dressed. I said 'family' because the following morning when I was shown over the house we came to the large dining room used for official dinners when he was entertaining in style or when the President, Kenneth Kaunda, and his entourage stayed. I do remember that we drank wine with the meal and at the end he poured five glasses of port from a decanter, one each for the two of us and one each for the servants whom he then toasted before we left the dining room and returned to the library. There we had a 'Nightcap' and further 'Chat' before the old chap went off to bed. Before he went he urged me to make full use of the room and its splendid contents and if I felt like reading for some time prior to retiring then please to make full use of the drinks available.

The following morning after breakfast we strolled around the vegetable garden, passing as we went the courtyard adjacent to the kitchens and utility areas including the cellar. There I saw for the first and only time in my life a huge cask being decanted into smaller utensils and eventually bottles. As the cask was labelled 'Portugese Produce' I assumed it to be of Port Wine. Sir Stuart instantly acknowledged the fact and in response to my enquiry said that he was laying down a new stock, starting with the 500 bottles contained within the cask. A somewhat different life-style to one that I was accustomed to! Whatever the case it is obvious that the whole brief visit was of enormous interest to me, the memories of which, some 40 years on, are still so vivid.

Sir Stuart died two years later. I never met him again. The burial service was attended by the Paramount Chief Chitimukulu as well as President Kaunda. I believe that some African Rituals were followed at the funeral service.

Clubs

As part of the fabric of social life in the Province the Clubs played their undeniable part. Whilst these are of European origin they provided a focal point for social and sporting occasions which were generally of great benefit to the local population. This is not to say that the Africans were welcomed. Because of the complex cultural and social diversity of their respective lives we were to learn that Europeans believed that the races in such situations were best left to their own devices. For better or worse this included those of Indian and Pakistani origin as well as the Africans. In some of the larger towns and cities Indian and Pakistani Sports Clubs were developed and strenuous sporting contests took place between them and the European dominated ones. Even the Roman Catholic Indians of Goanese origin enjoyed their own facilities. as was the case in Uganda at the time of the deportations by President Idi Amin.

In one respect the Clubs were a godsend in that they provided employment to numerous Africans who would otherwise have been confined to their villages, or in the worst case scenarios, the 'shanty towns'. Barmen and chefs, caddies and green keepers, sweepers and gardeners, drivers and tractor mechanics – many such people learned their skills because of and not in spite of the European presence in the provinces.

In the Northern Province I was able to learn the rudiments of the game of golf as both Abercorn and Kasama boasted very creditable courses, although there were 'browns' instead of 'greens' which consisted of sand, sometimes oiled, which when scraped along the line of the putt was quite useable. Unless the Club was rich enough to have the use of a watering system there was little point in trying to cultivate a 'green' to the fine grass carpet standard which would be required, as the hot season would preclude it. As it was most of the 'Bush' courses had fairways of coarse Kikuyu Grass upon which a preferred lie for the ball would be obligatory.

Generally the Clubs provided a variety of sporting opportunities from golf to tennis to squash to football to rugby, etc. etc., although in many instances the numbers playing a particular game were such that a separate Club from the parent one came into existence. This was particularly true of the mining towns on the Copperbelt where the wealthy companies provided unprecedented facilities for their employees.

In a social sense the Clubs held many dances, dinners and barbecues for fund raising purposes, but there were also non-sporting cultural events which were the highlights of the week or month for many members. For instance bridge was a popular game and the theatre sections attracted many aspiring thespians.

For better or worse we were prevailed upon to join this 'happy band' when we eventually settled into Kasama. Being only 12 in number it was a question of being a team of all the talents as everyone had to be more than just an actor or producer or stage manager or 'prompt' or 'props'. Every year the Theatre Association held two major festivals, one for one-act productions and the other – and major – one for full scale three-act plays and musicals. The adjudicator came for three weeks from London and normally stayed at the Festival Centre which varied each year but which had always been at one of the large and wealthy Theatre Clubs on the line of rail, but more usually the Copperbelt.

As a result of the Declaration of Independence called by the

Rhodesian Government led by Ian Smith ties with the South were being cut and the Zambian Government decided to switch the import of essential oil from there to the completely new and untried route through the north to Dar-es-Salaam in Tanzania. Petrol rationing having been imposed it was obviously impossible for the theatrical productions to travel so the adjudicator was required to go to them. It had therefore been decided that in our modest way a production could be staged at the Kasama Club. The play chosen was *The Rattle of a Simple Man* by Charles Dyer, requiring a cast of just three people. Such a tiny event in the life of the province but such a massive one for the ex-pat community. For Adjudication (and Opening) Night the audience had been asked to 'dress-up' and they certainly did their part in making the evening a glittering success. In the overall National Event we took the Best Actor award and lost the overall championship by one point!! A remarkable success story and one of which we were all very proud at the time.

Lusaka

When in Abercorn we had been satisfied with the Junior School standard at the small expatriate one presided over by Mrs Dixon, a kindly teacher of the 'old' school to whom the three R's were the foundation of all education. Upon our transfer down the line to Kasama the situation was not at all the same. Pam, being a schoolteacher herself, took a dislike to the set-up there and fretted that we must do our utmost to move to a different district if the opportunity arose, which it did six months later. A vacancy occurred in Lusaka for a District Inspector, the incumbent Gwyn Pritchard having been transferred to Broken Hill. The sudden transfer had occurred because the Inspector there had been killed in a road accident when on leave in the UK.

The transfer having been approved we arrived in Lusaka in the latter part of 1966 and were housed on a new estate at Olympia Park, a mile or so from the office near to the Ministry of Health. The District extended from Mumbwa in the West to Feira in the East and from Lusaka south to the Kafue River where it joined the Southern Province administered from Livingstone.

After the transfer from the Northern Province I returned some 'Props', which we had borrowed, to the Lusaka Theatre Club which over the next year or so became a fondly remembered home from home for ourselves and our cultural aspirations. If this sounds somewhat pompous I should perhaps explain that unlike so many amateur undertakings of this kind in the UK, performing perhaps two productions per year, there was a full-scale programme for a large and multi-talented membership which possessed its own theatre. The comparison should really be between a society using a Church Hall and one using its own 250-seat provincial theatre. This was fully equipped with sound and lighting decks plus property and costume sections, rehearsal rooms and social facilities. Yet if one was to see the early records and minutes of meetings of the Society which still existed in the Club's library it was possible to see a dogged determination to develop a European culture within the heart of what was commonly referred to as 'Darkest Africa'. With no corporate backing, as was the case with the copper-rich companies which funded such theatres in Chingola and Mufulira, the Society gradually prospered until it was able to fund – entirely from its own resources – a £50,000 development of restructuring in the 1960s.

Compare this with the fact that when it started, the railway from the south finished at Lusaka and the overnight passengers crossed the lines to the only commercial accommodation in town, the Lusaka Hotel. There, following dinner, a rudimentary set was erected and draped at one end of the dining room. A few hardy souls, founder members of the Society, performed under 'Tilley' lamps a one-act play, following which a collection was taken from around the room. 'A good night' was one comment in the minutes from those days, when the audience had contributed a meagre (by today's inflated standards) two pounds!

One could of course be just a social member but to enjoy it to the full required participation and in this respect both Pam and I were willing volunteers. I suppose in our time in the country we took part in probably 20 productions travelling with them to other Clubs and Societies upon either requests or for Festival activities. Neither of us wished to tread the boards so, except on very rare occasions, our roles were confined to either back-stage or production. I became a reasonably adept but strictly 'amateur' Stage Manager and Pam was a very diligent 'props' and 'prompt'. Mind you even she did not possess the nerve as did one young female props assistant to sally forth into the barber shops throughout the country and the South seeking 'Durex' signs and advertising material! This for a production of *Staircase* which had a set featuring a very seedy barber shop in the east end of London. She succeeded in her quest in Salisbury (now Harare).

The overall time scale for productions was that a 3-act play or musical would be performed on stage for a week before a paying audience, which was why the standard was so high. The next one would be near to dress rehearsal and the one to follow would be at play reading/line learning stage. Possibly the one following that would be at casting stage, probably in the club room or library. In between all this activity there would be a once a month 'Members Only Night' where aspiring producers could display their wares in a one-act play. This was performed under great difficulties because of the constant use of the stage. The members in the audience certainly knew their 'theatre' and many were the tears shed at the hisses and boos greeting a production woefully short of the high standard demanded. The reasoning was that the paying public had a right to demand the best and therefore, hard though it might be, the training and judgement given by the members was critical. I was fortunate in that my attempt (*The Monkey's Paw*) was greeted with approval and three months' later I was asked to produce a play for a one-week run for the public. I chose the comedy *The Odd Couple*, which was well received and enjoyable.

Over the years I produced both in Lusaka and subsequently in Malawi some notable successes with farces, which I always enjoyed, *A Flea in Her Ear* by Georges Feydeau and *One for the Pot* by Ray Cooney being memorable, and one or two 'bummers' such as *Sweeney Todd* – not the fault of the play but my ineptitude.

One of the many enjoyable aspects, as one might expect, were the numbers of extrovert characters that were on hand. Some of course were totally outrageous but others were of an extreme elegance and courtesy – almost like refugees from a Noel Coward comedy of manners. This is not to denigrate them but to admire and remember them with affection. One of them was a South

African, Lee Case, a tall elegant batchelor who affected a limp with a walking stick as a prop. His South African dialect was difficult to detect so much had he overcome it in his pursuit of the 'English Gentlemen'. A kinder man did not exist.

In the latter part of the Sixties and early Seventies the drop internationally of standards both vocally and visually from what was normally expected in society broke upon an unsuspecting world. Lee was called to London on business with a colleague and was invited to afternoon tea and cocktails at a somewhat 'swishy' apartment one Sunday afternoon. The hostess dispensed tea from a large silver platter inviting the guests to take such sugar and milk as was needed. She wore a topless outfit which displayed her large 'charms' to the assembled guests, most of whom – it being London – had seen it all before. Lee took it in his stride and when she bent over his armchair he calmly asked if she would kindly remove one of her 'boobs' from the tray as it was impeding his efforts to get at the sugar!!

The work was pretty much the same as in the North but as one would have expected, the Vaccination Programme having started in and around Lusaka, was much more advanced there than in the rest of the country. It had really got to the stage where maintaining the standard was the objective. The aim was then to vaccinate in the clinics all new-born babies and other patients, travellers at bus and railway stations as well as students in schools, etc.

It was made easier and was comparatively undemanding in the sense that communications and stores and vaccinating serum and cold storage and workshops and vehicles and staff were easily come by, which was only to be expected, Lusaka being the capital city. Co-operation had long been the standard amongst the comparatively sophisticated urban population, in contrast that is to the remote 'hit and miss' experienced in the distant rural areas.

Once the vaccination campaign was going smoothly it became a question of tracking down reports of alleged cases in the villages. In 99% of these there was an innocent explanation, the alleged disease turning out to be anything from measles to chicken pox to abscesses to worms to malaria and so on. Occasionally a report would prove to be anything but dismissive and one incident caused considerable concern.

The far eastern end of the district that I operated terminated at Feira, the conjunction of the Luapula and Zambezi Rivers where over the far bank could be seen the Portuguese colony of Mozambique. The little outpost was reached by driving 120 miles along the Great East Road, a fine tarmaced highway, then turning south along a very poor single track 'Bush' road for the 76 miles to Feira. Half way down the track one came to Katondwe Mission Station, where the White Fathers administered a school and agricultural training facility.

It was from this Mission that the report of smallpox cases in the district had emanated. The main house stood on a high bluff overlooking the church, school and workshops. There I was made most welcome by the Fathers whilst I established a base and drove all over the place tracking down the reports, mainly true for a change, and vaccinating as we went. Feira itself was a 'nothing' town, extremely hot and humid, where the goats appeared to live in the trees and on the thatched roofs of the houses. The little 'outpost' seemed to have established itself as a fishing village and crossing point to the far country. There was one house of substance for the tenancy of the District Officer, a post which had recently been 'Zambianised'. It was said that previous occupants had carried out their secretarial duties in the extreme temperatures and humidity by sitting in the shade in a large tin bath of tepid water with a board placed across it to carry a typewriter and papers.

When the day's work was done, I retreated back to the Mission where I had been allocated a bedroom, sparsely furnished as one might expect, but containing all necessities for survival! There was a small bathroom or shower as far as I remember and both candles and a hurricane lamp at the bedside. There was no 'loo', the edifice being reached along the path starting at the far end of the outside veranda which ran around the whole building. I did not explore the area that first day as we had been on the road since 5 a.m. and it was now approaching sunset. As it was I was glad to shake the dust off with a shower and brush-up and it must have been about half-past six when I ventured out and walked around the corner to see a magnificent and very 'African' view. Down the hill in the valley stood the church alongside the school. It seemed to be ablaze with lights and the chants were quite loud and clear as they echoed up to the house. Obviously the evening service was taking place but it was the sight as much as the sound that was spell-binding. As a background there were myriads of small lights in the villages around and along the valley where numerous cooking fires were being lit for the evening meals. The smoke from these rose in a perpendicular fashion in the hot still air which against the background of the setting sun and twilight sky with stars newly appearing seemed to me to be carrying the Church's messages to distant parts. A dream? An hallucination? A trick of the mind? Perhaps – but it happened and then black night descended and the vision was gone. What a strange and wonderful place Africa can be.

It was almost an anti-climax to see at the end of the veranda a very old Priest with a head bereft of hair but with a magnificent white beard stretching to the middle of his chest. He had his eyes closed and was telling a rosary of black beads, which I assumed would be in harmony with the prayers of the church service. He was leaning back in his chair with his eyes closed and was unaware of my presence until I discreetly coughed and apologised for disturbing him. When he arose I discovered that he was even in old age a very tall man. With suitable 'head-gear' and robes he would have been the epitome of a priest of the Russian Orthodox Church. In the half-hour or so that we spent together I discovered that he was indeed of Russian birth and had been a priest-in-waiting or apprentice, or whatever one is called, when the Russian Revolution of 1917 tore the country apart and forced the clergy into fleeing for their lives from the vengeful Bolsheviks.

He succeeded in escaping abroad where his Faith directed him to the world of the International Missionary. He thus ended up at a newly-established mission station in Katondwe with a mixture of similar 'priestly' refugees. There, their first task had been to construct the permanent buildings utilising local materials wherever possible. The fact that it still stood and was habitable and was used for all their domestic chores and private devotions was a tribute to all the trials and tribulations that they must all have faced. A similarity could be drawn with Sir Stuart's endeavours around the same period at Shiwa Ngandu.

When we strolled around to the dining room we were joined by several other 'White Fathers' who were all immaculately 'scrubbed' and shining clean (Isn't cleanliness next to Godliness?) as they returned from their days of labour. Whether these were in teaching or agriculture or spiritual affairs I never did find out but one person of outstanding personality headed the group. He was the Priest-in-Charge, Father Pavliecki, who was originally of Polish nationality. As a member of the Communist Party he had been caught by the invading German Army in 1939 and interned in Dachau Concentration Camp for the next six years. There he had been forced to tend the Crematorium, and dreadful sights he must have witnessed. In spite of his communist associations within the camp, which probably helped to save his life, he came to believe that there was a higher presence which was safe-guarding him for some unknown future. When he was released at the end of the war he joined the Roman Catholic Church and after Ordination volunteered for missionary work in Africa. Hence his presence at Katondwe, his only home. Tragically he was killed some two years later when the mission vehicle he was in was hit by a train on an open rail-crossing on a road near to Lusaka.

As we sat around a long scrubbed white table with Father Plaviecki at its head and ate a simple but generous meal, we started to converse about our lives past and present and hopes for families and the future. The talk continued over the coffee and even more so when the whisky began to circulate. One other priest that I remember hailed from Italy and had been sought after the war by the Communist Partisans in the mountains north of Trieste. Fleeing for his life he had eventually escaped south and again volunteering for missionary employment had found himself assigned to starting a mission from scratch some twenty miles from Katondwe. He was succeeding against all the odds, but with the assistance of several Lay-Brothers in a facsimile of the scenario at Katondwe over 40 years earlier.

All of this I learned whilst sitting after dinner surrounded by an international gathering of dedicated Catholic Brethren. It somehow made my upbringing in the Church of England quite insignificant, but their interest in me and my doings in life was quite extraordinary. I suppose that their paucity of visitors made them as eager to learn from me about life in the 'outside' world of Zambia as I was to learn from them about life in the 'enclosed' world of the mission stations. Inevitably and as one might expect given the background to most of their lives the talk turned to survival and its achievement in adverse circumstances. A fascinating evening.

One other event occurred during my stay at the Mission which I still recall with some amusement. When I left the Dining Room that first evening and proceeded around the veranda to my room I had to pass the head of the path leading to the privy (Chimboozy or Chim to the locals) and decided that as the moon was full I could easily see my way to it without a hurricane lamp. It was dark but breezy inside and after fumbling around I succeeded in urinating down the hole in the wooden seat. The following morning with a slightly more serious intent I made the same journey, toilet roll in hand. To my great astonishment I found that the 'loo' was of the long-drop variety but with an extraordinary variety in its structure. The hut, for it was little more than that in size, was built on a sort of raft constructed and wired for stability to the nearby rock outcrops but with angled timbers below securing the base for the users. What was truly astonishing was the height at which it stood above the valley. At the time I figured it for some one hundred feet. Having perched nervously on the hole and seen the drop where 50 years of use had turned the face of the cliff into one long brown scar, some visitors might well have become constipated at the thought of using it. There was also the thought that a 'Blow Back' was a possibility, since there was an up-lift of air at the cliff-face. No wonder I had thought it 'breezy' the previous night!

After three days' work and leaving a team of vaccinators in place to chase up all the contacts it was time to return to Lusaka. Before we left we were asked to take a family of patients, some four in number, two of whom were suffering from leprosy, with us to the City Hospital for onward transportation to the nearest 'Leprosarium' (a specialist medical centre) lying some 90 miles north of Lusaka on the road to Broken Hill. At about 4 p.m. we were free to start the journey home and somewhere around dusk we reached the main road. It must have been around 9 p.m. when we passed Olympia Park and I was dropped off at my home. Simon, the Driver, was given instruction to take the patients to the Hospital and then go home leaving the Land Rover at the nearby Police Station.

I remember the film of red dust on the surface of the bath water and an ice-cold Castle Lager on the side when there came a knock at the door and Pam poked her head around. 'Simon has returned,' she announced, 'and desires converse with thee' or words to that effect. It transpired that the hospital had declined to take on board our Leprosy patients and effectively told Simon to buzz off. When we returned to the hospital I could see in the A & E what appeared to be a Casualty Clearing Station in a war zone. The sweating and struggling medical and nursing staff were trying to cope with a massive influx of patients from the shebeens and shanty towns and I realised that I could not have pitched up at a worse moment, it then being about 10 p.m. and the last Friday night of the month when everyone in employment got paid.

There was one dead body partially covered by a blanket on the floor, two men half sitting against the wall with blood oozing from arm wounds and a woman in some sort of vomiting condition. What with the milling and shouting relatives all demanding attention, it was not much wonder that Simon had been told to 'buzz off'. I could only explain to a Sister and the Medical Officer that we were only delivering the patients for onward transmission to the Leprosarium. Since Simon had already driven some 300 miles since dawn that day it was out of the question for him to do another couple of hundred. I had given the patients some money for food so that they could wait at the hospital for transport, and since they had already been in transit for a week then a few more hours would make little difference to them. Reluctantly they agreed to accept the responsibility and thankfully Simon and I departed for our respective homes.

Pam and I had been married for ten years when we got engaged. Perhaps 're-engaged' would be more correct. Somewhere in those ten years Pam had lost her original engagement ring, a simple Georgian diamond and gold one which had been purchased from an antique shop in 'England's Lane' off Primrose Hill in Hampstead. I make the point about it being 'antique' because in those days a Purchase Tax had to be paid on new jewellery but not on second-hand.

There was a restaurant outside Lusaka, formerly called the 'Blue Lagoon' but which under new (Indian) control was renamed 'The Copper Chalice'. Some alterations had been carried out and my help and advice had been sought by the owner as to the legal requirements and food safety and hygiene within the kitchen and store-rooms.

Pam and I went to dinner there on our wedding anniversary as guests of the owner, Pam being totally astonished when the bill was torn up at the table by the owner. An announcement was made to the assembled diners when a waiter bearing a decorated gateau on a tray arrived at the table. Pam's day was complete when I gave her a new engagement ring, a gold and sapphire one which she still possesses.

Another event which also had its origins in the Asian community, was when I met the larger than life 'Harry' Amin, the owner of the Grand Bottle Store and Bar in Lusaka. I believe that his real name was Harishanan Amin Patel, but to all and sundry he was known as Harry. He developed an interest at another Bar in Kafue some 25 miles south of Lusaka, and again I was asked to advise on the alterations. As a result I together with Pam was invited to Harry's Birthday Party, to be held just after Christmas at his house on the outskirts of the city.

We had already made our plans for the Festive Season and were going to spend four days at the Victoria Falls Hotel but would be returning on the day of the party. A description of the Victoria Falls in those days and a comparison with today requires a study of its own, as it cannot adequately be described in a narrative such as this. Suffice to say that as a family holiday it was fabulous.

The long journey home was difficult from the midway point because of violent storms en route so that we were late by some two hours when we eventually found our way to Harry's house. Because of the delay two things had happened. The ladies and the gentlemen had separated into two distinct parties, the children being with the ladies. In retrospect this might have been the norm as it was an Indian household. The second thing was that the curry had been spiced up as we were late and no other European invitees had come. Since Pam would not have been comfortable surrounded by Asian ladies chattering mainly in Gujarati she was invited to join the men-only table rather like a queen-bee! We all sat around a large dining table, some eight or ten of us, and in the centre of the table was not a floral arrangement or similar which one might have expected but a large enamel bowl of ice. Each guest had his preferred drink in front of him so that when I asked for a Lion Lager a glass was produced and a case was placed behind my chair for my sole use. Pamela asked for a gin and tonic and was rewarded with a bottle of gin on the table and a case of tonics at her feet. A request for lemon was met with a slight delay and I suppose that one of Harry's numerous offspring or nephews was despatched into the garden to gather a fruit from the trees in the orchard. Having got off to such a start it was not long before the alcohol took effect and the talk began to flow. Much of it was hilarious, led by the extraordinary mimicry and vocal talents of one who was described to us as a Trainee Brahmin Priest.

The spiced-up curry was delicious but a glass of whisky to finish the proceedings tasted like an ice-cold glass of water. It was a lovely evening and the following Sunday I was invited to come out again to the farmhouse where Harry intended having an open house for his friends and family. I was instructed to bring along our youngest son because there would be myriads of infant sons and nephews with whom a cricket match was to be arranged.

There I sat with Harry on the garden swing, enjoying his generous hospitality whilst Matthew, who appeared to be the youngest there, played for his team. There seemed to be some local rules in operation because no matter how many times he was obviously 'OUT' the delivery would be called a 'No Ball' and he would be allowed to continue. This until he had genuinely struck the ball and had scored a run. As he also held a catch the Asian youngsters appeared to hail him as the 'Man of the Match', at which point the match having ended he was delivered, all four years of glowing youth, to his somewhat, by then, glowing father!

Some twenty years or so later when Matthew was undertaking a course at a London Polytechnic, one of the students whose parents lived in Ruislip (part of my old local authority district prior to going to Africa) and with whom Matthew became friendly at the time, turned out to be a niece of Harry's. Matthew said that the talent for spiced-up curries still existed in the family!

The Copperbelt

After a further year spent teaching and training at the School of Hygiene in Lusaka I was posted to Ndola for the remainder of my contract.

The Copperbelt Province was different to the others in that it contained the copper mining and refining towns, all of which had their local authority status and separate Public Health Departments. Even the mines themselves maintained extensive clinics and medical services for the well-being of the work force. Part of this organisation was that of the Environmental Services applying themselves to the health and safety aspects as well as the normal food hygiene, water supplies, pest control and so on. With a workforce of thousands living in mine properties and compounds coming as they did from all parts of Africa and beyond, the health, well-being, safety and morale both of the employees and their families was seen as an essential part of the production process. A day's sickness of one employee was counted as a loss to the mining company – particularly if it was preventable, hence the high standards prevailing and insisted upon. Incidentally all services were provided for free by the companies.

My job, as far as was possible with both limited resources and mining company interests as well as the local authorities to contend with, was to service (if that is the correct term) the remainder of the province in an environmental sense. Known in all reports and documents as 'The Peri-Urban Areas of the Copperbelt' it stretched from Ndola in the south to Bancroft (shortly to be renamed Chililabombwe) in the North near to the Congolese Border. Off to the east was Mufulira which was some ten miles from the border crossing into the Congo Pedicle.

This extended for 55 miles which had to be crossed before re-entering Zambia after the ferry crossing over the Luapula River which marked the international border. It was a wearisome business trotting from customs and immigration posts but it was infinitely more acceptable than travelling the very long southern route through Kapiri Mposhi and Mpika to Kasama in the Northern Province before doubling back to Fort Rosebery (Mansa), the provincial headquarters of the Luapula. To complete the picture the western edge of the district bordered both the North Western Province and the northern part of the Central.

The 'wearisome' problem that I mentioned of going through customs and immigration in and out of the Congo and in and out of Zambia at either end of the 'Pedicle' was even more protracted when we last made the journey from the Cape to Malawi. By that time the border between the 'International Pariah' Rhodesia and Zambia was well and truly closed at the bridge crossing over the Zambezi at the Victoria Falls. The only way forward was to drive fifty-five kilometres along the riverbank and face customs and immigration into Botswana. Then drive a quarter of a mile to customs and immigration out of Botswana whereupon we arrived at the ferry.

Transported over the river we had to pass through customs and immigration into Zambia and then drive back the fifty-five kilometres along the Zambian side of the river to the Victoria Falls, to see the same bridge we had last seen four hours previously. Wearily there was still the long drive to Lusaka, yet another 'rest and be thankful' stop on our sojourn to far distant Malawi.

Cemeteries, burials and exhumations

As part of any training course in the environmental services there should be an element which is devoted to the funeral rites and disposal of bodies in the society in which one lives. Sometimes these overlap in that the practices of the various Faiths are imported from other countries. Whatever the case the principles remain the same, i.e. the final disposal must be carried out in such a way and with as much dignity as possible so as to protect the living population from harm. Much will depend upon the beliefs of the destination of the 'Spirit' of the dead body. In some the body simply has to be buried as quickly as possible because of the heat and rapid decomposition, as in the Moslem countries of the Middle East, in others the disposal is by fire (Hindu), in others the birds of the air (Pharsees) and the beasts of the desert (Kalahari Bushmen) will be incorporated into the rituals. Then there are the problems of Witchcraft and Voodoo where parts of a body, particularly of a distinguished deceased, are required for initiation purposes. These practices are much more common in the world than one might surmise.

This explains the compromise for instance between ritual and beliefs and witchcraft in the burial practices carried out by one community. When the Chief dies the burial site is prepared by diverting a stream from its normal course and digging a grave in the exposed bed. To ensure continuity of the Spirit to his successor the top of the skull is used as a vessel from which a potion (ingredients secret) is drunk by his successor. The body and 'cup' are then buried in the grave and the stream restored to its normal course. The site is totally obscured and lost and any grave robbers are thus deterred. Something of a similar nature takes place when the Paramount Chief of the Bemba, Chitimukulu dies. His body is hung over a smoking and guarded fire in his hut for some 15 months, prior to burial at a secret location known only to the senior members of the tribal council, the hut having been burned to the ground.

At the London end of Northolt Airport, at its junction with the A40, is situated the Polish War Memorial. It is dedicated to those pilots of the RAF stationed there during the war who lost their lives fighting in the ferocious air battles over London during 1940 and 1941. In the 1960s I attended my first exhumation at the cemetery in Northwood where the Polish War Graves were situated. The body was to be exhumed and taken back to Poland and the documentation alone from the various bodies was impressive. It included finally a Certificate from the Bishop of London to say that the process could go ahead but that the transporting of the body should not endanger the health of the public during its journey to its new resting place, due decorum and reverence being observed at all times, etc. Once the coffin is removed together with its contents, it is placed into a zinc-lined oversized one waiting by the side of the grave. The extra lid then has to be soldered to the casket and the final wooden lid screwed down. An infallible system, even though at times short-cuts have to be made because of unforeseen factors, e.g. the weather, the state of the coffin and remains and the like. The process is not supposed to start until the cemetery is closed and unauthorised members of the public have departed. On one occasion the sexton (grave digger) placed a screen around the site and started work at lunch-time. With the rain pouring down and the forecast very bad he figured that visitors would be few and he could get on with the work unhindered.

It proved so and by the time I arrived with the undertakers at the official time of 6.30 p.m. the exhumed coffin was already on a stand waiting for the oversized coffin to arrive. Whilst the soldering and sealing process should be carried out on the spot I agreed that it could better be carried out in the funeral director's workshop, having due regard to the extremely 'damp' weather. With curtains drawn on the hearse the transportation was carried out without any more fuss. The main factor which I had to assess as an Environmental Health Officer was whether there was a risk to the health of the public. I concluded that as the deceased had died from natural causes and that the original coffin was still in good condition a variation in the standard procedure could be allowed.

In the original case of the Polish pilot the lid of the coffin had become detached from the walls and it was possible to see the contents. They consisted of a uniform stuffed with bags of sawdust. Evidently there had been a massive explosion and probably fire in which the body had been totally consumed by the heat. There had been, one supposes, a ceremonial funeral, the only way in which the death could be honoured. It was of no concern to us and we merely observed the procedure of sealing the coffin inside the zinc-lined one and seeing it start the journey to the grieving and no doubt devoted relatives in Poland.

Independence was declared by Ian Smith, the Head of the Rhodesian Government to the south. He announced it to the world by quoting the Saint Crispin's Day speech from Shakespeare's *Henry V*. This had the unfortunate result of the Rhodesians being termed 'Smith's Crispins' by the International Press. It also had the result of making the Zambian Government determined to cut the traditional economic and commercial ties with Rhodesia. The result was that the offer by the Chinese to build a railway from Zambia to Dar es Salaam on the coast in Tanzania was accepted. The line passed through the Northern Province and it was there in Kasama that the Provincial Health Inspector at the time, Tom

Hinde, received a request to issue a Death Certificate for a labourer, the body lying in a camp staging area along the line some distance away. The deceased could then be 'exported' home.

Taking a member of the medical staff with him Tom duly found the camp and was escorted to the service area warehouse at the end of which was a large cabinet deep freezer. When opened the man's frozen solid body could be seen in a sitting position at one end, fully dressed in the standard uniform issue complete with cap. The Red Booklet of the *Thoughts of Chairman Mao* was clutched in his frozen hand.

The condition of the body meant that no examination was possible, nor was it necessary as the man had quite clearly died of a broken neck. The circumstances were of no concern to Tom but what made it a memorable event as far as he was concerned was that the rest of the freezer unit was full of frozen chickens which accounted for the fact that the body was squeezed up at one end. Presumably the chickens were destined for the kitchen. As Tom remarked to me 'When one thinks about it in a practical way, the contents of the freezer consisted totally of dead bodies, but aesthetically . . .?'

One of my colleagues in Africa had once been employed in the North London Borough of Finsbury when a very old church had to be demolished and the site cleared following considerable damage during the Blitz. Catacombs were involved and great difficulties were encountered in moving old stone coffins, very often lead-lined, stacked in alcoves and on shelves since the time the church was built sometime in the Middle Ages. The lead-lined ones had corpses in them which were incredibly well-preserved but as hard as iron to the touch. All of them had to be re-located to a cemetery outside the Borough, a thankless task but made simpler by the fact that the original interment records had been lost in the bombing of London so that documentation was kept to a minimum.

I little expected to be asked by one of the most powerful mining groups in the world to extend the scope of my limited expertise in cadaver disposal to study the legal and practical obstacles in closing a cemetery, exhuming the bodies and re-interring them at a new location some miles away.

The request came from the mining company at Chingola and in outline consisted of a desire to obliterate from the map the site of the old European Cemetery on the outskirts of the town, which had been closed in 1950. Since then the waste overburden, mainly soil and clay, from the smelting process had been growing and spreading to such an extent that it now nearly surrounded the old cemetery. Considerable expenditure had to be employed every year to keep the piles of earth at bay since they were up to 50 ft in height and ran through the 'Bush' for miles like hunting tunnels thrown up by gigantic moles.

An elderly engineer who had lived all his life in the district took me there and showed me round as he explained the mining company's difficulties. Essentially, of course, they could simply abandon the old place, remove the headstones and within a year or so the site would be covered naturally and lost forever. There were however certain legal, historical and moral objections to this course of action. In the first place it was consecrated ground (a legal entity) I understood. It was also a visual historical record of the European presence in Chingola since its early days as a mining community, some 50 years before. I was told also that some of the bodies were the ancestors of local families still living there who would be singularly averse to any action which might treat the graves with anything but the level of decorum and respect which one might expect under normal circumstances, and this did not include the dumping of the mine residues on their distant relatives – even in death.

As I walked around and read the headstones I realised what a treasure trove this was for any historian, local or otherwise. A whole family wiped out by Blackwater Fever – mother, father and three children. Wartime road accidents and RAF personnel killed in air crashes, but the graves were not considered the concern of the War Graves Commission since this was not a War Zone but was only used for training purposes. Those I had seen in the cemetery in Abercorn some two years earlier were those of soldiers killed in the 'Battle' of Abercorn against the Askaris and German Battalions led by General von Lettow-Worbeck and were genuine war graves. I think that they might have been those of members of the Seaforth Highlanders apart from the German ones, but as I took no notes it is impossible at this distance in time to be certain.

One grave which I looked at and pondered over for some time concerned a young man of 21 years of age who died on Christmas Day in 1945. What on earth happened in this case? I asked the engineer. To be that age, I thought, full of the sap of life and to be buried on that day of all days was too awful to contemplate. My companion explained that he was there when the event happened.

There had been a drinks party around the pool of a resident that morning. The young, fit and daring macho men all had 'bangers' of one sort or another and thought a ten-mile dash down the road to the Hippo Pools on the Kafue River would be a capital way to expend their energy, the Pools being a known swimming and picnic spot. The young man who died had the fastest vehicle and could well have been the best driver. At any rate he was the first to dive into the pool, and a crocodile got him. The 'remains' were recovered later in the week. So sad.

Investigations from my office unveiled a nightmare can of worms of both a legal and practical nature. Exhumations could for instance be carried out but as one might expect only with the approvals of the ecclesiastical authorities and the Minister of Health on the advice of the Director of Medical Services. Before these could be officially sought the preliminary work had to include an official 'Search' for the relatives and/or antecedents. Further, there had to be a detailed plan prepared as to the actual site and numbers involved, the exhumations themselves, the workforce to be employed, the proposals for safeguarding the bodies as well as protecting the health and well-being of the local population, the transportation arrangements and finally the details of the re-interments. When I discussed these difficulties with the Mining Officials I discovered that even with using company facilities as much as possible to cut costs, certain obstacles remained which were well-nigh impossible to resolve. For instance trying to trace relatives from burials of 50 years previously, especially if, as in the case mentioned before, the whole family had succumbed to Blackwater Fever.

One problem arose in those tentative discussions which would never have occurred to me but which was uppermost in the mind of one senior engineer, and that was who was to physically undertake the work. Whilst he had numerous semi-skilled drivers and excavators and mining staff who were all African under his control, there was no possibility of using them. Their fears of burial grounds and spirits and witchcraft and so on ran far too deep and he had been told bluntly that it was not possible. He had considered using the Europeans on the payroll but that meant that there would be no supervising staff at various levels, which meant that a whole section of the production process would have to be shut down because it was against the law and union rules.

There was only one solution as far as he was concerned, and that was to employ a workforce which had no connection with the country whatsoever. The Company had other mining interests in both Rhodesia (Zimbabwe) and South Africa where the workforce was of predominantly Zulu or Ndebele stock. He knew from experience that they would tackle any role which other Africans found distasteful and had no fear of the witchcraft element since they had no beliefs in other 'Gods' and would seek the protection of their own who were far more powerful in any case!

The cost – a pinprick by mining standards – was reckoned to be somewhere between £5,000 and £10,000, using Company facilities. The preliminary report which I drafted was submitted to the Permanent Secretary in Lusaka, copied to the DMS and Chief EHO, and that was the last I ever heard of the problem. I went on four months' leave shortly afterwards and upon return embarked upon a further series of postings stretching from Solwezi to Fort Rosebery (Mansa) to (finally) Kawambwa in the north of the Luapula Province.

African beliefs take strange twists at times and what would be thought a simple enough item to a European would have quite different responses from a different section of society. The first occasion I recall resulted in a full scale riot between the students at the School of Hygiene when the Lhosi faction from Barotseland brought two tortoises into the kitchen after their evening meal and when the coast was clear of the staff. A Zambian version of a midnight feast in the dorm. They had barely commenced cooking when the Bemba students from the Northern Province charged in and demanded that the cooking of the tortoises be stopped. The riposte that the Bemba were just as partial in their own way to eating locusts was completely ignored and the resultant fight whilst not serious in physical injuries was a bit devastating for the kitchen. Suffice to say that overnight security was strengthened, the kitchen was declared strictly off-limits and a new set of cooking utensils seemed to solve most of the problem, although the inherent distrust of the two participants could never be completely ignored.

I well know that kitchens can be off-limits to anyone not authorised to use them and heaven help anyone who uses the facilities without that authorisation from the person in charge. I once boiled some snails from a village water point in the largest cooking pot that I could find without seeking permission or advice from my wife, i.e. the person in charge (for want of a better term). The roof fell in when she found out. That I was doing my best for the health of the local population as I was officially required to do seemed to have escaped her. The fact was that I was intending to send the eviscerated shells through the post for identification purposes to both the University of Zambia in Lusaka and the Natural History Museum in London for cross-check purposes.

In retrospect I suppose the clinching factor in my fall from her grace and favours was that (a) I had not discussed the problem with her and (b) the snails I collected came from a Bilharzia infested stream. The resulting fracas calls to mind the lines from an old Phil Harris song. 'Woodman, Woodman spare that tree. Chop not a single chop. It's the only tree my wife can't climb when she gets after me . . .' Be warned chaps when you start the brew in the kitchen without permission!

Having strayed completely off line I suppose the best way back is to relate a somewhat bizarrely humorous funeral that Pam and I were witness to in Blantyre in Malawi.

John, a cricket devotee and some time umpire, had developed a brain tumour, but following exploratory surgery in Johannesburg it was declared inoperable and he returned home to die some two months later. The widow, having spent money on the South African venture when she should have sent the poor man home to England, now had no funds available to despatch the body there. She resolved to have him cremated, but the nearest crematorium was in Harare in Zimbabwe. This again was too expensive, and having refused to bow to the inevitable financial constraints and use the local cemetery as a normal family would do, she resolved upon a Communion Service in the local Anglican Church followed by a cremation at the Hindu Burning Ghats at the back of the railway sidings in the adjoining town of Limbe.

Members of the cricket team who prior to his death had been coerced by his wife into gathering at his bedside to sing his favourite songs and discuss the fortunes of the cricket team – this while the patient was completely unconscious – were further cajoled to act as pall bearers. Pam and I were aware of all this but still felt a degree of pity for the deceased and his somewhat odd family, so we arrived at the small and well-filled church believing that at last the on-going ordeal was over but . . . well read on!

We were all kneeling when the coffin preceded by the priest in communion robes came down the centre aisle. As it passed my pew I could quite clearly see the outline of John's face under the wobbling and unattached lid of the coffin. The Cricket Captain that year (1980) was Bob Renshaw, a good friend still, who was one of the pall bearers. He told us later that when they collected the body from the hospital mortuary the coffin produced by the undertaker was too small, or perhaps the body was frozen with ice. Whatever the reason the lid would not screw down.

The Service proceeded, but within ten minutes the priest stopped the proceedings, went over and whispered to the widow at the front of the church, and then promptly disappeared into the Vestry. He emerged a few moments later having changed his garb for that of a priest conducting a funeral or black communion mass. Once this had been established the service and prayers began again. It all seemed interminable but probably was over within an hour or so from the time we entered the church.

Not so for the pall bearers who generally speaking were of the Anglican Christian persuasion. Upon arrival at the Burning Ghats the carers of the bodies there wished to remove the body from the coffin and place it upon the pyre. The coffin could then be re-used! As it had been paid for already this was out of the question, apart from any aesthetic aspect. The coffin and its contents were then prepared for cremation in the Hindu fashion by pouring over and smearing the body with ghee (refined butter) to assist in a successful burning. With the flames starting to engulf the coffin the pall bearers felt that they had done their duty according to the family's wishes and retired to the Club for a well-earned scotch or three.

A week later, there came a visitor to the office of one of the chief pall bearers. He was carrying a cardboard box with what were supposedly John's ashes, which his widow had requested so that she might take them back to England when the family left. Eric, the recipient, opened the box and decided that a large piece of thigh bone and some of the skull in a cardboard box hardly constituted 'ashes in the urn', which the widow was expecting, so he did a very sensible thing. He sorted out and disposed of the majority of the bones and purchased an African-style urn at the local curio market. He filled it with what was left of the remains, sealed it and passed it on to the lady concerned the day prior to her departure, reasoning that there wasn't enough time left for further difficulties to arise, and in this he was correct, thank the Lord.

North Western Province

Solwezi, not to be confused with its Congo (Zaire) counterpart of Kolwezi, lies some 50 or 60 miles inside the provincial border from the northern part of the Copperbelt, the nearest towns of any consequence being Chingola and Bancroft (Chililabombwe). The farthest point of the province measured as the crow flies is 550 miles from Solwezi ending at a tiny outpost called Chinyana Litapi. To get there one travels the main road via the towns of Kasempa and Kabompo where after nearly 400 miles in a Land Rover travelling over dirt roads there is the welcome sight of the Government Rest House high on the hill overlooking the river.

The following day the journey is resumed and Balovale on the banks of the wide Zambezi River is reached. The town is so named because of the Lovale Tribe whose Paramount Chief Ashinde lives at his 'Kraal' a few miles up the river. He occupied a fine bungalow behind a woven reed fence some six feet or so in height which was decorated by the skulls of the lions he had killed during his lifetime. All this Pam learned when she and Matthew, our youngest son then about seven years of age, were invited by the Chief to tea when they paid a courtesy call upon him. To put things slightly more in context: I was transferred to the Province in late 1970 and shortly before completing the tour of duty in 1971 Pam and I and Matthew went on tour with the 'Boss', my good friend and Provincial Medical Officer, Harry Bwanausi.

Together with the Principal Medical Assistant Chris Mundia, a tall, handsome Lhosi originally from Barotseland (now Western Province), the intention was to visit all of the health centres and hospitals and out-station clinics in that part of the Province. We were 'Out' for about ten days in all but the day that Pam and Matthew remember was when they enjoyed the hospitality of the charming and dignified Chief Ashindi. Photo displays, albums and medals were all at the ready because he had been honoured by the Queen at Independence.

Meanwhile the remainder of the touring party ferried across the river and set off across the Zambezi Flood Plain the last 55 miles to Chinyama Litapi. I should point out that it was the dry season and the floods had receded leaving behind a layer of sand up to axle depth which necessitated the Land Rover travelling in low-ratio gearing and 4-wheel drive both there and back. The whole journey was endless and we used up the 40-gallon drum of petrol in the process. It was only possible to make the journey in the dry season and I was forced to enquire what happened to very sick patients who required hospitalisation. The answer was that their relatives would transport them, paying money to anyone who had access to vehicles as the Health Centre there had none. In the rainy season the only means of transportation was by bicycle, riding where possible, wading where there was no other way and sleeping on the termite mounds above the rising waters. The journey to Balovale would take a week. It was said that if the patient could survive the journey there was a good chance that treatment would succeed.

The great Zambezi River and both its major and minor tributaries play a huge part in the life of Central Africa. Its most dramatic outpourings are seen at the Victoria Falls when in full flood but throughout the whole vast area the River was steadily brought under control for its immense power potential. Kariba Dam was built in the 1950s and 60s followed by the Cabora Bassa in the 70s both generating immense hydro-electric benefits to the region. Several smaller dams and power stations followed, harnessing the power for instance of the Luapula Valley waterways.

The first at Kariba between Northern and Southern Rhodesia, now Zambia and Zimbabwe, was probably the most dramatic construction played out against the politics of the time. Part of the development was the re-siting of all the villages within a forecast area of the rising waters once the Dam was completed. A very difficult problem was that of the wild animals. Some were very good swimmers (elephants and hippos) but others (big cats) were not and even those that could fend for themselves in water would possibly be found swimming in the wrong direction once they discovered human being in boats in between themselves and shore-safety. When one considers the incredible variety of beasts involved the mind strains to believe that any rescue at all could be attempted, but it was. Under the planning name of Operation Noah many brave souls from both sides of the river gave their utmost to save as many of the stranded animals as possible. From comparatively 'gentle' bush babies to ferocious baboons, from exhausted antelopes to dangerous mambas, the rescue work went on. A documentary film was made of the work which I once saw broadcast in Africa, but because of the political scene it was never, as far as I know, given much exposure in Europe, although my wife tends to disagree.

One of the tributaries of the Zambezi is the Matanda River just outside Solwezi. On a beautiful Sunday afternoon three lay brothers from the local mission station went fishing in a boat which had a small outboard motor. Because of the strength of the current it was not easy to manoeuvre and this contributed to the ensuing disaster as the boat drifted between a hippopotamus and its calf. The boat was attacked and overturned and one man was savagely bitten and killed outright. Of the remaining two, one was drowned in the river as he tried to reach the bank and the third succeeded in scrambling ashore some distance away from the tragedy.

Harry Bwanausi's two post-mortems did not take him long as both the causes of death and the circumstances were easily ascertained. Even a layman could hazard a guess at the cause of the first one since there was only half a body left over from the mauling by the hippo!

My problems on that Monday morning were slightly different. On the outskirts of Solwezi was a Government Dairy Farm managed by a Dutch Volunteer. He came and asked whether I could carry out a post-mortem on one of his cows which after a few days of being listless and off its food had been found dead in the field that morning. There was no local Veterinary Officer and I was the only qualified Meat and Food Inspector anywhere around, and though the request was a little unusual it was certainly not unique. The animal was lying in what I care to describe as the 'cartoon' position for its demise. In other words it was on its back with all four legs pointing to the sky. It was already gassing up and was bloated but there was no sign of blood around its orifices, thank God, so that Anthrax could fairly well be discounted as a primary cause. The first thing to be done was to open up the carcass and upon the first cut a loud extrusion of gases occurred with some noise rather like a balloon deflating at a party. It did not faze the onlookers of whom probably some 20 or so had assembled by this time, a free show was never to be scoffed at in Africa.

It was difficult to strip and properly examine the internal organs because of the amount of blood retained within the body, but from whatever lymphatic glands I could reach and the general appearance of the flesh there had been no fever, which was a great relief to the Manager. If Red Water Fever for instance had been present then it was possible that the whole of the 56-strong herd might be incubating the disease and would have to be destroyed. Fortunately it was not.

Cutting further into the 'deceased' I unearthed the liver and kidneys. It was then patently obvious as to why the animal had died. A large nail had been swallowed at some time or other and had penetrated the stomach wall and succeeded in infecting most of the organs of the abdominal cavity. The liver was particularly affected with multiple abscesses in the tissues which in turn had spread to the stomach walls and hence the kidneys. The official cause of death was 'Bacterial Necrosis of the Liver and Organs' and you may wonder why I have detailed this episode in such detail.

The main reason was that both the Manager and myself had serious doubts as to what would happen with the carcass once a decision had been made as to its disposal. Free 'nyama' or 'meat' was not to be passed up lightly by the African staff but we had visions of poisoning half of them should we allow diseased meat to be taken. On the one hand there would be rejoicing and many thanks, on the other condemnations, enquiries, police involvement, witchdoctors and so on. We both knew that merely burying the animal was not a solution as it would be dug up in the night and carved up around the villages. It was therefore with some relief that I could show the assemblage the oozing pus dribbling from the internal organs, and equally that the Manager could state quite categorically that all of the internal parts would be burned whether they had abscesses in them or not; and to assist combustion the burning would take place in a pit where the whole mess would be swamped with petrol and diesel prior to ignition.

It then fell to me to state that I agreed entirely with the Manager but that I was prepared to release the carcass into the hands of the African foreman who would be in charge of its distribution and disposal. In this I was comforted by one thought which was that there was no sign of a generalised spread of the infection. Knowing the African way of cooking over a small fire i.e. boiling the food I was pretty confidant that there would be no food poisoning outbreak amongst the staff and their families. Nevertheless I held my breath for the next 48 hours, but all was well.

Pause for thoughts of fish

Since I hail from Grimsby, that great fishing port of the early part of the twentieth century, now sadly left derelict and struggling to find a new role in life, I suppose it would be counted inevitable that since I was almost weaned upon the food I should have retained a liking and taste for fish in all its forms throughout my life. My blushing bride of 1957 was rapidly converted once she was aware of the delicious bounty provided by the fish market and my father's labours. Apart from Grimsby fish, which Father continued to send on a monthly basis through the Post right until we left for Africa in 1965, we have always had access to fish and fish markets.

One might have thought as we did in leaving England that we were saying good-bye to such a delicacy but we were to be wonderfully surprised at what we found. The great lakes and rivers, to say nothing of the bountiful oceans surrounding the continent, provided a variety of fish unmatched I think in the Northern hemisphere. At least as far as I was aware the fish-world at home was bounded by haddock, cod and plaice with a sprinkling of skate and sole thrown in. Seasonally there would be cod roes − never the soft herring ones − and the odd crab to please Mother as well as those fried-up delicacies, with which our daughter was weaned to the taste, cod tongues and cheeks. In his retirement years my father still cycled to the Docks when well into his seventies to retrieve the unwanted cod heads from his old employer as these would by then have gone to be processed into fertiliser. He had discovered that a local fishmonger was very keen to obtain as many pounds of tongues and cheeks as Father could produce. In three years by this simple trading Father put away £1,000, of which as he said to me 'The Taxman knows nothing'. Smoked haddock and kippers, locally processed, were always a delight.

Fish and chips, whether wrapped in the *News of the World* or *The Times*, having gone, we set about devouring as much as we could of that spawned by Africa, and during the next 25 years the rest of the world of our travels. Our first taste and one of our favourites was Nile perch, closely followed by fresh water bream. Mozambique Prawns in all their majestic forms we did not discover until we lived in Malawi some years later. Catfish, whilst fat and meaty, were never to our taste being very 'muddy', which wasn't suprising since they grubbed around in the bottom silt and detritus of the waterways. Kapenta, that little anchovy-like fish, was caught commercially, much to the disgust of the local fishing communities but to the delight of the increasing populations of the towns and cities. Dried and/or smoked fish was always on sale in the markets where Kapenta was a popular local dish. Dried Kapenta with a (hot) tomato dip was used at many a cocktail party in European society.

The fighting tiger fish with its ferocious teeth and incredible aggressiveness was not considered a 'European' dish and was usually given to the African staff after the battle of landing it. The difficulty with preparing and cooking it was that its skeletal system consisted of hundreds of small Y-shaped bones rather like wish-bones on a chicken which were very tough to remove. Once these had been overcome the flesh was quite tasty. Pam then hit on the brilliant idea of mincing the whole together and from the resultant mix she made fish cakes, which were delicious.

The Luangwa River in the Eastern Province harboured a fish with a nasty poisonous spine protruding from its dorsal fin. They were sought-after delicacies by the Africans, who from years of living on the river had the dexterity to disarm them and ready them for the pot. One of our party had the misfortune to be stung on his lower leg as he reeled in his catch. Three days later he was still in considerable pain, although recovering. The fish were called 'Squeakers' by the Europeans as this was the sound they made as they were pulled from the water.

Some years later we lived for three and a half years on St Helena, that lovely, rocky and isolated island in the South Atlantic, famous for many reasons but known internationally as Napoleon's home for the last six years of his life. There Pam was taught to make small, savoury fishcakes the St Helena way from the local produce of 'Jacks' and barracuda. They were equally nice whether served as cocktail party starters or as a main course. We once paid host to a party of ravenous golfing/sailors from a Royal Navy Oceanic Survey Ship, either the *Hermes* or the *Hecate*. I do remember the platefuls of these delicacies that were scoffed with the pre-dinner drinks, but it was not for these that Pam received an endorsement of her culinary skills. The replete and satisfied matelots voted her 'The Cheesecake Queen of the South Atlantic' because of the sweet that was served that night.

When living in the Luapula Province we often went to the fish market some 20 miles away at Kazembe – the fish being sold directly from the dug-out canoes of the fishermen. The Luapula Valley was ever hot and humid so it was always pleasant to sit outside in the shade at Rachel's Bar drinking an ice-cold lager and enjoying one of her partly dried and cooked fish but also served cold. For the life of me I cannot remember the names of these small fish but I do remember how delicious they were.

One of the great joys of our lives has been to have wined and dined in so many different places of the world. At all times fish and fish dishes have played a prominent role. From the 'Fruits de Mer' of the Channel Islands to the 'Andaman Sea Food Basket' of

Thailand. From fish braivlais (barbecues) on the shores of Lake Malawi to fish curry in England cooked to perfection by a well-seasoned former tea planter from Assam.

Apart from the delicious pickled fish in South Africa, the ice-cold and huge oysters in Cape Town were memorable, as was the serving of fish in a frying pan in Seaview. The policy of the restaurant was 'Kill It and Grill It' but I think that they were merely following my mother's never to be beaten skill of frying fish as she said 'With a light dusting of flour – NEVER BATTER – and fry sharply'. 'Batter' in her view was a disguise for inferior fish. She was probably right.

Although I was well travelled as far as eating fish was concerned I never came across Fish Soup until I visited Spain. Fish pies were also to be savoured, not least in the City of London. The lovely country of Portugal spewed over with its piscatorial delights. Their Dover Soles were magnificent and much of their shellfish dishes left but lovely tastes in one's mouth. I was to discover some years later that due to the demands of the vast increase in package holidays Portugal had to import shellfish. Where from? Why Orkney, the islands in the far north of Scotland, where I was by then the Chief Environmental Health Officer.

We were on holiday with Ethel, my mother-in-law, and our daughter, Victoria, and decided to have lunch at the fishing port of Sagres. There Pam thought it would be nice to have a crab starter, Portugese style. One large crab is used and a soup/stew is made with the flesh and it is served in the shell. The participants then partake of the offering, eating as well those gorgeous breads baked locally with copious amounts of water and Vino Verde to cleanse the palate! Pam ordered the crab and it was brought over for us to see prior to preparation and cooking. It was a large green-back, still alive and waving its legs and claws at all and sundry. Ethel turned around to see this animal which we intended eating. Have you ever heard or seen the expression 'Eyes standing out like chapel hat-pegs'? Mother exactly. Great hilarity but as always Ethel tried it, liked it and swore by it ever after.

Looking back I can find numerous 'fishy' incidents which could be related, but one will suffice for the moment. In the Luapula Valley was a large freezer and processing store operated by Irvine

and Johnstone Ltd, the main purpose of which was to freeze-dry
the fish kapenta, for transportation and sale on the line of rail, but
particularly in the Copperbelt. The return journey brought frozen
foods and dry goods for sale to the few outlets in the Province. A
friendly expat called Jack Lynch when calling there one day spotted
what he thought was a salmon. Just why a Scottish salmon had
found its lonely way to a store of the African fishing industry was
never revealed, but Jack bought it anyway and brought it up to the
house. He suggested that if Pam was willing we could have a
dinner party on the following Saturday night using the salmon as
the main course.

There was only one serious problem to that, said Pam, having
studied her recipes, as she had never cooked a salmon before – the
lack of a bottle of white wine. I was duly instructed to scour the
villages and stores for such an item but in three days of searching
I discovered ne'er a drop. On the Saturday morning I was
instructed to drive to the Provincial Headquarters at Mansa. It was
the dry season and the gravel road had recently been re-graded
with most of the pot-holes having been filled in, but there was a
snag. The distance was a little short of 120 miles. The times of such
a journey could vary considerably, depending upon the time of the
year and the state of the road. The longest for me had been about
five and a half hours under a rather ferocious African storm,
conditions which were fortunately not present on the day of the
request but which unfortunately denied me the last excuse for not
undertaking the journey. To add to the (mild) confrontation there
were further limits placed upon the trip in that (a) I was not to get
involved with Chimon Patel in a discussion about cricket –
Indian, English, Test Matches, etc. and (b) I was not to seek
comfort in the arms of old golfing cronies over a beer or three at
the Mansa Club, but was to come straight back with the bottle of
white wine to be obtained at the Patel Syndicate Store which
Chimon master-minded for his grandfather, the founder of the
business.

In the event I was back home by about 2.30 p.m., my only lapse
from grace being the fact that I did have a beer at the Club whilst
the car was being filled since it was right next door. Whilst the
main reason for going down the line was the Bottle, I had been

given a shopping list, all of which could be filled at the Syndicate, but nevertheless family folk-lore persists in the tale of the round-trip of 240 miles for a bottle of wine to cook a salmon for a dinner party in the middle of Africa. One might well ask why one didn't phone around the Province to narrow the search as it were, but there was no access to the communication systems of today, in fact they had not been invented! The dinner party was a great success.

This experience, i.e. the cooking of the salmon, was recalled when my brother-in-law arrived in Orkney several years later with an eleven pounder which he had fished for and caught on the River Tay on his journey through Scotland. My sister and his brother, whose birthday it was, were with him. The salmon was the centre-piece of the birthday dinner that night, the white wine being much easier to obtain.

Kawambwa

When we returned from leave in 1971 I found myself posted to Kawambwa District, about 120 miles from the Provincial Head-quarters, Mansa (formerly Fort Rosebery) in the north of the Luapula Province. Whilst it was certainly the most remote and from the European point of view the least populated of the nine postings I had it was also the most enjoyable both professionally and socially. The Europeans in the town consisted of our two selves and two Dutch Volunteer Nurses plus the Linesman i/c of the electricity line to the power station. With his wife that made a total of six in the little town. We all faced difficult problems from time to time, not least where they involved staff or politics. There was only one small 24-bed hospital which was fully utilised but all local Big-Wigs demanded transportation to Mansa where a large hospital and greater facilities were available. This screwed up the limited transport available for the out clinics.

I was once hauled in front of the local Special Branch which was acting in the belief that the 'party' held one Sunday afternoon was a political 'party' and not a social gathering. Such was the fear of possible opponents of the regime. The first time I ever saw a 'rigged' election, apart from the usual bully-boy tactics of stopping people voting who were not card-carrying UNIP members, was in the first part of our nine-year stay in Zambia. A UNIP Official was haranguing a group of villagers in the days when the chief opponents of UNIP were the ANC led by Harry Nkumbula. The man had a sample ballot paper with the contestants listed and alongside each photograph was the official symbol of the candidate, approved of course by the ruling party. One must remember that with a largely illiterate population (86%) visual symbols were the norm, but to put a bottle of Castle Lager against the picture of Kenneth Kaunda and a Fisi (Hyena) against that of poor Harry and invite the population to mark its preference was an obvious political scandal. Kaunda as one might expect won by a landslide and then backed by the overwhelming success of his Party, persuaded Parliament to ban all other political organisations. For a year or two it lasted as a solidifying ploy. Once the financial rape of the country was complete and the funds ran out, this fact along with the collapse of 'jobs for the boys' created an undercurrent of resentment about the *'apambwambas'* or fat cats with many a cry of 'It was better under Colonialism' by the downtrodden.

There were other Europeans in the district, there being a large Secondary School with expatriate teachers on the road to the valley. The large hospital at Mbereshi contained a variety of nationalities, although the majority of nurses and ancillary staff were Zambian. I think we did a survey once of nationalities around the town and district and counted 19 different expatriate ones. These were all contract workers paid for under 'Aid' schemes devised by their own governments. They were brazenly sought by the political bosses; being needed, so they said, to counter the 'evil effects of Colonialism', as was the plea made to the supine powers at the United Nations. Under the onslaught of all the 'incomers' and the Zambianisation policy the administrative structure of the country rapidly declined into a shambles since all and sundry demanded European levels of pay and living standards.

Housing alone created many grievances. I even had to complete the building of the house in Kawambwa after we moved in to the habitable bit, but by then I had been in the country for six years and knew what to expect. Some newly arrived 'expat' families had to be accommodated in Government Rest Houses for many weeks when these were designed for passing through and over-night stops for government employees and their families. When Pam and I arrived in Lusaka in 1965 the Rest House there was still immaculately run to a 3-star hotel standard, albeit for European Officers. There was a separate one for African staff who required different types of food, sanitary accommodation and facilities for 'extended' families. Come Independence the cry was for equality, which in the event meant downfall and dismay for all. Not one of the 'village' wives brought to the Capital by rapidly promoted husbands or party bosses had the remotest idea as to how to accustom themselves to large bungalow-style houses with electrical power as the heating, cooking and lighting source, Open wood fires, cooking pots and candles had been the standard in the villages. Many a brand new cooker was ruined by an untutored wife lighting a fire inside it to heat her cooking pots on the rings on top.

It was a variation of this simple factor which was a problem at the Secondary School in Kawambwa. The bulk of the new boarding intake came from simple village schools and homes where pit latrines were the norm. Water was carried from streams, wells or springs in the vicinity and so was a precious commodity, not to be wasted on sanitary arrangements. The new students had to be shown how to use a water closet, a flushing system, a hot and cold water system, a shower unit and so on. The Health Assistants of the Department spent up to a week on this work every term. The worst manifestation of the problems faced by the staff unless this 'training' was carried out lay in the fact that the new intake used the WCs as they would the village latrines which they had been used to all their lives. They stood on the seats and squatted and excreted from that position. This rapidly turned the unit into a disgusting and stinking cesspit of fly-breeding excellence. The few who dared to use the flushing cisterns were at first frightened to death at the rush of water. This created even further problems because with the blocked drains the water overflowed and ran all over the concrete floors. The scared students were too embarrassed to report the situation to the maintenance department.

Prior to Independence a development to cure these difficulties had been designed in the form of an Aqua-Privy. Essentially these were a cross between European, African and Asian cultures in the form of a septic tank linked to a drainage system. The single unit was covered by a concrete slab which had foot pads to assist in squatting to relieve oneself. There was an overhead flushing system and the unit could also be used for showering. In a practical sense they were excellent but the new education authorities decreed that the children must be taught to use European facilities and not these last vestiges of Colonialism. Hence they fell into disuse.

Another difficulty which we encountered was that taps on wash-hand basins were being broken with monotonous regularity. It was much more prevalent in the girls' washrooms than in the boys', and one particular factor accounted for all the trouble. From an early age the girls had been used to heavy domestic chores, i.e. the hewing of wood and the drawing of water, to say nothing of pounding the mealies into a flour which when cooked would form the basis of their staple diet, sadza porridge. It was therefore relatively easy for young women of powerful physique and extremely strong hands to turn a tap off and snap it from the joint by applying too much strength to the faucet in question. The basic resolution required tuition but we never entirely cured the problem.

When I was employed at the University of Malawi a few years later I came across a variant in the 'strength' of African women. There was a student called Grace on the Chemistry course. It was the last name that should have been bestowed upon her. In truly African fashion she was called 'Gracee', an extension hardly likely to appeal to fans of Miss Fields of Rochdale. One afternoon it seemed that there was a dispute involving the said 'Gracee', and eventually the problem was wormed out of the other students. Each student was entitled to have his course fees paid by Central Government funds which also paid the University for his food and travelling expenses to and from home. The students received no money to support themselves except for six Kwacha (about three pounds some thirty years or so ago) paid to them as pocket money on the last day of each month.

Whilst 'Gracee' was undoubtedly bright, and had a perfect right to be on the course, she was nevertheless no credit to it having broken numerous burettes and pipettes and a variety of other scientific instruments. In short she was clumsy but she was also a very large and powerful creature, her best feature being her face with its perpetual smile whenever she faced trouble with the authorities. In short no one on the staff had a bad word to say against her. What we did not know at the time was that she burned internally and smouldered on the outside with resentment against her fellow students, mainly men, who constantly laughed at her clumsy endeavours to be a simple scientist.

She devised a perfectly sound scheme of revenge, albeit requiring a degree of effort on her part. She decided to rob her fellow students. On pay day she sought out everyone she could get her hands on and take 50 ngwee (half one Kwacha) from each one. For this price the boys could have sexual relations with her wherever there was bit of privacy around the Polytechnic. It mattered not that the lad had not laughed at her. She was determined to have the cash out of him and if he refused she would beat him up and take it from him – always with the offer of her compliance on the table so to speak. She even hunted down those who had escaped her clutches the previous month. Obviously the Authorities had to take action and she was quickly expelled, much to the relief of the suffering fellows.

The road to the west out of the little town of Kawambwa led to a Government Agricultural Station but about 14 miles out a by-road led to the Experimental Tea Scheme founded and organised by two English expatriates. They had both been recruited at the same time, had arrived almost simultaneously, under the same terms and conditions and for the single post. This fiasco had arisen because one had been recruited by the (then) Ministry of Overseas Development and the other through the Crown Agents. These stupidities occurred more often than one would be led to believe and could originate equally well in London as in the Developing Country, a term much despised by the settlers (mainly farmers) of 3rd or 4th generation European stock.

An instance I recall was seeing a post advertised internationally for an officer to serve a three-year term on the 'Island of St Helena in the South Pacific with air-passages to and from the island'. This from the Foreign and Commonwealth Office in London when the island lies in the South Atlantic, can only be reached by sea and the nearest airport (RAF) is about a thousand miles away on Ascension Island!

The two expatriates had both been planters on estates in Asia; one of them had been in rubber I think in Ceylon but the other one was the genuine article involved in tea on the vast estates in Assam since he left the RAF at the end of the war and chose to remain in the sub-continent. He became a good friend of the family and still is although we have rarely seen him since the splendid curry lunch laid on for the family when he was Custodian of the Ruins of Cowdray Castle and lived in the Roundhouse there. He lives in retirement in Midhurst and we still correspond.

I mention Peter at some length because he came to our aid at a very trying time for the family, a period of some two months in around 1972 when Pam became seriously ill with Hepatitis A. She was mainly bedridden for most of that period and needed careful nursing throughout. The main concern was to get the diet right and this was not easy when fresh vegetables and salads were needed each day.

Our plight was of course made so very much more difficult because there was only the small and over-used African Hospital which was incapable of treating and nursing a case where the patient was a European. The difference in foods and languages and standards of basic hygiene would have been a very serious impediment to her recovery from this severe illness. The sickness involves the liver and a jaundiced condition develops which in extreme cases can result in liver failure. Hence the need for fresh vegetables until the liver can be gently nursed back to full function.

When Peter was clearing the land for the tea estate he also realised that the black 'Dambo' soil uncovered was excellent for growing vegetables for his own use and that of the estate workers. Apart from this we had developed a system of sending a Land Rover to the State Cattle Ranch at Mporokoso where a beast would be shot and bled before it was brought back to the tea estate for the carcass to be butchered. As I was also a Meat and Foods Inspector that was my responsibility. I could also get fish from either Kazembe or down at Ngwewere on Lake Mweru, so that we were well-supplied with the necessary ingredients for any meal. At the time of Pam's illness all this infrastructure was in the process of being developed.

At the height of this problem I had to arrange to pick up the children as they flew in to Lusaka from England for their mid-summer school holidays. Lusaka was over 500 miles away, so it was a sizeable nut to have to crack. It meant leaving Pam, still bed-ridden, alone and with only the House Servant, the faithful and very much respected Peter Chiwaya, to organise the household. There was one West Indian Nurse who was a real strength to Pam and she appeared daily from her duties at the Hospital. Thank God for her because the Asian Doctor Hussein was pretty useless.

The family car at that time was a Peugeot 404-Estate of inestimable worth. It was in this that I set off for Lusaka and promised Pam that I would be back, God willing, by the following Thursday some six days later. One difficulty was that the boys arrived two days earlier than Victoria and we had to stay with friends while I busied myself around Medical Stores, Government Stores and the Ministry of Health HQ. When I collected Victoria at 8.30 a.m. at Lusaka Airport I still had one call to make so it was about half-past ten when we finally hit the road to the north on that memorable Thursday run for home.

I explained the situation to the three of them that there would be a long day's motoring, the provisional stops being at Broken Hill (Kabwe) and somewhere along the road to Mansa, unless we had enough 'juice' to get there on one-tank. Facing us was the ever difficult problem, never solved, of the faster you go the more juice is used and time is gained but the slower you go less juice and hence less expense is incurred but because of the time factor overnight stops might be needed. In the real as opposed to the theoretical world our first task was to start with a full tank and one four-gallon Jerrican also full for emergency purposes. We topped up at a garage in Kabwe, some 86 miles up the road, and set off again for Mufulira another 150 miles away. A further 25 miles brought us to the Congolese Border crossing. Customs and Immigration out of Zambia, 200 yards and another queue for Customs and Immigration into the Congo (now Zaire). Forms to be filled in and checked and passports and identities to be verified. The car and luggage to be opened up and searched – twice! All of this took time and we still had to travel across the Congo Pedicle to reach the ferry crossing over the Luapula River in time for the last boat of the day at 6 p.m. We reached the river at about 5 o'clock and joined a line of vehicles, all of them African wagons piled high with the usual assortment of passengers and animals and charcoal and goods and timber and beer and as usual grossly overloaded. They were a danger in daylight but dreadfully more so when they crawled along at night, usually devoid of rear lights and a terrible menace to all other road users.

Once parked in the line I joined the queue to the Congolese Border Authorities for the usual paper pantomime and petty officialdom for permission to exit the Congo. One should not be too harsh on those officials, dealing as they did with a crowd of shouting and pushing bodies, all of them claiming to be a relative or friend of a friend, with excuses to match the purposes of the journeys undertaken and so on. Overworked, underpaid and very often months behind with their pay coming from Kinshasa. Independence and the rebellion and fight for power in Katanga Province had done nothing for these minor officials but it was at this point with time getting on and sunset rapidly approaching, and with the depressing thought of a night to be spent on the river bank, that fortune suddenly smiled upon us.

The man in charge of all the chaos, or so it seemed to us, detached himself from the madding crowd, came across to us in the queue and politely asked whether we could take his brother with us to Mansa. We had no reason to refuse and with that we were whisked through Customs and Immigration with a smile and courtesy which had been unthinkable an hour earlier. We returned to the car and a young man joined us with his luggage, which fortunately was very little. Having settled ourselves back in the car we were suddenly waved out of the line and down to the river bank to catch the last ferry of the day.

We still had to get back officially into Zambia but officialdom made no problem for us and at last with all obstacles being cleared, apart from the 200 miles still to travel, we set off up the road to Mansa. Half way there I had to stop and use the reserve petrol in the jerrican, but once in the town I found the garage still open, it then being about 8 p.m., and was able to fill up. We snatched a quick drink with a packet of crisps at the Mansa Club next door and then embarked upon the final leg up the escarpment, across the 'Dambos' to the only fast track of road (about 20 miles) recently re-graded with good gravel, into Kawambwa.

When we pulled up at the house, the bedroom curtains parted and a frail face appeared at the window. Whilst I had warned the children that their mother had been and was still seriously ill there was a momentary silence in the car which ended with them piling out to her welcoming arms and the start of her long recuperation. It having been a long and very strenuous day I left the off-loading of the car to Peter and enjoyed an ice-cold Lion Lager, probably sitting at the bar in the 'Elephant's Nest'.

This was rather a nice thatched roof affair which I had built over the concrete patio at the rear of the house. Known to all our friends it became an absolute essential for any social gathering of more extensive scope than a mere dinner party, but was in regular family use for 'Sundowners'. I have always thought that the troubles of the day should be put to rest within the family when the sun goes down. This is especially true for the little children for whom kiss and make-up is a vital part of life when they snuggle down for the night. As far as we adults are concerned, face to face over the bar with a calming drink to savour does more to resolve the stupid quarrels and inanities of the day – rather like having a double bed – than anything else I can think of. Head to head one is forced to communicate and hurt and rancour can often be easily soothed away.

Being without a job Pam decided to improve her culinary skills. She had always been a good cook but now she set about the task in earnest. I have mentioned the fact that I had access to meat and fish and vegetables – the basic ingredients – so all that was needed in a sense was guidance. This she found in the *Robert Carrier Cook Book*, the definitive tome of its day which I had bought for her as a birthday present with some prescience long before we had ever heard of Kawambwa. In the two years spent there she became a very fine exponent of the art and one which came into full blossom some years later when we lived on the remote island of St Helena in the South Atlantic.

Kilwa Island and the Luapula River

Lake Mweru is about 200 miles long and some 30 miles across at
its widest point. At its southern end it flows into and becomes the
Luapula River. It is one of the smallest of the African Great Lakes
and supports numerous fishing villages along the shore. There were
probably about a dozen junior staff scattered along its length
starting at the only place of any size, Nchelenje, the terminal point
of the 60 miles of road joining it to Kawambwa. At that point the
road swung to the north following the line of the lake to its far
meeting at the end with the Congolese Border. By then one would
have been about 170 plus miles from home, about three hours on
good gravel roads with easy corrugations in the dry season but
anything up to five or six hours at the height of the rains.

Loading up the LWB Blue-coloured (WHO-supplied) Land
Rover took several days. Having to take a thousand different items
ranging from bicycle spares to pencils to mealie meal to paraffin to
candles to uniforms, I think you will guess that by the time we left
Kawambwa at 5 a.m. the vehicle was loaded to the axles, with
springs at their limits. Obviously the travelling personnel sat in as
much space as was possible, and one always had to remember the
fuel for the return journey, a constant problem in the distant rural
areas.

Despite the difficulties outlined above there were occasions
when I would have a light load and could for one reason or another
dispense with the services of my usual driver and I would take the
vehicle myself. In that event Pam was able to accompany me. One
of her remarks made as we turned for home at the far end of the
Lake has stayed with me all these years. 'Who are the fools around
here?' she said. She was referring to the fact that at all of the villages
we passed the inhabitants were lying mainly fast asleep in the shade
of their huts prior to sun-downer time when the canoes would be
readied for a night's fishing on the moon-lit Lake. We then had a
long way to go over rutted and water-filled pot-holed roads and
would arrive home some time between 7 p.m. and 9 p.m. tired
out. But it was part of the job. The problems were there to be
overcome and there was a great deal of satisfaction when one
achieved success in a particular case.

It should be remembered that there was still a world-wide search going on for the remnants of that crippling and vicious disease, smallpox. With something of a start of disbelief I received a message that there was a case on Kilwa Island lying towards the Congolese shore of Lake Mweru. There was no way of communicating with the island other then by hand, the message had taken a week to reach me, so there was nothing for it but to go there and see for myself. This was not as easy to arrange as one might imagine. The only Government vessel that could be used for such a trip was the fast Police Boat lying at Nchelenge. A trip down there and a chat to the Officer-in-Charge went well. 'Yes' we could use the Boat and 'Yes' the Police Coxswain would be made available for the trip, but there was a snag. We would have to supply the petrol as there was nothing in the town and the Police Service could not spare any of their own. A date was agreed and I was introduced to the Police Sergeant-Coxswain, Enoch Simbotwe, one of the most memorable Africans I have known.

He was a stranger in a strange land because he was a Lhosi from Mongu in Barotseland, but was immensely respected in the district because of his innate courtesy, good manners and fine bearing. Not every outsider in a tribal sense was readily accepted into a Bemba heartland. In my time in Africa one other Lhosi springs to mind for similar reasons. He was the Principal Medical Assistant in Solwezi and my next door neighbour, Chris Mundia, who once took the boys shooting wildfowl where they got covered in leaches. Having been brought up on the River Zambezi and its flood plains, Enoch was an expert waterman who because of this upbringing had developed into a powerful human being. He was slightly under 6 ft in height, which had placed him upon the reserve list of paddlers for the Royal Barge. This was used by the 'Litunga', the King of Barotseland, on ceremonial occasions, the most importance of which was the 'Kuomboka Cermony' when the King moved by water from his home in Mongu to his Winter Palace above the rising flood waters of the Zambezi. To the chosen paddlers it was a great honour, one much sought after and a lasting disappointment to Enoch that he never attained it. To make up for this he was blessed with a superb physique which together with his watermanship made him an outstanding Coxswain.

On the day of the journey to Kilwa Island we left early and we were in Nchelenje by 8 a.m. Another hour spent in fuelling the boat and stocking it with both metal jerricans full of petrol and one plastic one full of water and we were away. The twin Yamaha outboards cleaved a fine creamy wake across the Lake, with Pam and I sitting like smug cats in the stern on this most beautiful of African mornings. Enoch handled the steering and tuned the engines with ease whilst the fourth member of the party, Lefan Kamfwa, the Senior Health Assistant, sat beside him

We had been going about half-an-hour when the boat took a huge ninety-degree turn to the left, as we land lubbers say, which put us onto a new course to port heading for the mouth of the Luapula River. Enoch shouted an explanation to us over the noise of the engines. There was apparently a Congolese fishing barge operating in Zambian waters which he had spotted as a dot on the horizon. As we drew closer it was possible to see that it was no ordinary fishing vessel but rather a collection point for the numerous dug-out canoes now seen scattering at the approach of the Police Boat. The operator of the barge was a character right out of the novels of Hemingway, Maugham and Greene. The visual picture is complete if you ever see the film *The African Queen*, starring Humphrey Bogart as Charlie Allnutt, except that the character we saw that morning at the top of the gangway as we boarded the vessel was coloured, had a variety of gold fillings in his teeth and was not only filthy greasy, he was exceptionally so and was exceptionally subservient and 'Uriah Heepish' to boot. In short he was not a very likeable individual, even should one have a morbid interest in villains and their ilk.

The mouth of the river was a protected area as many immature fish fed there on the rich food provided by the delta waters. Enoch proceeded to lay the law down to this individual in no uncertain terms. In Army jargon he 'tore him off a strip' as he appeared to be a persistent offender. Threatened with confiscation of his boat and incarceration in a Zambian gaol (no one disputed things with Enoch) he became a cringing, whining wretch and was more than relieved (I almost expected him to pee himself with relief) when a decision was made to impose an instant fine instead. This took the form of a 'Fish Tribute' for the Police Mess in Nchelenje, Enoch himself selecting the best from the holds. The last we saw of the vessel and its memorable Master was as it slid round the back of Killwa Island on its way into the safety of Congolese waters. I should perhaps point out that the International Boundary was such that Kilwa was very much nearer to the Congolese side of the Lake with only a channel between it and that country.

Freed from his police duties Enoch set course for the island, now clearly visible. We made landfall at the nearest fishing village but only at the third one did we receive the directions we needed. The suspect 'patient' lived about a quarter of a mile up the escarpment from the beach where the boat was secured. The path at the top took us past the reed-constructed fence surrounding the house/houses of the Chief, whose name I forget. I do however remember his framed MBE fixed to the gate post for all to see. It had been presented to him, probably by the British High Commissioner in Lusaka, on behalf of Her Majesty the Queen, at the time of the granting of Independence. The accompanying text spoke of the Chief's 'Loyal and Faithful service . . .' of which he was immensely proud. Seeing as it was in this still remote part of Africa, it was certainly a moving moment, representing as it did in such a small way the finer aspects of Colonial rule.

The village was clustered beneath the shade offered by some magnificent mango trees where the fruit was not only much larger but about a month more advanced than on the mainland. This probably had something to do with the very hot and humid conditions. We were given seats under the trees and great was the crowd of villagers who squatted around us, many of whom – especially the young ones – were seeing a 'white' man for the first time. Some of the older children happily pushed the younger ones forward who howled with fright even when our arms were rubbed to show that the (white) colour stayed and we were not dressed up witch doctors. The patient and a few others duly arrived, but it was clear from the outset that the problem was not one of smallpox but of scabies, caused by the Itch Mite, *Sarcoptes Scabiae*. The island clinic was about five miles away but at the other end of the island, the outward journey to which was not only tiring but fraught with other difficulties of which accompanying a sick patient covered in scratches and sores was only the start. The return would have been even worse as the medicine, Benzyl Benzoate, applied liberally to the affected areas of the body, dries white on the skin, which in turn would scare any simple islanders to death.

Once the examinations were over the discussions took place in true African fashion with everyone joining in, as to what was to be done. The Chief accepted the situation and promised to do his best to secure a safe journey for the patients to the clinic. We were inclined to the view that the best way was to get a message to the Medical Assistant at the Clinic, who we were assured had the prized possession of a bicycle, explaining the position and asking him to attend. I therefore wrote a note for the Chief's messengers to carry to him.

There was then a flurry of farewells with much hand-shaking and when it was my turn I apologised for my impoliteness in not bringing a gift for the Chief, as was customary, but he assured me that the visit was a gift in itself. Lefan pointed out that we had fine fish in the boat and he was sure that some would be sent to the Chief. For my part I asked whether it was possible to obtain some of the cape mangoes, high above in the trees. Young boys vied with each other to obtain the best for the visitors and we duly departed laden down with mangoes and good wishes.

Half way down the path to the boat there was a tiny hut and out of it came a very old African. It was obvious that he had been a robust and strapping youth, but the ravages of age had done their worst. (Who coined that miserable phrase about growing old gracefully?) Over his bones, for there was little more than that, was draped a British Army khaki overcoat. He held in his hand the tiniest bunch of spring onions, that he had obtained from his garden. He fell to his knees by the side of the track and held them out to Pam, a gesture so sincere and so genuine in gratitude for our visit that she was hard put not to cry. With the crowd of villagers singing and chanting around us we made our way to the boat.

The moon had appeared by the time we reached Nchelenje which would have been about 6 p.m. We then still had 60 miles to go and reached home somewhere around 9 or 10 p.m. What a day!

It would be difficult to improve upon experiences such as these and one should not be misled into thinking that they were an everyday occurrence. Far from it, but they are recounted because of their abiding interest and as a balance to the countless hours of wearisome journeys over miles and miles of 'Bloody Africa', as the saying goes. I can still taste the dust. Oddly enough I can still recall the smell of Africa as it used to hit one as soon as the plane doors were opened. As for the heavenly scent of rain on the hot, still air at the end of the dry season, this will stay with me forever.

One other event is worth recounting of the time spent in Kawambwa. It occurred when Pam was in the process of recovering from her very serious bout of Hepatitis. A survey was required of the villages spread along part of the Luapula River which marked the international border between Zaire (Congo) and Zambia. It was as usual for smallpox vaccination purposes as part of the on-going WHO programme to eradicate the appalling disease and its affects from the world. The after-effects of Pam's illness were still very much in evidence, particularly her two or three stone weight loss and her very 'white' appearance caused by her being bed-ridden for so long. As the trip was scheduled to take place over the best part of a week this time we were to use the large, slow diesel-engine Police boat. Since this was capable of carrying passengers and supplies, it was agreed that Pam should come along for part of her rest and recuperation process. I figured it was the least that the Government owed to us for their unsympathetic approach to our problems during her illness. One of these had been to report me for disciplinary purposes for being off-post when I left Pam in her sick-bed and drove the 500 miles to Lusaka to pick up the children as they arrived from England for their summer holidays. Most unpleasant.

What particularly is recalled to mind is again our splendid Coxswain, Enoch Simbotwe. I remember sitting under the stars with the boat tied up at a distance from the shore to avoid the worst of the mosquitoes when he suddenly said, 'There is a boat coming'. This when only the natural sounds of the river's night life were audible. Sure enough five minutes later a two-man canoe swept past silently on the current. He told me that he always knew because his 'friends' told him. His 'friends' turned out to be the frogs. Whenever there was movement or business on the river not to their liking they always dived and stopped croaking until the real or apparent danger had passed. As their croaking was otherwise constant throughout the night their warnings were as good as and probably better than any electronic device.

We had organised the trip so that messengers were sent 24 hours ahead of the boat to alert the villagers to the impending arrival of the vaccination teams. There was no other means of communication in those parts and to arrive unannounced would not only have alarmed everyone it would have been a gross discourtesy. The people would simply have faded away into the surrounding bush.

On one occasion when inadequate notice had been given we turned up at a school after lunch and then tried to explain our intentions. There was a lot of whispering amongst the students as we tried in vain to get one of them to volunteer to be the first to be vaccinated. It was of no use and one by one and then in a mad rush across the desks they disappeared through the window openings, all thirty something of them. We were delayed by a further day as the messengers and vaccinators rounded them up and demonstrated the techniques to be employed. When the class was re-assembled and the job successfully undertaken the master explained that there had been a rumour floating around that all their teeth were to be examined and if faulty in any way they would be pulled out. The final straw was when they saw the large bucket being carried by the Senior Health Assistant, Lefan Kamfwa. It was a medical stainless steel one and they knew that in the medical centre it was always full of blood and used dressings and so on. Hence the panic.

We slept in the village huts wherever provided but otherwise stayed on the boat because of the mosquito problem. After several days we turned around for home and half way along the river Enoch decided to take a couple of hours off so we headed for a thatched river-bank beer hall on the Congolese side. There we sat for a couple of hours drinking 'Simba' Beer, except that in Pam's case because of her recent illness it had to be Coca-Cola. It was most enjoyable sitting in the shade against the dwarf walls, there were no windows, and feeling the cooling effects of the gentle breeze after the heat of the river.

One memory of the river is of passing numerous stripped carcasses of crocodiles, the unwanted parts, as the licensed hunters required only the skins. It was suggested to me that these bodies would provide food in the river for the fishes and perhaps an occasional crocodile so that it was not as bad as it looked to European eyes. In other words everyone benefited – except of course the original crocodiles which were easily hunted and shot as they lay in the shallows or sandbanks. The protruding eyes glowed red in the light of a torch and provided a perfect target for the kill. Their skins were scraped, salted and sent to the nearest Cold Storage Board abattoir. There they were measured, valued and purchased, then packed along with the skins of slaughtered animals for trans-shipment to the tanners and manufacturers of the outside world.

Peter Chiwaya

Before I embark upon a 'Zambian Summary' I feel upon reading the above that I have not done justice to one Peter Chiwaya, our very much loved and respected House Servant for most of our time in that country. His family came from a village on the Samfya Road about ten miles out of Mansa. I seem to remember that he had numerous sisters but he was the middle one of three brothers. Reuben was employed within the Post Office at Mansa and Simon the eldest was the driver allocated to me when I first arrived at the hospital in Abercorn. He eventually transferred with me to Kasama, and Lusaka, which is where we first came across Peter. When we had difficulty in finding a House Servant, Simon told me that his brother had been taught to cook and clean by a Scottish lady in Mansa but was now employed within the team as a vaccinator. Once approached and appointed Peter then and for the next nine years proceeded to exceed all our expectations not only in his duties but in his loyalty and understanding of our needs. I would that I could say the same for ourselves because there were times when the demands and responsibilities placed upon him were far in excess of what one would have expected. Many were the problems to be faced when I was transferred from post to post, sometimes even when I was on leave and he coped with the burden of travelling to a new district or province burdened not only with his own family's goods and chattels but also our own worldly possessions. He once got stuck in the Congo Pedicle in the wet season for four days with a broken down open 7-tonner laden with household goods on his way to yet another posting, this time in Mansa. He came with us from Lusaka to Ndola, back to Lusaka, to Solwezi, to Mansa and finally to Kawambwa and never once did I fear that he would not turn up, possessions all intact.

It is however not for all the transfers that I remember this fine man and his concerns for our welfare in a general sense. He it was who was left in charge of the house when I had to depart on the long round trip to Lusaka to collect the children when Pam was suffering from Hepatitis and in bed for two months. I described earlier that I was away for a week and with no immediate means of communication (the nearest phone was 120 miles away in Mansa) for help and advice, so much of the normal running of the house was left to him. For this alone I am forever grateful.

It is however on a more direct and personal level that I shall remember him. It occurred in Solwezi when Pam had returned to England to arrange for Matthew to join his older brother, Simon in school at St Lawrence College in Ramsgate. I was due for leave shortly after but in the intervening period a telegram came from Pam telling me that my Grandfather (Fred) Tonge was extremely ill and was not expected to survive. He was then in his 94th year and quite clearly was the patriarch of the family. To an African mind this carries very serious implications. When three days later I received the news that he had died Peter, who was already aware of the first telegram, knew that I was depressed and upset and the reasons why.

That night at about 11 p.m. after I had gone to bed and was half asleep I came fully awake when I heard the outer door being unlocked and footsteps stumbling around the lounge. I went through and put the light on to find Peter tumbling over furniture in the centre of the room. He stank of 'Chibuku' or 'Pombe' or 'Shake-Shake' or whatever it is now called. He had been down to the local shebeen which he would normally only do once a month so it had to be something serious for this to happen.

He blinked and saw me for the first time. He then proceeded to stagger his way across the room and whether he intended to or whether he just stumbled I am not sure although I prefer to believe the first, he placed his arms around my neck. He told me in a drunken mumbling and with odoriferous (it sounds a bit better than 'stinking', which the native beer certainly invokes) breath how he had been out to the beer hall to get drunk for me since I could not go to my village to pay my respects to my grandfather, the Bwana Mkubwa of the family. We Europeans pay lip service to paying respect to the deceased but in his beliefs unless I did this I would be thought by the family to have contributed to the death, this being even more important because of the age and seniority of my grandfather. I found a large torch in the kitchen and led him to the back door where I showed him the path home, and off he stumbled, weaving his way to his house, having done his duty by me and called to tell me about it.

I then put out the lights after securing the doors and returned to my bed, whereupon I burst into a very tearful stupor, but eventually sleep came. I was awakened at 6.30 a.m. by Peter with the morning cup of tea. Nothing was said by either of us.

When we finally left the country I found him a post as a cook in the local authority rest-house since, as he explained to me, 'The heart is too hurt when you go'. The house in the village in which he was to live bulged with every kind of household utensil that we were not taking with us. With a brand new bicycle and an extra month's salary in his pocket, the parting was still a fraught and tearful one, as we said our farewells.

Zambian summary

At the risk of repeating myself, for I might have been on song about this earlier, I just wanted to mention my feelings about hiring servants. The word 'servant' seems in these politically correct days to be frowned upon and is much derided. Nevertheless I feel I have been a 'servant' all of my professional life and have never felt the need to be 'subservient', which is what many people seem to interpret from the status. My first Chief, Herbert Brant, put the matter in a nutshell when he found me being less than polite to a local ratepayer. 'You are a Public Servant. Why? Because the public pays your salary and is entitled to be respected and deserves a polite response in its dealings with the Council employees'. The same applies in all walks of life. The taxi driver is employed to serve you, as is the waiter, the post office counter clerk, the shopkeeper and so on. When, therefore, we came to Africa, Pam and I had no trouble with the concept of master and servant. The terms of employment were agreed upon and generally speaking were much sought after. The provisions included a basic wage, a free house, a bag of mealie meal per month, school fees and uniforms for his children plus his own working clothes throughout the year. The anti-colonialists, usually personified by schoolteachers, without even trying to understand, scoffed at these sort of living and employment arrangements which had evolved over many generations and mocked them with the word 'paternalism'. The Africans should be taught to stand on their own two feet and should not be held back by this colonialist approach of master and servant which was a constraint upon their march to FREEDOM! Such was the attitude then prevailing of the newcomers to the country which often manifested itself even further when they included the servants in their evening meals.

Having completed three 3-year contracts with the Zambian Government and my services being no longer required, we left the country to return home. Old timers in the country when we first arrived had warned us not to stay more then a maximum of three years in Africa. It will get under your skin, they had said, and be like a perpetual itch buzzing around your body. In short you will be in love with the place and wherever you travel in the world you will always retain an abiding affection for the continent.

We therefore had no desire to leave but as an expatriate with an expiring Work Permit there was really no option. Being on expatriate contract terms gave certain benefits, particularly with regard to salary and final gratuity, one of which was the assistance given towards boarding school fees for children receiving full-time education in England. They also had the benefits of flying out to Africa three times a year during the school holidays. Effectively this meant that Africa became 'Home' and England the place where they went to school. It also had the effect of leaving the three of them with mixed feelings all round as to the 'benefits' of a boarding school education. They all survived the experience and Pam and I are sure that overall the standards of education, the travel, the overseas experiences, etc. more than balanced the books to counter the loneliness of separation for us all. The enforced separations and joyful reunions have always made for a close-knit and warm and loving relationship within the family, which exists to this day.

The agony of decisions to be made for the education of their own children now rests with them, thank goodness. Any detailed views upon their own education must lie with them, but as always with parents, 'We done our best' as we saw it at the time.

Contracts and travel

There is a school of thought that says you could always have stopped your wandering ways by ending your contracts and returning home to a life of standard local government tedium and bureaucracy, but this would not have been for me or for Pam for that matter. By the time we got to Malawi we were well beyond those sort of inclinations and feelings and in addition the children were well settled in their schools and enjoyed the experience of 'Africa' being home and 'England' merely the place they went to school. Whilst I did on one memorable occasion take a job in London (Southwark Borough Council to be exact) it only lasted a couple of weeks and I resigned in order to go off to the Middle East for three months to work for the Americans.

Completing three 3-year contracts meant that we obtained unprecedented opportunities for international travel. In the case of Zambia it meant travel to and from the Dark Continent at the beginning and end of each contract. In this way we became familiar with the ins and outs of flying and cruising, long before there were the long-haul jets and package tours of the present day. The era of mass travel had not even been thought of let alone brought into operation.

It was therefore with great anticipation that we set off for Europe in 1968 at the end of our first contract. We routed ourselves via Kenya and Greece (Nairobi and Athens) and enjoyed the experiences thoroughly. Then England. In retrospect we had scheduled too much leave (four months) than was good for either us or the families. It culminated in doing endless rounds of 'arrival and hello' visits, then 'staying' visits and then 'farewell' visits around the British Isles from our rented accommodation near Guildford. This put considerable stress upon relationships and family ties and we vowed that the next time we arrived home we would take half the leave entitlement and choose a base where people could visit us. As it turned out three years later we offended my mother when we took the family off for a month caravanning on the Continent with only a brief week-end 'arrival and hello' visit!

Inevitably in the three years working on the other side of the globe a totally different life-style had developed, with sporting and social habits singularly at variance with those in England. Simply put the beer tasted ghastly, warm and sweet in comparison to the ice-cold sharp-tasting lagers of Africa. The pubs were not open at the right hours, i.e. when one was thirsty in mid-afternoon or early evening. People went out for a drink at 9.00 p.m. or thereabouts when we were ready for bed.

I remember Mother and Father trotting off to the Conservative Club in Cleethorpes one Saturday night at 7.30 p.m. in order to safeguard seats for themselves and their friends in a corner of the dance floor when there was a 'Turn' (comedian or singer) performing. We arrived some minutes later to find the upstairs bar not yet opened whereas the downstairs one (Men Only) was. Father promptly hauled his willing son off for a beer or two with his cronies downstairs and Pam was left parched with Mother and her elderly friends. She was not best pleased.

At the end of the leave in 1968 we put Simon into boarding school at St Lawrence College, Ramsgate, Kent. It was the start of 15 worrying years trying to give each of the three children as much equality in terms of educational opportunities as we could manage with our limited financial resources and fluctuating international exchange rates for Sterling. It was not easy, but then I suppose the same things happen to all families who care about the future for their offspring.

Whilst we were well aware of our problems, one aspect that we never thought of was the strain that half-term school leaves could place upon everyone. The school would be closed for a week, the children passed from Ramsgate to Guildford to Shrewsbury and so on, to say nothing of the burden placed upon various family members for meeting and greeting and despatching them to and from a variety of airports and railway stations. Even with the use and expense of 'Universal Aunts' it was always a difficult time. I freely apologise for the thoughtless difficulties caused to any members upon whom we placed too much of a burden.

At times the boys stayed with the parents of friends from the school who lived nearby. On one occasion Simon and Matthew stayed at a poultry farm in Kent after returning a weekend early from Africa. Simon had a bad dose of D and V. He was diagnosed as suffering from 'suspected cholera'. I think his reported projectile vomiting attack on the doctor instigated that diagnosis! The farm, its produce and inhabitants were promptly placed into quarantine until the all-clear was given some days later.

When a contract has been successfully completed and no renewal is in the offing then upon return to England it becomes a search for work. It is not immediately obvious in one's elation at the family re-unions and holidays and new cars and sometimes new houses and investments and so on. After a month or so with all rejoicings out of the system, reality sets in and the future has to be squarely faced. In my case, in the desire to work outside England, and missing already the life in Africa, the obvious starting point was the Overseas Development Administration edifice at Eland House, Stag Place, Victoria, London. The second calling point was at the Crown Agents, very often not recognised as a separate company but one in which the Government had a large shareholding. Its basic function was to act as a 'Buying' Agent for Governments world-wide. Its recruiting arm was an adjunct to its prime objective although the recruitment of personnel was regarded as just another sought-after commodity. The third starting point was the Inter-University Council for Lecturers and Teachers and Technicians for Affiliated Teaching Establishments World-Wide. In the meantime one would naturally be searching for overseas contract posts in whatever newspapers or journals were readily available. Then having found the post that one was seeking came the tiresome business of completing reams of application forms and passport details and security declarations and so on and so on. If one was lucky then an interview was forthcoming, following which one might or might not be offered the position sought. It is always galling to find oneself as 'first reserve', just in case there is an unforeseen problem with the 'appointee', although I should point out that on two occasions I have been offered posts on the rebound when exactly this event did arise.

In each case it had placed the employers in serious difficulty and their first thought was to turn to the 'reserve'. Each time I was readily available and was immediately appointed to the newly vacant post. In one instance it resulted in over five years employment in the desert in Saudi Arabia, and in the other being offered the post of Lecturer in Public Health at the University of Malawi.

CHAPTER 3

Malawi 1974–80

MALAWI IS A BACKWATER, being one of the smallest of the African nations. It has extensive agricultural interests, particularly tea estates, a large lake some 350 miles long and 50 miles wide, but small by African standards, for certain fishing interests. Centred upon the lake the tourist potential is quite remarkable but the development has to be slow because the present infrastructure – hotels, transport, game lodges, boats, trained staff and so on – is quite incapable of withstanding a mass tourist agenda. Further it has suffered financially and by mal-administration in much the same way as other newly independent countries have, so that the present prospects are not particularly good.

One odd thing post-independence that has to be recorded is that the President, the Ngwazi (Leader) Dr Hastings Kamuzu Banda, was quite obviously a good old fashioned dictator. Whilst the rest of the African leaders of the time paid cynical lip-service to democratic ideals, he quite clearly and openly ruled by decree. For instance he made sure that the agricultural labour force stayed in the rural areas under the 'Bully Boy' tactics of the Malawi Young Pioneers, the youth wing of the Malawi Congress Party. Note the initial letters, i.e. MCP. In Europe at the same time of when I write, there was a great 'Feminist Revolution'. Led by such as Germaine Greer, who should have known better but probably made a fortune out of leading the revolt with slogans such as 'Burn Your Bras' and 'Male Chauvinist Pigs'. Again note the initial letters i.e. MCP. The much-impugned males of the world took this as their slogan in revenge. Shirts, sweaters, vests and tattoos became commonplace as did ties picturing pigs with the letters MCP below. A newcomer to the country and university was met at the airport and came through Customs and Immigration wearing such a tie, which was not spotted. It was promptly snatched off him in the Arrivals Hall and hidden, much to his bewilderment. The political gaffe was gently explained; as was the fact that there was a large and growing Islamic faction in the country to which porcine ribaldry, irrelevant in Christian dominated England, was tantamount to hurling the first gauntlet in the next Crusade.

Certainly the President held elections, for selected candidates of the only Party allowed, the voters being paid up members of the Congress. Parliament consisted of a half-day address by the Ngwazi followed by ten days of sycophantic praise by the Members for the pearls of wisdom delivered from on high by the President! In so far as it kept Malawi afloat in the turbulent times of the wars in Angola, Mozambique and Rhodesia (Zimbabwe) prior to their gaining independence, the policy worked. It was also aided by the fact that Malawi continued to trade with South Africa and willingly supported the scheme – WENELA – was the acronym for the organisation but I cannot now decipher it, which recruited volunteer workers for the mines in South Africa. It was always interesting to see the end-of-contract miners arriving at Chileka airport in Blantyre carrying stuffed suitcases and new blanket rolls as gifts for their families at the end of their two years away from home. A sight which was replicated for me at Heathrow on many occasions when I flew in from Saudi Arabia at the end of another contract. There was never a shortage of volunteers, whichever continent one was gainfully employed upon. In Malawi's case it was of benefit to all concerned. Under the scheme the Malawian Government received payment for the work in international credits – gold or sterling (the South African currency being Rands) – and made payments to the local families in Malawian currency (Kwacha). The miners, fed and housed in much the same way as the expatriate contract workers in the Middle East, were given wages every month and upon return to Malawi their leave pay and end of contract bonuses were waiting for them in the local banks and post offices. No wonder the scheme was popular in a country geared to agriculture.

The economies of the adjoining countries suffered by supporting the Freedom Fighters and it was interesting to see the visitors to Malawi, from Zambia in particular, gasping at the sights of loaded supermarket shelves and bulging food stalls at the markets. We counted ourselves to be very lucky to be in this little oasis as the international war clouds swirled around.

Personally I believe that marrying the Western World political systems with the Paramount Chiefs and their responsibilities with due allowances for the Settlers, as was being developed by the Colonial Service, was the way forward; but the times they was a-changing and 'colonialism' was a dirty word, especially to the Americans, so independence was granted to many ill-prepared and under-prepared colonies. 'INTERNATIONAL AID' would solve all things was the cry, whereas real development only comes from the blood, sweat, toil and tears of personal commitment. The Colonial authorities administered vast areas of Tribal Trust Lands with the help and approval of the Paramount Chiefs, from which European settlement and development was barred. A serious point largely overlooked and mainly forgotten in today's world. Perhaps a descendant of mine will turn out to be a historian who upon reading this will feel intrigued enough to start researching a true account of the effect the Colonial System had upon Africa. I suppose one could start by reading Thomas Packenham's *The Scramble for Africa*, which is concerned with international wheeling and dealing, the fight to obtain colonies and land for mining and development. What I would wish to see would be research into the 'British' Colonial Service and its various triumphs and disasters within the countries concerned. How often have I heard the cry from local Africans 'It was better under Colonialism!!' When President Mugabe started his policy of stealing and re-distributing land I remember comments made by two Zimbabweans, one a taxi driver, the other a caddie, both employed at the busy tourist centre of Victoria Falls.

One said 'What do I want with land and farming. I am a town boy I am not a farmer and I know nothing about it. I am a good taxi driver and I earn good money from the tourists here, which will not happen if the tourists all run away'. Substitute the words 'taxi driver' by the word 'caddie' and you have the African case against the Mugabe reforms in a nutshell.

The Polytechnic

The Polytechnic in Blantyre was one of three colleges comprising the University of Malawi. The others were both in the old capital city of Zomba some 40 miles distant. The Polytechnic buildings had been designed and erected by the Americans with scant regard for local weather conditions. They were thus able to funnel a breeze up and down the corridors to combat the humid conditions found in say Florida and the Gulf of Mexico. The trouble was that the site was 4000 ft up on top of the Central African Plateau and had precious little in the way of sea-level humidity but plenty of dust-generating heat spirals. The place in short was incapable of being cleaned with dust and dirt swirling around the corridors every hour. Building design faults were incapable of eradication, the only solution being to raze it to the ground and start again, but there being no money the Malawians were stuck with it.

The Americans do not operate very well outside their own country. It has been said on more than one occasion that they or their Governments do not know where the rest of the world is and one can well believe that this is so. I do not think any of us would be much different if we were to sit comfortably in the middle of the richest country on earth.

The other thing that strikes one about the Americans abroad is their absence of either knowledge or curiosity about the countries they live in. Stimulated perhaps by the examples set by their Presidents and 'Air Force One', the Americans take America with them wherever they go. Working for them some years later in Saudi Arabia and stated purely as a simple example, it was a common sight to see large truck/trailers arriving at the camp mess halls bearing the legend 'TEXAS BEEF', having been trans-shipped all the way from the States when a perfectly acceptable alternative was available in Southern Africa and Europe. 'Acceptable' that is to everyone except the Americans.

Similarly their naivety was something to behold at times. In Malawi an agreement was reached with the American Peace Corps for a detachment to work in the rural areas improving the lot of the local people by building model villages. Within a year most of them were living in huts the like of which the villagers were perfectly capable of building for themselves. Even worse was the fact that they decided in the face of much advice to adopt the African way of life, with 'bonding' being a prime objective. Whatever may be said about a 'love in' or 'hugging and kissing' à la United States, it is most definitely not African. With a strictly conservative leader it was only a matter of time before the Government took action. Sure enough the President declared that he needed overseas aid to uplift the Malawians and it was not for the donors to come and live like the poorest of the villagers indoctrinating them with the worst of their own cultures. Out went the Peace Corps en bloc.

The 'conservative leader' mentioned above had also decreed that women, including expatriates, were not allowed to wear trousers, unless they were of Asian cultures, and must wear long dresses with sleeves at all times. Men were not allowed to grow their hair longer than the lower lobe of the ear. Many were the startled new arrivals at the airport being handed a pair of scissors and told to go and cut their carefully barbered locks in the toilets before they could be allowed into the country.

An incident occurred when a local expatriate resident whose hair had grown 'illegally' long was accosted by the police and physically escorted to the barber shop. On the way he pointed out several others in the street similarly breaking the law. The policeman agreed and took them all under his wing to get their hair cut. The prime suspect was not the most popular of men that afternoon with his fellows but the rest of the population found it extremely amusing.

I do not wish to imply that Americans individually cannot be the nicest of nice people with a generosity of spirit difficult to match. Fortunately I have met many of them and admire so much of their attitudes and outlook. Unfortunately their tendency metaphorically of never using a Forty-Five when a Bazooka is handy seems to dominate so much of their culture and lifestyle with the winning philosophy being their only thought.

The work was not unduly taxing, more especially since I had the benefit of two congenial colleagues to work with. David Broad, a Chemist, was the Head of the Department, but the Senior Lecturer in Public Health was John Channel, an old Africa hand who had served many years in Uganda.

David was an interesting character blessed with a sharp mind and even more the gift of hand and eye co-ordination when it came to sporting prowess. Never having played the game before he came to Malawi, his first Handicap at golf was 11. By dint of playing and practising regularly he eventually came down to a 4 but then became bored with the game. As a change and a challenge he took up bowls. Two years later he was a member of the Malawian Team at the Commonwealth Games in, I think, Australia. When he returned home he dropped that particular sport and decided to spear-head a challenge upon the 1,000,000 and 1 Darts Record as featured in the Guinness Book of World Records. The event, staged for charity by the Round Table Society, was held over the next four or five days non-stop by players at the Blantyre Sports Club. They achieved their aim but were beaten shortly afterwards by a 'Pub' team from England.

Not satisfied with this, David finally made a solo attempt upon the 'Most Trebles in 12 Hours' Darts Record, which he achieved, and to which his photograph bears witness in the Record Book over the paragraph recording the event.

My specialised brief was to lecture in the field of Meat and Other Foods and to this end I spent many hours at the Cold Storage Board Abattoir working with the students and Meat Inspectors, of whom the Senior, Mr Siteema, taught me a lot about the practical aspects of the work but above all how and by what criteria cattle carcasses were graded for marketing purposes. The cattle came for slaughter from three sources. (1) Farms and Estates (2) Government State Ranches (3) Rural Areas (Chiefs/Village Headmen) The first two would submit their animals when they were judged to be commercially viable and would obtain the best grades and hence the best prices when sold. To obtain enough cattle from the third source was always the problem for the buyers. The difficulties arose from the fact that cattle in the Tribal Trust Lands were regarded as valuable assets more precious than money. The Cattle Buyers (Cold Storage Board employees) had a tough time in trying to persuade the owners to part with their cattle. Just enough would be sold to cover immediate needs, e.g. school uniforms and fees for their numerous off-spring. Even then the scrawniest and thinnest animals would arrive at the abattoir. I should point out that these cattle were the original beasts found in the villages which even when full of worms and herded by the young boys but otherwise left to fend for themselves were as tough as old boots, to which the grading of the carcass bore witness.

Increasing Government subsidies for sending more animals for slaughter made not the slightest bit of difference and indeed usually had the opposite effect of obtaining fewer beasts! The same problems arose in Zambia and I remember Chief Shakumbila's observations upon the increased subsidies when I was there. He had many 'Afrikander' cattle, as the village beasts were called, kept mainly on the Kafue River Flats. 'Why should I get rid of more of my valued cattle when I can get the same amount of money as last year for sending in fewer of them?'

The grades used for the dressed carcasses were (a) Choice (b) Prime (c) Standard (d) Commercial (e) Inferior. It should not be implied that 'Inferior' was in any way unfit for human consumption. Neither should it be inferred that 'Commercial' meant that the meat was only good enough for manufacturing into sausages and pies by the purchasers. Most of this type of meat was sold at a lower price because of the grading and then was taken to the local markets for sale to the bulk of the population. Neither the Africans nor the Europeans ever saw eye to eye as to the best parts of the carcass. Normally we would be happy with a fillet or so plus the liver, occasionally the kidneys and a large piece of top or silverside. Sirloin was a rarity because the African butchers did not know how to cut it.

I was once told by an African hunter that we Europeans discarded the best parts of the meat when it was still fresh. He was referring to the practice of cutting open the body of a newly hunted antelope, stripping out the intestines and extruding the contents and without any more ado other than chopping them into pieces, boiling them up for immediate consumption. Utilising the contents of the abdominal cavity for use as tripe or sausage or black pudding casings requires a more elaborate preparation for European tastes. The scraping and washing and preparation of the stomachs and intestines for tripe and sausages, even the haggis, is now beyond the 'ken' of domestic and farmhouse talents and is left to the commercial world.

Fortunately being a trained and qualified Meat Inspector has stood me in good stead over the years, not least in Africa and the

Middle East. Mind you I was not required in Saudi Arabia to examine the carcass of an elephant, chopped up and on the back of an open 7-ton truck in the pouring rain as I was in Zambia. In Saudi the Pakistani workforce killed in a poorly designed although newly built 'slaughterhouse' – the up-market term of 'abattoir' would be insulting! The practice there was for the slaughterman and his assistants to round up the fifty or so sheep to be killed, and barefoot, with no protective clothing whatsoever, set about the killing and bleeding of the animals. With 50 dead sheep covered in blood and all breathing their last spumes of air and blood, the place was a mess. However much one railed against the practices the Saudi Authorities seemed to accept them without too much fuss. Perhaps we were too near to the desert! Providing nice white overalls and helmets and headgear and boots made little difference as they rapidly disappeared and one suspected that they found their way back to the villages and towns in Pakistan and India.

One aspect of the work at the Cold Storage Board was that it was a first class place to see so many of the diseases and conditions afflicting the beasts of the field which have in so many instances been eliminated in Europe. Many, many types of parasitic infestations, infectious diseases such as Tuberculosis and acute and chronic disorders resulting in multiple abscesses (Bacterial Necrosis) of the liver and kidneys. There were on the other hand infections which were unheard of outside Africa, e.g. the much feared Red Water Fever which could decimate a herd in a matter of days.

The fact that so many different diseases and parasitic conditions existed made practical demonstrations easy, none more so than when I undertook a subsidiary teaching assignment at the behest of a friend, Mike Smith, who conducted training courses in Hotel and Catering Management for one of the international organisations. These immaculately dressed trainees had a fascinated, although somewhat morbid interest in the worms and flukes and abscesses and warbles and so on that I demonstrated every Friday afternoon in the term. They would have run a mile rather than see the killing and dressing operations at the abattoir.

Local holidays and home leave

One aspect of working at the Polytechnic, which was the envy of many expatriate employees, was the generosity of the leave entitlement. Under the terms of the Overseas Aid Scheme Local Holidays and Home Leave I was entitled to accrue four days' leave for each completed month of service, to be used at the end of the Contract, in my case two years satisfactory service. After the first two years I was offered a one-year extension and then a further year before a final two-year contract. I therefore remained overseas for four years, much to the delight of the children at their boarding school in Ramsgate. They were flown out three times a year, at Christmas, Easter and the Summer Holidays, which precisely mirrored the closing of the Polytechnic for the local holidays. These did not affect my overseas entitlement in any way, so that the family as a whole enjoyed the best of both worlds.

After nine different postings in nine years spent in Zambia, some of which were many miles from an International Airport, it was a relief to live in Blantyre with the Airport at Chileka being only a dozen miles away. I possessed a 504 Peugeot Estate Car which was quite capacious and with a roof rack added could carry a large amount of luggage. When the children arrived we were able to load it with all manner of camping gear, the large frame tent, the cooking utensils, the fishing rods, cold boxes and such for our relaxing sojourn of a week or ten days at one of the camping sites at Lake Malawi. It was always a joy to be there, after which we would return home. The social and sporting life was dominated by the Blantyre Club, of which we became enthusiastic members. For (then) £75 a year family membership one had access to and played golf, cricket, tennis, squash, football, rugby, hockey, bowls, billiards and snooker as well as having the use of a beautiful swimming pool. Socially there were five assorted bars in addition to an attractive and well appointed restaurant (The Copper Bowl) where we first enjoyed magnificent prawns from Mozambique and were introduced to 'Portuguese Steaks' as they were known, served piping hot and sizzling, streaming garlic aroma as they were brought through the restaurant by the waiters. Welcome-home-nights and farewell-nights were always spent there with the family as well as any other nights we could find an excuse for.

Strangely enough all these magnificent sporting facilities are now under-used, the team sports especially so. Why? The advent of international communications and satellite TV broadcasting, particularly by Sky Television. This country can now show all the sports channels and Malawi is no exception. The members have turned into 'Watchers' and are no longer 'Doers'. All very sad.

By the end of the academic year 1980 the Government was not able to fund the courses any longer, having judged (rightly) that both it and the Local Authorities now had sufficient qualified Health Inspectors to see it through future years. Indeed it had been a difficult enough job trying to find them employment over the previous couple of years. As the course was closing it became necessary to seek further employment and this could only sensibly be done in London. There were serious thoughts about a total migration to South Africa and I actually received a phone call from Mafeking, then the capital of the 'Homeland' of Bophutotswana, offering me a job within the Cold Storage Board / Meat Inspection and Grading Area, which I did not pursue. Hindsight, as they say, is a wonderful thing and I have often wondered how life might have turned out working there, with its close affinity to the internationally known 'Sun City'.

We therefore packed up our goods and chattels and departed for the UK. In the intervening years Simon had been accepted and was enjoying his Degree Course in Zoology at Bristol University. His first serious love affair starting at school had progressed so far as to have him visit his girlfriend's home in Bermuda and we actually met her parents for dinner at the Piccadilly Hotel. She came to Africa I seem to remember a couple of times.

Victoria had left school and having taken (successfully) English, French and German at 'A' Levels had perversely opted to study Law and was accepted at Chelmer College in Chelmsford in Essex.

Matthew still had one year to go at St Lawrence College and since I was no longer gainfully employed within the Overseas Aid Scheme I could expect no help with the Fees. As things turned out Shropshire County Council made a one-off payments to assist and although it only covered part of the fees it was certainly a help. Moving house within the United Kingdom is expensive enough. Moving internationally can easily treble such financial burdens. It

13. *Simon, Victoria and Matthew at Victoria Falls in 1968*

14. Health Campaign in a village in NW Zambia

15. African village in Ndola

16. *Author, with beard, doing his barman bit in the 'Elephant's Nest' at our house in Kawambwa*

17. Malawi wild life: Victoria had no fear of chameleons — unlike the Africans

18. Malawi wild life: Simon with mamba which had been killed by the locals while trying to eat a bush-baby

19. Saudi Arabia: visiting the Wadi behind KKMC in1984.
We are loading the guns for target practice

20. Saudi Arabia: Pam braving the sand dunes

21. *Disembarking at St Helena*

22. Jamestown, St Helena. One of the few places with access to the sea

23. St Helena: the author on foot in search of a pig to be inspected

24. *Orkney: cruise ships in Kirkwall Bay seen from the author's garden*

was so in this case and we went through a sticky patch before I went off to Saudi Arabia.

Yet again I obtained a job on the re-bound because persons appointed turned it down at the last minute or, as was the case in Saudi Arabia, the appointee returned home very quickly having stated that in his view the job and living conditions were impossible. These were not helped by being on a 'Single Status' Contract, as the mind-set of the Security Guards and particularly the Religious Police was particularly directed towards and probably against the concept of large numbers of single people let loose upon the land.

The difference between married and single status was not fully appreciated until Pam joined me some 18 months later, when we had a pre-fabricated, trailer-style home but which, however humble, was regarded with different eyes by the security services. It was there to be protected, as was the family, as decreed in the Koran.

PART 3

Saudi Arabia, St Helena, Orkney Islands 1981–2002

CHAPTER 4

Saudi Arabia 1981–86

THE SAUDI ARABIAN GOVERNMENT, oil rich and mega-dollar rich
beyond dreams that anyone can comprehend, decided in 1973
that the Western World (its main customer) was not paying enough
for its oil. The Organisation of Petroleum Exporting Countries
(OPEC) therefore doubled the price. Millions of dollars flooded
into the Kingdom and were shared out between various 'Princely
Supplicants' for thousands of different enterprises and services.
Government projects were prioritised and the development of the
mainly barren and desert lands proceeded. Security was needed to
protect the oil fields, and with the influence of the Americans
predominating, the decision was made to construct two 'impreg-
nable' bases at Yanbu (Navy), Ta'if (Air Force) – one, as can be
seen, on the Red Sea Coast and one south of Jeddah (both
presumably also sited to give some protection to the Holy Cities
of Mecca and Medina).

There was a third base allocated for the Army to protect the
northern frontier and this was sited in the Ab Dibdibah Desert
about 90 kilometres from the Kuwaiti Border. Starting from scratch
a fortified base was decided upon which would house 76,000
personnel, including families. The scheme would be master-
minded by the American Army Corps of Engineers but the work
would be undertaken by giant American Corporations, notably
Bechtel, Morrison-Knudsen and Siyanco. Recruitment for the
masses of personnel involved took place throughout the world, but
the main administrative structure was the same, i.e. Americans,
Western European and OTCN (Other Third Country Nationals).
Salary levels reflected this division of nationalities but were
generally on a par with the standards in the home countries. Each
of the companies endeavoured to fulfil a contract drawn up by the
Corps of Engineers which specified the number and classification
of the workforce to be employed. Some contracts which required
highly qualified and skilled staff, e.g. medical services and elec-

tronics, had to be undertaken and headed by American and Western employees although subsidiary staff could be OTCNs.

King Khalid Military City

The cantonment was to be called 'The King Khalid Military City' or, as one might expect, 'KKMC' for short. The total workforce was some 20,000 and to minister to their needs was a monumental task in its own right. Starting from scratch in a barren desert, a base camp and airstrip was constructed, but before this could be done the most essential survey work had to be undertaken to seek a massive, constant and guaranteed water supply. This was located several hundred metres below ground and was apparently trapped glacial waters from a previous Ice Age. The forecast was that the level would fall some four feet overall in 100 years when the City was in full operation. To conserve water even allowing for these generous promises was still a concern. To that end the foul sewage system was linked to a Treatment Plant, the final (purified) effluent being carried to a Water Purifying Plant which then provided domestic supplies to the houses and encampments.

Trees and shrubs were planted throughout the area of the main City, each of which was logged by computers into a root irrigation system and received its apportioned amount daily, any surplus or malfunction resulting in a trickle of water being returned to the underground reservoir whence it all originated in the first place. A most ingenious system, but with many scientific pitfalls along the way. For instance the obsession with treating the sewage in the first place to a high level of sterility. This resulted in a low level of Rota-Viruses on the filters which were literally starving to death because of the lack of 'edible' food. Another unexpected sideshow occurred when the temporary sewage ponds were put into operation prior to the main treatment plants being ready. This treatment system consisted of three enormous lagoons, the sewage being fed by gravity from the first to the last over a series of small and shallow rapids. The combination of air and the oxidising effect of the sun was sufficient to treat the waste. By the third lagoon the water was pure enough for birds to feed upon it. The City was accidentally sited on one of the main north-south migratory routes. Crossing the desert regions was a strenuous time for the birds and thousands upon thousands of infinite variety descended upon the water. It was a pleasure to be watching them in close up from the mobile hide of my company vehicle. The discovery of a large lagoon where they could both rest and feed before continuing their journey was a godsend for the birds. I hope that at least one man-made lake still exists, but I doubt it as they were all scheduled to be closed down once the main sewage treatment system came into operation.

Duties and responsibilities

The purpose of my professional life was to ensure that as far as I was able the workforce would remain in a fit and healthy state so that 'Production and Schedules' as laid down by the Corps of Engineers would not be interrupted. For the first three months I was literally a one-man band and could only scratch at the surface of the problems encountered. Getting to grips came later. The company that I was employed by, Hospital Corporations of America (HCA), in view of the previous incumbent's experience, had offered a three-month contract to me basically to size-up the situation. This I did and it was sent off to the Headquarters in New York. Subsequently I was offered a new 12-month contract to go back out and set about trying to implement the Company's contractual obligations in preventive medicine. It was an uphill task but I managed to cobble together the rudiments of a Department, the basic structure of which remained intact for the next five years, so I suppose I left some sort of foundation behind me.

Events took a somewhat unexpected turn a few months into the year when either HCA or its 'Princely Partner' fell from grace and favour and the company contract was terminated. The Medical Services Contract was awarded to another American company, Charter Medical, based in Macon, Georgia, which with its Saudi Royal connections formed the local operating business of 'Saudi Medical Services'. The result of all this was that I was offered a new contract on a 12-month on-going basis with an immediate inducement to work for the new company, a Head of Department ranking and a vastly increased budget to truly reflect the importance of the Preventive Medicine scenario within the new regime. Above all else and in keeping with my enhanced role I was offered a 'Married Status Contract'.

These were as rare as 'hens' teeth' as the saying goes and it would not be amiss to say a little about the difference between 'Single' and 'Married' contracts as they existed. In the case of the former, both the Security and Religious Police could raid their quarters at any time on the look out for illegal gambling, drugs, alcohol, pornographic materials and even simple cheese-cake and girlie magazines. In the latter case, a married home is a sacred and venerated place and only the intervention of the local Emir and Religious Police can void the tenets of the Koran, that within the home a man can do as he wants. Extremely he can with impunity beat his wife, drink alcohol, sleep with the family goat or whatever else takes his fancy, but once outside the home he falls into the same 'arrestable' category as anyone else.

Unless one has served in Saudi Arabia one cannot comprehend the paperwork involved in not only being allowed into the country but actually being employed there. Add to that the complications arising from being granted 'Married Status' and the list of required documentation stretches beyond belief. All primary documents, i.e. Birth Certificates, Marriage Certificates, Professional Qualifications, etc. had to be Certified by the Foreign and Commonwealth Office in London and then translated into Arabic and duly copied for the Saudi Authorities prior to submission. The endless journeys to Dammam and back that one had to make, the standing in line with a personal Arabic-speaking interpreter, the apprehension generated by fear of a mis-translation and refusal to accept the application, the relief generated when approval was given locally to pursue the issue of a married status visa in London, the queues at the Saudi Embassy in Belgrave Square, more queues at the Saudi National Bank, and a final one to accept the return of our passports with the Visas stamped therein. The whole process took about six months from start to finish.

My opposite number in the Corps of Engineers was Bob Lopez, and he it was who had the unfortunate experience of having to arrange the transportation of a body, that of an American who had died suddenly of a heart attack on the base. Involving his employers, the local police, the American embassy, the medical services, the translators, the Saudi administrators in the province, the immigration authorities and so on ad nauseam. He had to obtain the signatures of 57 people before approval could be given for the body to be shipped to the States. The final act was to ensure that the man's passport was fixed to the outside of the coffin with the page showing an Exit Only Visa stamped in it!

A major part of my responsibilities was to keep the workforce free of preventable diseases and thus not impinge upon production levels as laid down by the Corps of Engineers. It follows that apart from general living conditions the main ingredients to be considered for a healthy life style were the purity of the water being consumed and the quality of the food being eaten. One should not forget the air being breathed but we lived in an extreme environment of dust and heat and cold so it is rather a specialist subject of its own. You will note that I have not mentioned infectious or contagious diseases, but these were of little moment except oddly enough for chicken pox, that childhood disease of the Western World, which rampaged through part of the workforce hailing from Sri Lanka. It struck these adults quite severely and eventually a whole barracks block had to be used as an Isolation Unit.

One also had to be aware of the possible threat of rabies, which was an endemic problem. It gained much more in importance when we discovered the Korean Community had a practice of keeping hidden – both in the mess halls and underneath their barracks – numerous dogs. Usually being fattened up for the annual Moon Festival when delicacies of the canine variety are an item. I believe that they can be eaten at any time of the year. Since we were forbidden to shoot or poison animals we devised a method of dealing with the problem which was as efficient as it was humane. Once we had trapped or caught the animals they were placed in a sealed wooden killing box on the back of a Toyota Pick Up where a length of hosepipe led directly to the exhaust pipe. Half-a-mile down the road the carbon monoxide had done its job. The carcasses were disposed of in an off road pit out in the surrounding desert. Since I was one of a rare breed of persons who has seen a human case of rabies and had known the disease at first hand in Africa I had no desire to see a replicated scenario in Saudi

Arabia. I had no choice but to carry out this distasteful chore, which incidentally appalled the Thai (Buddhist) members of staff, so that the work was done by the European, Filipino and Pakistani employees.

The work was undoubtedly complex. At any one time there were up to 50 mess halls serving the 20,000 workforce, of which some 30 odd were for the Korean construction companies. The largest of these would produce 1,000 meals every day for companies as diverse as the great corporations of Hyun Dai and Sam Wan with every type and economic class of company in between. The one common feature was their devotion to 'Kimchee', a fermented vegetable soup comprising everything from cabbage to seaweed with a heavy garlic presence. Certainly not to Western tastes, but it was produced locally, unlike the food for the Americans, which was entirely trans-shipped from the States in trucks bearing the legend 'TEXAS BEEF' on the side. Their compound was strictly guarded and admittance was by invitation only, the main reason being that to the envy of all other workers, alcoholic liquor was allowed and the personnel even had their own Club for social purposes.

It was too risky to brew when living in the Single Quarters but when Pam arrived a false wall was built into one end of a bedroom wardrobe, behind which shelves rapidly became packed with fermenting bottles of grape juice. In the on-site supermarket both red and white grape juice could be bought and on the adjoining shelves sugar and yeast were stacked. The rest was easy and recipes were freely traded. I recall that we made some very pleasant table wines as well as an extremely acceptable 'Sherry' of the Bristol Cream variety. Beer was a little harder to come by but a Dutchman made a good brew which used marmite as a flavouring base. This rapidly went off the market when the Saudis discovered the use to which it was being put. I was also given a recipe for 'Carrot Whisky' but never had the time to make it.

The big American bases belonging to Aramco (Arabian-American Oil Corporation) provided grain stills in each bungalow, the end product of which gave the user a potent liquor needing to be cut twice before consumption. Its local name was 'Sadiqui' (Arabic for 'Brother') and this was the base product for the illegal trade operated by the (mainly) Filipinos. The penalties were severe in any case but woe betide anyone caught selling or involving a Saudi in the business. The strict Sharia Law would then be applied in all its savage and cruel certainties.

It is sometimes difficult for the outside world to understand the ways of the legal system in Saudi Arabia. Westerners are used to the criminal or civil cases being thrashed out in open court, which never happens there. Instead all the evidence both for and against is gathered and placed before a travelling magistrate. He will have at his disposal the official reports of investigations, the statements of aggrieved parties who are seeking redress for any injuries, and pleas from the accused of innocence or mitigation. This is of particular importance to 'foreigners' – particularly non-Muslims, whenever road crashes are the subject of the claim. Damages are normally three times higher for Muslims than for Christians. Unless damages are paid by either the employing company or the accused's family then the miscreant will stay in jail indefinitely. Any punishment will also have to be served.

In KKMC the large American base was surrounded by a security fence and two main gates at the north and south ends of the compound controlled the traffic both vehicular and pedestrian in and out. At about 5.30 p.m. on most nights which was at dusk and it was somewhat cooler, the wife of an Army officer was in the habit of going for a run outside the fence. In spite of being warned she insisted on running the five miles around the base, going out of one or the other of the gates and returning by the same one some 50 minutes later. Almost inevitably two Saudi soldiers lay in wait for her and she was stripped, beaten and ravaged by the pair of them. They then went in to hiding in the vast Saudi Barracks.

The alarm was raised when the woman failed to return and she was found staggering along the wire trying to reach the safety of the main gate. The primary investigation, including a medical examination, showed the truth of the woman's story and it then became a search for the criminals. 48 hours later their hiding place in the barracks was discovered and they were held in custody. To Western eyes it would seem to be an open and shut case and probably a mandatory 25 years to life sentence would have been pronounced. Under Sharia Law the sentence for raping a Saudi woman is death but the victim in this case was not a Saudi.

The visiting judge having gathered and considered all the evidence found that there were mitigating circumstances for the accused. First, the woman had been warned not to go beyond the security fence on her evening run. Second, she was not dressed appropriately for Saudi Arabia when outside the American Compound. Third, the provocative nature of her attire would have aroused desire in the simple minds of the soldiers concerned and would thus have initiated the attack. Fourth, even though she was neither a Saudi nor a Moslem she should have been aware that in her dress and demeanour she was committing offences strictly forbidden in the Koran.

Her 'attire' consisted of mini-shorts and a bra-less top, enough to send any Saudi wild with desire! In spite of all this she was still entitled to her say prior to sentencing as undoubtedly a criminal act had occurred. She asked that the same sentence should be passed as under Sharia Law, precisely death for the accused and compensation payments for herself. Taking all factors into account the Judge decided that if any compensation was to be paid it should be a matter for consideration between the American and Saudi Military Commands. The men would not be executed but would receive a period of imprisonment plus 800 lashes each. This part of the sentence is not physically as severe as it sounds As the whipping is carried out with the lash being wielded with a copy of the Koran tucked under the armpit. Its main purpose is one of humiliation and it is carried out in stages over several weeks. A full parade of military personnel is there to witness the punishment. It would have been permissible for the victim to have witnessed this part of the punishment but the lady in question rapidly departed for the States.

To monitor the workforce under the three broad headings – water, food, air plus the more obvious ones of the living and working conditions, required staff, and I so structured and built up the service that there were about 25 mixed nationality personnel working in the Environmental Services. After a year building up the Department it became fairly obvious that one aspect which had been overlooked when the company contract had been drawn up was that of Health Education. On my next leave I recruited a specialist Environmental Health Officer to set up such a Unit. His name was David Quirk and professionally he did extremely well. The scheme he devised and set up for a multiplicity of languages, nationalities, food and feeding habits was such a success that when entered for the Domestos Health Education Competition in London, a Highly Commended Certificate was awarded. The Committee seemed to believe that we held an advantage over the other entries, backed, or so it was thought, by vast amounts of Saudi money. Whilst there might have been an element of truth in this it was as nothing compared to battling for contract variations (Departmental finances) and local recognition by the company, Corps of Engineers and the Saudi Ministry of Defence (MODA). Then too the writing of the scripts and translating from English into Saudi, Urdu, Tagalog (Filipino), and Thai was a time-consuming affair. Remember also that Arabic reads from right to left across the page and starts at the back of the book, which makes lecturing tricky.

Saudi medical services

It was a new experience working for the Americans. Particularly was this so when the monolithic and autocratic American Army Corps of Engineers was employed by the Saudi Ministry of Defence to design and build the City. All contractors were made to feel inferior in their efforts to comply with their contracts. Instant removal from the site was the immediate response to difficulties encountered, although a Labour Disputes Court did exist.

The American obsessions with systems produces results in a constant and steadfast way but makes no allowance when things go wrong. One is given a structured brief and this is one's Bible. Sometimes an unforeseen problem arises and the expectation is that you will draft an amendment to the Management Procedures which will be approved by top 'Brass' and which then becomes part of the' Bible'.

The Procedures are inviolate and must be followed. Tunnel vision is the result and wherever possible (which means every time) you must cover 'yo ass' with paper, as an American colleague once said to me. Should you observe a problem which is out of your remit and if not dealt with quickly will reflect badly upon the Company then you might attempt to tackle it. If all goes well and you get the Company off the hook, then your stock with the employers and your resulting annual bonus will rise in line with each other. On the other hand . . .?

I once did step into a problem which my immediate boss, an American doctor, thought he could deal with. It was a food poisoning outbreak in a Korean Mess Hall. I knew at once that his approach was totally wrong and over his head I went to the Chief Executive and explained my predicament, whereupon I was told to go and pick up the pieces but was also warned of the consequences if I was wrong. Both subsequent reports were sent to headquarters in Georgia. It seems strange in retrospect that a local matter such as this could be projected into an international setting, but one has to remember that the company medical services contract was worth millions of dollars with an extremely suspicious paymaster who demanded the most meticulous of reports upon incidents such as this.

Once the reports were received in Macon in America, a noted epidemiologist was called upon to adjudicate as it were, and he was prevailed upon to come to Saudi Arabia and study the problem at first hand. Having done this and returned home his final analysis was sent to the Chief Executive. It completely approved of the action I had taken after seeing the difficulty arising, and I was an extremely relieved employee to obtain such a commendation.

One Doctor who had a serious dispute with the Chief Medical Officer was unceremoniously taken from his work by the Security Guards and driven to the landing strip where a light plane was already waiting. Flown to Dhahran, he was escorted to an international flight to New York and flown out with three months' pay in his pocket. His goods and chattels from KKMC were forwarded to him at a later date.

I must confess that I have never had cause to regret my overall basic and hands-on training at Cleethorpes BC. At least by the time I was 21 I was (professionally) a rounded article, although with two qualifications still to go, not quite the finished article. The combination of work, night school and day release courses was the norm in those far off days. Many of the professions have now abandoned in-service training, exchanging them for degree courses.

These, in my profession, seem to consist of vast tracts of social awareness training which is of little value when Mrs Smith's drain is blocked and causing an overflow nuisance in the local park. To be fair neither the Food Standards Agency nor the Environmental Agency were created until the mid-nineties and took many duties away from local authorities. The modern environmentalist complete with, in my view, a nebulous degree then has to find his way in the professional world with only his wits to help him. If he is lucky he will have found his feet by the age of 25 or 26. In comparison by that age I was professionally qualified as well as a qualified Meat and Foods Inspector after a further year's study, I had spent two years in the British Army, seen service in Northern Ireland and Egypt, left home, got married and had become a father.

I reluctantly comment upon the standards displayed and allowed of grammatically incorrect letters and reports which reveal an awful lot about the quality of the modern primary and secondary school teaching. As I write I find the whole subject depressing. If the basics are not taught properly then how on earth can English language and literature, history, geography, mathematics be studied at a more senior level, and as for the degree courses, particularly for the sciences and engineering, the law and accountancy, one can only fear for the future. Nuff said.

Life in Saudi Arabia

Many people have commented upon the imagined oppressive life-style that we led in Saudi Arabia. Stories of difficulties lose nothing in the telling and usually the recipients are only too willing to judge and condemn without even trying to understand the problems that the expatriate encounters. One always thinks too, of the attitude of the international media and its voracious appetite for depressing or alarmist stories. 'Good news doesn't sell newspapers' unless there is a dramatic human interest angle e.g. escape from Saudi jail hell, my dog was be-headed in mistake etc. etc. Providing one keeps within the law and confines oneself to the strictures laid down by that law and one's obligations to one's employers then

even if living in single isolation one should live well. A person
basically subdues all normal feelings for the Western way of life and
looks forward to the next leave. Exactly as being a new conscript
in the British Army, the first three or four months are the worst
and infinitely better if one is lucky enough as I was to secure a rise
from the ranks sufficient to be offered a married status contract.

With a busy office and large workforce to direct and supervise
and as one might expect difficulties with the American Military
(Corps of Engineers) from time to time to contend with, a six-day
working week of 48 hours and the endless paperwork and
bickering that goes with living in Saudi Arabia, and particularly in
a desert with its environmental and climatic extremes, one might
wonder just how successfully one's wife might adjust to living
there. After all, I had had a year to establish myself and get used to
the desert, its privations and benefits, so I was a wee bit
apprehensive about taking Pam with me, great comfort as she
always was and is to this day. Living in a trailer with no veranda
or garden is not quite the same as living in a beautiful African
home.

I should have known. Pam would have staunchly survived the
Black Death, I believe. So much common sense has she, which
combined with an inner strength of purpose and self-belief sees her
through most of life's crises. Whilst there was never any such crisis,
acclimatisation cannot have been easy for her, and I was greatly
relieved that she settled into the way of that particular world with
her usual graceful ease.

No better way exists of demonstrating this than to describe a
visit made to a Bedouin Tent Encampment (the Black Variety) in
the Wadi outwith the confines of the camp. We were invited to
spend the afternoon there together with the Chief Executive of the
Company Tom MacDaniel and his wife Sandy. The large tent was
divided into two living areas with a shaded open end adjoining the
men's quarters, and acting as a sort of communal lounge. There we
men were plied with endless cups of tea (Chai) throughout a long,
hot and frankly boring afternoon. We were offered trays of fruit
for refreshment and given an air rifle to take pot shots at tin cans
tied to nearby bushes for amusement. We lounged at long length
upon the carpets spread on the sandy floor with cushions to bolster

our aching and unaccustomed Western society backs. Meanwhile Pam and Sandy were being 'entertained' by the ladies in their quarters. She said that they were a cheerful bunch, the most abiding memory being that the children as young as eleven or twelve wore the veil and at the slightest sound of a man's voice they were smartly dropped into place, hiding all the facial features. There was curiosity shown about the Western style of dress and no doubt the afternoon passed with a little more interest in each other than could be demonstrated by the men. The climax came after a butcher was summoned from somewhere or other and then disappeared for a while to remerge dragging a reluctant sheep behind him. This was tethered to a post and no doubt after a prayer was said it was duly despatched by the age-old sacrificial method of cutting its throat. After being skinned and eviscerated the carcass was taken off by the women to be cooked.

Family prayers were always said at sunset (about 6 p.m.) followed by the evening meal. At this point a large platter was borne in upon which lay the newly cooked sheep, which was curled around a bed of boiled rice. Various salads and seasonings were set around the dish and we men were invited to participate of the meal. We knelt or squatted around the 'feast' eating only with our right hands and tearing off pieces of meat which we ate with our bare hands. At the end when all were satisfied the remains were taken away by the women. Meanwhile Pam and Sandy had been regaled in similar fashion in the women's quarters except that they were dining mainly upon the organs and entrails prior to the remains of the carcass being brought in. Pam said that she quickly learned to reciprocate when a particularly juicy piece of intestine was offered to her by finding similar titbits with which to respond. Somehow we all survived the experience but agreed that it was not a life-style which had much appeal for us softies from the Western world.

One can see that I would be fully occupied throughout the working day, but for a wife with no employment other than to attend to household chores settling in would have been difficult. It was made easier by the fact that socialising between sexes was permitted in the Mess Hall, which one must confess always provided the most magnificent choice of meals. Both of us have a natural curiosity as to the places we live in and a natural bent for making friends and acquaintances, which ingredients are the foundation for our firmly held belief that what matters in venturing into a new society is what one puts into it and not what one takes out. This is what Pam set about doing, and eventually came to enjoy Saudi Arabia with all its aggravations, pitfalls, climate, dust-storms, religious fanaticism and the like. There was an immediate benefit to be seen upon her arrival as we were immediately moved into a three bedroom trailer home in the married quarters section of the 'Workers Compound', as the Corps of Engineers had labelled it.

Their own tightly controlled piece of KKMC was a complete model of an American Army Base complete with permanent homes, gymnasia, tennis courts, indoor and outdoor arenas, swimming pool, tarred roads, commissariat and so on. They even had a nine-hole golf course carved out of the desert, although strictly speaking this bordered the outer fence. Competitions were extended to include such Western Europeans as myself, whereupon I happily won twice over the next few months. As the working day was from 8 a.m. to 5 p.m. over a six-day week, floodlighting was common over the outdoor sporting facilities, i.e. tennis and basket ball courts and football pitches (ungrassed), but golf courses were too big for this. Competitions only took place on our one precious Friday off.

I should perhaps point out that the 'civilian' Americans I worked for lived in the same trailer camp as Pam and me. It was the American 'military' with their civilian acolytes who had the superior living quarters and social arrangements. Since they were all permanent employees as against the contracted and transient ones on site such as ourselves I suppose it was only natural that they placed themselves at the head of the queue.

Occasionally it was possible for the 'Brits' to extract the urine as the saying goes, although chances were rare. Called to account by one arrogant executive in a Company Management Committee for pronouncing the word 'schedule' in a British way instead of the harsher American style, I gently apologised for my shortcomings. These included inadvertently lapsing into Standard English Pronunciation as I had been taught to do. I expressed the hope that over time the committee members would be able to understand. The Chief Executive roared his approval amidst the general laughter.

The Corps of Engineers approved a scheme devised by an administrative 'nugget' to set up a quick response team for general emergencies. The team would be composed of a plumber, bricklayer, electrician and a couple of labourers driven around the site in a purpose-made vehicle workshop. The Fast Response Team as it was officially known was quickly renamed the Rapid Response Team since the British response to the original was to refer to it as a FART. One up to the European expats.

Being placed at the 'head of the queue' became quite normal as a courtesy by the Saudi authorities for married couples and their families. It was most noticeable when one was travelling. Single men could not travel in the same vehicle as married women except with the permission of the husband. A wife incidentally could not travel on her own except with the written approval of her husband, the thought of which gave Pamela a few palpitations. It was only of consequence once when she went with a group of wives to visit the caves at Hoffuf on the fringe of the Empty Quarter in the south. Apart from that whenever we left KKMC we were generally together and in the Company's vehicles.

Established in a hotel in either Riyadh or DKD (the three towns of Dharhan, Al Khobar and Dammam which adjoined each other) we were given family rooms as opposed to single ones for lone travellers. There were special areas in the dining rooms for the married families, separate times for swimming in the hotel pools with no allowance for single men and women to enjoy the water together. Above all there were separate buses provided for the families with darkened windows and luxurious seats, most notably seen at the airports. One should point out that the hotels were the last word in luxury and the food was a sight to behold. In some there was even a bar, although only soft drinks were dispensed. Apple juice and fizzy mineral water together made a mockery of the real stuff but was known as 'Saudi Champagne', and everywhere one could obtain the American non-alcoholic beverage of 'Near Beer'. 'Iced Tea' was also a popular drink at the dining table.

Once inside the International Airport the separate facilities were immediately obvious and since I had suffered the long and dusty journey on my own on numerous occasions I was more than happy to be ushered with my wife from the back of the line of weary single souls to the front. There to be escorted to our seats and settled without the usual struggle. 'Saudiair' was tops in this respect and with excellent In-Flight Services it catered for its passengers extremely well.

During my time away in Saudi, Pam had attended a TEFL (Teaching English as a Foreign Language) Course in Cambridge. As one might expect with her intellect she passed with flying colours. This led unexpectedly to an unusual teaching job in the desert. There she was not allowed to teach male students, although the need was desperate for many of the international workforce. As there were no female employees in the 'workforce' category this avenue was blocked. Nevertheless, the senior management teams of the various Korean companies had married status contracts and frequently had young families with them. Pam was therefore approached with regard to teaching privately some of those infant children the complexities of the English Language. The children came to the trailer on a regular basis and the whole venture was a moderate success. I still remember her 'star' pupil. A five-year old boy, one Kim Soo, who was exceptionally bright even by the Korean meritocratic standards and is probably by this day running one of the giant Korean corporations, if not the country. Needless to say Pam enjoyed the work and the pin-money!

She also enjoyed the international flavour of the various visits and meetings of the wives, usually arranged by the Americans. These were devised so as to coincide with specific demonstrations featuring a national culture. With such talented ladies as Korean, Thais and Filipinos it was not difficult to see and admire their skills in origami, fruit cutting and flower displays. The industrious and multi-talented Americans were undoubtedly the leaders in the field of handicrafts and hobbies. The massive influx of immigrants from throughout the world into the States brought into the country the enormous variety of skills which were then passed on to succeeding generations of the families. On the Corps of Engineers Compound where the recreational and sporting facilities were second to none the vast sports hall was used for the Springtime and Autumn Fairs, raising funds for service charities. Even though Pam has always 'dabbled' in handicrafts of various kinds, cross-stitching and oil painting, silver work and (if it can be included as such) her life-long interest in cooking, she was, like me, astounded at all the jewellery making, gemstone polishing, chocolate goodie coating, patchwork, quilting, model making and whatever else one can think of.

Several years later we were on holiday in the United States and stayed for a couple of nights in Palm Springs. One evening the central street was closed to traffic and a vast handicraft market was erected. We were somewhat blasé about American handicrafts but even we were astonished at what could be done. After a wonderful evening's viewing and exploring the various stalls we dined upon a superb charcoal-grilled steak, an American speciality. Taking a last look around the street we came across a tobacconist/gift shop displaying the most extraordinary clock in the window. Electrically driven, open cased and with gear wheels revealed and (supposedly) driven by little brass model men pulling levers, the whole open concept is an extreme optical illusion but fascinating to watch. They were not a mass produced item, so we were told, but were made to order by a company in Arkansas. The chance was too good to miss and the result was that after some months the clock arrived and now sits on the mantelpiece, keeping perfect time after seven or eight years' service and providing an endless source of amusement and speculation by children and adults alike.

Inevitably in a document such as this one is forced to be selective and recount only the major (to Pam and me) memories. Hundreds of incidents and events have to be discarded, and in this day and age of mass travel, to detail all our overseas holiday and business trips would evoke a bored response from the reader. Employment in Saudi Arabia and with both of us living there opened the door to world travel limited only by one's personal finances and time available. The financial basis was secured by the fact that we were entitled to two return tickets to London every four months to enjoy our three-weeks accrued leave.

This was payable in cash and we could negotiate any deal we liked with the (mainly) Pakistani travel agents. The end result was that we visited Hong Kong, Bangkok Thailand and Singapore and even returned to Malawi with the family – apart from Matthew who remained in London when our first grandchild, Clare, was born. On several occasions we returned to England but we became fixated on overseas property and Portugal as our preferred country for long term prospects of retirement.

Portuguese intermission

Portugal came about because of Pam's brother David, who with his wife, also Pamela, had 'discovered' it many years previously when the huge developments in Spain were catching the eye and when the Algarve in southern Portugal was relatively unexplored and certainly not developed. His comments and views about the Portuguese people, our allies for the past 600 years, the climate (Atlantic rather than sweltering Mediterranean), the unspoilt nature of it all and above all else the wonderful seafood impressed us greatly. Little was I to know that once the 'Mass Tourism Age' was upon us I would be employed in the Orkney Islands whence masses of shellfish would be shipped to the Iberian Peninsular and sold there to feed the ravenous tourists as the local industry could no longer cope with demand.

Once we visited the country we were firmly hooked and fell completely in love with it, and for that matter still are today, although the vast villa developments on the Algarve would have put us off had they existed then as they exist now. The Algarve fortunately is only the southern province of the country, albeit a beautiful part protected from the fierce northern winters by the Monchique Mountains and hence an all-year-round holiday destination.

At this point in our lives (1984) an event occurred in the United Kingdom which was to have an extraordinary impact on our future life. The half-year event was the Miner's Strike led to its bitter end by the General Secretary of the Union, Arthur Scargill. Financially crippling to both the Union and its Members it may have been but for us two it was the most financially rewarding of our lives. By the time it started I was into my last year in Saudi Arabia working for the Ministry of Defence (MODA), supervising a Health Service Contract. I was as usual paid in Riyals, the local currency allied to the American Dollar. Again as was usual I was paid in cash per month in the exact amount I had been contracted to receive. The point being made here was that there were no deductions. Neither for rent nor water nor telephone nor food nor transport, nothing was deducted. Having received the due cash in hand I was able to go to the local bank and exchange the money for a sterling draft to send overseas. All very simple and neat, but for us it depended upon the value of the exchange rate. During the six months of the strike the value of sterling fell dramatically against the dollar and at its height one dollar (4.5 riyals) nearly equalled one pound sterling. The result was that my salary nearly doubled in value and the amount saved was such that purchase of a property in Portugal became a reality.

In many ways the purchase of a small villa in Praia da Luz in the Western Algarve was both the best and worst of purchases. Best because it became a holiday home for many of the family and worst because it blinkered our vision as to the likely direction that our lives might take. This was particularly true of the contract system by which I had been employed for many years. We should have seen beyond the end of the existing contract and calculated the risk of it being either renewed or extended. When the contracts were good and the bonuses were paid out, the worth of the employment became obvious. There were occasions when companies lost contracts or their worth was reduced overnight by 20% or similar due to a fall in the price of oil (Saudi Arabia) or revaluation of the local currency or sterling (Africa). Slings and arrows, as they say. The one way of avoiding this was to 'cash in the chips' and resume our lives in the UK, with me taking a post back in Local Government whence I came all those years ago. We decided not to do it and again a strange sort of event intervened and influenced our decision-making.

Following the Miner's Strike the severe grip of recession took hold of England. With three million unemployed it was a desperate time for job seekers, of which Victoria was one. She had studied Modern Languages (English, French and German) up to A-Level standard but had then applied to read Law, was accepted at the University of Essex, and graduated at the time of the great recession. After some months of trying and living with her grandmother in Shrewsbury she had only been able to obtain locally a junior clerical post.

Owning the property in Luz Bay near to Lagos on the Algarve in Portugal became the focal point of getting her 'launched'. Knowing the country a little I reasoned that recession or not there would be the usual influx of holiday visitors so that there would at the very least be a chance of picking up a holiday post within the Luz Bay community. Her chances would be immeasurably increased as she aspired to a level above that of waitress, bar tender or time share agent. I therefore proposed to Victoria that she should go to the Portuguese Language Institute in Lisbon, staying there for three months, after which she should head for the Algarve as well-equipped as anyone could be to seek her fame and fortune. It all worked out extremely well and far better that any of us could have imagined. Having completed the course Victoria headed for the villa, which was managed for us by the Luz Bay Club whose owners, Barry Sadler and Joao Moreira, were responsible for a large staff of maids, cleaners, maintenance personnel servicing the needs of an international clientele owning some 200 properties. The owners invited her out to lunch at the 'O Poco' (The Well) Club Restaurant. It would have been early in 1986. She had scarcely been there a week or so when this happened. The two owners explained that they were in somewhat of a quandary as to what action to take regarding the vacant post of Manager of the villa complex. The problem arose because they had had to terminate the employment of the English incumbent because of a health problem. Should the vacant post be advertised in London and Portugal there would be a flood of applicants, possibly not resulting in an appointment until the end of the season, which was unthinkable.

Knowing the Tonge family's commitment to the country in general and the Algarve in particular they had decided on a radical course of action and were prepared to offer Victoria the job in spite of her inexperience. She had filed a CV in the Club's office upon arrival. The benefits included a beach apartment, not big but very nice, entertainment and lunch allowances, and the post was permanent and pensionable. This was the start of four very happy years of employment as she took precisely ten seconds to accept once she got over the shock of the offer. For us it also meant that there was a member of the family locally who could look after our interests in the villa, its lettings and maintenance needs, when we were not in residence.

This worked well while we were regular visitors from Saudi Arabia but became less so when I went down to St Helena in the South Atlantic and Victoria returned home. The family (both from the Tonge and Lineton sides) as well as many friends enjoyed their holidays there, but the situation changed when we did not return to mainland Europe on leave for some 18 months or so. Expecting to have a net credit in the Club accounts which would contribute considerably towards a lengthy holiday we found we were in debt as there had been no lettings to offset the cost of the maids, cleaning, painting, refurbishment, maintenance and administrative charges. A depressing start to a family reunion. The villa was a three-bedroom end of terrace house with a veranda facing the sea. The bedrooms as was usual were on the lower floor reached by an attractive but tricky spiral staircase. Two bathrooms were on that level. The kitchen was situated next to the dining area and large lounge which fronted on to the terrace. Overall it was a very nice holiday home and it was distinguished from the others nearby in that it had a uniquely paved patio garden which consisted of a 'horseshoe' design worked into the stone. It was easily explained once one was aware that the house had been built as a retirement present by the wife of a famous jockey of his day, Harry Carr. He had won the Derby on the horse 'Parthia' in 1959, and I bought the villa from his widow. It was called by the way 'Casa Henrique', a literal translation of which would be 'Harry's House' or more colloquially 'Harry's Place'.

When we settled back in the UK in the Orkney Isles I sold the house, having enjoyed its use through good times and bad for some seven years in all. It had provided a base not just for holidays but for us to explore the mainland of Portugal from the south to the north and from the east to the west. It is such a lovely country and the variety of its towns and villages and cities and mountains and river valleys and coasts is a constant delight. To add to those features one would be remiss not to mention the food and wine, particularly Port which although 'invented' by the British is Portugal's claim to be featured in any viticulture 'Hall of Fame'.

Contracts became difficult in Saudi Arabia and changed hands at company level frequently which destabilised the staff, and I was fortunate in obtaining a post with the Ministry of Defence, or MODA as it was more well known, as the Director of Medical Services, a grand title which meant little more than being the punch ball for anyone to have a go at, as the post stood between the warring factions of the Ministry and the Saudi Army, the Corps of Engineers who detested the supervising contractor, out of whose monies I was paid. A particular target by the Corps was my immediate boss, a former lecturer in the American Air Force (by mistake 'awarded' the rank of Lt Colonel, according to the personnel at the Corps). The company, which had to comply with its contractual medical service obligations and justify itself to everyone, was in a particularly unfortunate position. One can well see that there was ample scope for misunderstandings and mischief making particularly amongst the senior staff on site. They spoke perfect English but 'fought' each other in Arabic, and there was always the utmost difficulty for the Europeans in trying to understand the root cause of the problem which had arisen.

Suffice to say that I survived a most difficult year but was relieved to receive notification of a vacant post within the Overseas Development Branch of the British Government on the South Atlantic island of St Helena. The post was that of Senior Environmental Health Officer and was for three years' contracted service, with 'Home' Leave granted after 18 months. Naturally it was married status otherwise I would not have considered it. Shaking the dust off and returning to England was a pleasure.

CHAPTER 5

St Helena 1986–90

W HEN I OBTAINED THE POST of Senior Environmental Health
Officer on the island, I was told that travel arrangements
would be made for the next voyage of the RMS *St Helena*. Having
heard nothing for a month I enquired and was informed that the
ship's complement was full for the June trip, and I would have to
wait for the next sailing in September. If on the other hand I was
prepared to fly to Cape Town I could board the ship at the start of
her return voyage to England. The reason? South Africa was
subject to world sanctions and opprobrium for its racist policies.
The British Government could not be seen promoting travel to
South Africa. On the other hand if an employee requested it then
it could be arranged. The ship's round trip took about six to eight
weeks to accomplish. It started from England (Bristol) thence to
Tenerife, Ascension Island, St Helena, back to Ascension, on to St
Helena and then to Cape Town, South Africa.

The return voyage was pretty much the same, except that the
'Shuttle Service' between St Helena and Ascension Island was not
repeated. It had to be a part of the outgoing service because many
Islanders were employed on that Island and in the Falklands
following the war there. In addition the only airport in Mid-
Atlantic was that controlled by the RAF on Ascension Island, St
Helena being far too remote and mountainous, so it was said, to
have such a facility. The Airport was also shared by the American
Military and Space Agency as it was the first down-range satellite
tracking station from Cape Kennedy. Neither Ascension Island nor
St Helena had port docking facilities, both on and off loading of
vessels being accomplished by 'Lighters' while the ships were at
anchor in the bay.

The moving of the cargoes was as nothing compared to the
movement of passengers, as they had to disembark from the mother
vessel onto motor launches, and in the case of Ascension onto boats
manned by very skilled watermen. These had to be manoeuvred

as close to a single flight of steps where 'Catchers' were stationed. When they shouted 'Go' one was expected to step off the boat and not look down. At times it was like stepping into a void as one would be far below the level of the catchers. The swell and surge of the Atlantic Ocean was the problem and timing was all. Landings were easier at St Helena where there was a broad set of landing steps with overhead hanging ropes for assistance. Even there problems could occur, as instance the dunking a new Governor got in his ceremonial uniform upon his arrival from England. The town band was brought to a halt, the welcoming committee stood transfixed with horrified expressions and the Islanders roared with laughter and applause. Collapse of stout party!

From the ship and as one approached the steps in a small boat the view was somewhat daunting. The valley between the two sets of opposing cliffs was where Jamestown was situated. The 700 ft rock faces, dark and some would say sinister but certainly overbearing, dominated the landscape. As we landed we were aware that the wharf and quayside were lined with spectators silently appraising us. As we had some quarter of a mile to walk to the Customs and Immigration Control this was an action not to be undertaken lightly. Once clear of the formalities we found ourselves on the seafront promenade and journeyed the further quarter of a mile to the Consulate Hotel where we were installed for a few days. The native inhabitants as seen on the Wharf were of the black, white and polka-dot miscellany of colours, the result as one found out of the extraordinary mixing of various races and nationalities from many lands over the centuries.

The voyage from the Cape to the Island was undertaken by the (old) RMS, a passenger/cargo vessel of some 4,000 tons which was somewhat cramped and lacked a great deal of leisure space and facilities, particularly a sun deck. On the other hand a large plastic tank which when hoisted onto the foredeck and filled with sea water served as a rudimentary swimming pool, ice cold when south of the island and meeting the cold Humboldt Current from the Cape and warm enough to hold the 'Crossing the Line' Ceremony courtesy of the Gulf Stream when to the north. It was always a little bizarre to see it floating astern when off-loaded in harbour.

Having stated the obvious limitations, the food and drink and services were excellent. The bar was a natural focal point when opened at lunchtime and in the evenings, and when closed the integral lounge served its dual purpose of a place to relax with a book or games of cards, of which the noisy one of 'Euchre' was the most popular amongst the Islanders and 'Bridge' amongst the Europeans. Evening meals were very pleasant affairs with the ship's officers playing their parts as hosts at each table. Whilst they were always friendly they were always Ship's Officers, but some of them were more memorable characters than others, as one might expect.

Out of courtesy one must always start with the most senior of them and that would be Captain Martin Smith. He was a most pleasant man who had sailed into the Island on many occasions and he it was whom I first heard referring to it as the 'Island of Free Love'. The reason seemed obscure at the time but became blindingly obvious the more one got to know the place.

The more outgoing of the officers, perhaps because of his job, was Geoff Shalcross the Chief Purser. He it was who was the first port of call for any disgruntled passenger with a real or imagined grievance. A sense of humour was essential and Geoff had this in spades. He was also in charge of the daily sporting and social events, of which the 'Horse or Frog Racing' Evening was probably the most popular. A percentage of the bets placed went to Ship's charities. Pam's brother, Glyn, a CPO in the Royal Navy, sailed in the RMS when it was commandeered for service in the Falklands War. The volunteer civilian crew then included both Martin Smith and Geoff Shalcross.

The first thing to think about St Helena is its location and history. It lies some six days sailing from the Cape and three days from Ascension Island, well off the normal track for the original sailing vessels in the middle of the South Atlantic. Even the Foreign and Commonwealth Office in the modern age seemed to have only a hazy idea of where it was, referring to it often as 'St Helena, South Pacific'. Once the uninhabited island was discovered by the Portugese its value was immediately obvious. There was a stream of constantly running fresh water and a grove of 1,200 lemon trees nearby. The British as usual got in on the act and fought off both the Portuguese and Dutch to claim sovereignty.

Over the years it became a stopping place for vessels of all kinds. It became particularly useful for the British Government as a dropping off point for slaves freed by the Royal Navy from the 'Black Birders' heading for the American colonies and prior to their repatriation to Africa. It was also used at various times to house both Zulu and Boer prisoners from the wars in Southern and Central Africa. With all this movement of peoples one could almost overlook the input of a Chinese mining element as well as the British Military at various times, which in its most famous role undertook the guarding of Napoleon in his exile there.

All in all one can easily see that the procreation of the various peoples of the world in this small outcrop of land (only some 50 square miles) has resulted in a melange of skin colours and features the range of which is quite astounding to newcomers. Black, white and polka dot would at the best be only a generality of immediate observation. As steamships overtook the sailing vessels so the island lost its importance and the 6,000 inhabitants were more or less left to their own devices, although it did develop a flax industry.

The Island is the tip of a long extinct volcano which has left it with incredibly mountainous vistas dominated by the two peaks of Mt Acteon overlooking Mt Diana. To see the relevance of their names you must look up your Greek mythology. The main (only) town is Jamestown, which lies at the end of a long valley and fronts the Bay where all ships have to berth. At the end of the valley two roads climb the cliffs on either side, Ladder Hill and Side Path, each snaking through numerous hairpin bends and passing-places hewn from the rock walls. Vehicles meeting each other had a certain right of passage. The one coming down hill had to back up hill to allow the other one through, a relic of a by-gone age when horse drawn carts were the norm. At the head of the valley lies Napoleon's first lodging, known as the' Pavilion at the Briars'.

The roads discharge onto the upper (plateau) area, although this is a misnomer since they continue to be beset by breathtaking falls and hairpin bends ad nauseam, Each turn in the road bringing ever more beautiful views. In the hills lie villages and hamlets which grew up around the flax industry and have fallen by the wayside into smallholder farming since its decline. They bear wonderful names such as Guinea Grass, Blue Hill, Sandy Bay, Half Tree Hollow, Two Gun Saddle and the grandest address of all Plantation House whence the Governor emerges at 8 a.m. each morning to descend from the heights to his office overlooking the Bay in the Castle at the foot of Jamestown.

Some of the dwellings might be no more than a quarter of a mile away from each other as the crow flies but by road they are three or four miles into and out of the other side of the valley. As its importance to the economy of the world fell away so the Islanders scratched a living on the land or in animal husbandry (back yard pig or goat keeping) or relied upon the social services for their daily crust. Many men left for work in the Falklands or Ascension Island or United Kingdom before their British Citizenship rights were outrageously revoked by the British Government (now thankfully restored).

Physical communication between the villages was always difficult by foot and travel by motor vehicles was rare and expensive so that co-habitation in small hamlets was generally the norm. When I advertised for labouring staff I was surprised at the response from all over the Island. Little did I know that one reason they all had was that they had never seen the other half of the land from where they had lived all their lives. The refuse collection vehicles covered all the districts and made wonderful viewing vehicles.

The babies being bred from such a small gene pool led to many physical disabilities. I think the rate was about six times higher than in England. It is from this point that the reader should cast his or her mind back to the comment about the 'Island of Free Love'. The child-bearing girls, who matured very quickly (we employed a House Maid who had had eight children by three different men, the first being at the age of 14, and who was herself a grandmother at the age of 33), were well aware of the problems associated with bearing children from such a small integrated society as existed. There was never any stigma attached to girls having children out of wedlock. The only thing it proved was that the mother was capable of child bearing and would therefore be a suitable marriage prospect.

It is clear from all this that when visitors came from outside the Island, especially when young, single (and not so single) healthy males, there was no shortage of girls parading their attractions. The courtesy calls paid by the Royal Navy ships and those of the French Navy were viewed with great anticipation. Sporting events, from football, cricket, and golf to shooting were the daily attractions but the evening dances at the community centres and social drinking at the various bars were occasions not to be missed for the local girls and visitors alike.

On a sporting note the Islanders were fine performers at most events and as an example I can remember a mason (bricklayer) called Leon Crowie who played golf off a Scratch Handicap – his second course for handicapping being the larvae-strewn one on Ascension Island. The remarkable thing was that he played with only two clubs in his bag, a driver and a four iron, with which he also chipped and putted. A dispiriting scenario for normal hackers with a full complement of clubs and accessories.

Duties and responsibilities

Some time in the far distant sailing-ship past, goats had been left upon the Island, no doubt with the intention of providing supplies of fresh meat to add to those of fruit and water already in existence. The plan back-fired with a vengeance as the free-ranging animals literally ate the Island bare of all its trees and shrubs and denuded the thin soil of its grasses. Until the twentieth century little effort seems to have been made to curtail them and it was not until the flax market collapsed, upon which the local economy depended, that thoughts of the great minds in London turned to re-forestation and the stimulation of the lagging agricultural sector. Quite clearly nothing could be done until the goats were brought under control. It became illegal to keep goats other than in pens, the free ranging variety being fair game for anyone inclined to hunt them down. As an alternative to the goat problem, pig keeping, subsidised by the Government, was introduced and back-yard pig sties on the smallholdings was the norm by the time I arrived.

For many years fuel for the Island had been shipped in from the Cape in 40-gallon drums. Once empty these containers had a value for fencing and storage purposes until they rusted and rotted, became worthless and were tossed aside to litter the place in their thousands. Similarly hundreds of derelict cars lay by every house and wayside and village. All manner of rusted and worthless bits of tools and machinery were scattered throughout every farmyard and vegetable patch and flower garden. I labour the point because the despoliation of this beautiful land lay on every side. The fault of allowing such conditions to grow and multiply was not hard to pinpoint. It lay squarely upon the public health and cleansing authority, although it was the result of indifference and localisation programmes by the colonial Governors as much as anyone else.

Prevention is better than cure should have been the slogan. It was not and the problems were allowed to accumulate under the lack of law enforcement and poor laissez-faire weak management. The attitudes of contracted expatriate staff did not help. To put it mildly we were worlds apart in our attitudes to what constituted advancement and development of the Island. They did not mind so much me organising the clearing of rubbish and the cleaning of the streets providing it did not interfere with or disturb the age old ways of doing it or as was more likely not doing it. The local 'Saints' were the cause of many nuisances, no matter how much they offended against the Public Health Ordinances of St Helena Island. I stress that fact because we were not dealing with my views and prejudices but with the laws in existence there which had not been enforced for many years. It seemed to be useless to point out that practices they were prepared to condone on the island would have them complaining bitterly to the local Environmental Health Department if they occurred next door in England.

It would have been impossible to install a 'New Clean' attitude into the people without starting with the tools close at hand, i.e. the Staff, over which one had to become the dominant yet respected head. Within the first six weeks one had been sacked, two had resigned and a further two street sweepers had been so 'bollocked', if one will forgive the use of an old fashioned term, that (to quote a local Councillor, John Musk), I turned them into 'decent citizens'. They seemed to think that leaning on a broom handle gossiping with the passers-by was the most that could be expected of them each afternoon. The basic trouble was that no one took an interest in either the job or their appearance or attitudes and as a result the work-force was not highly regarded by anyone on the Island. Specifically everything was 'plum wore out'. The boots, the working clothes, the vehicles, the work-schedules, the working practices, the attitudes – all of these needed rapid attention.

I re-equipped the Department with new working clothes, although some eyebrows were raised at the resulting scene. I decided that the colour orange was both aesthetically pleasing and yet dramatic enough for the population to identify the staff wherever they were working and the vehicles in use. The resultant blaze of colour – even the new litter bins erected throughout Jamestown were orange – was startling to the local population. More comment was made about the new orange overalls and coveralls (for the female labourers). They were even seen at the community centres on Saturday night dances so popular did they become. Changing the heavy black boots worn by all the Island's labourers for steel re-inforced protective footwear in modern designs again created a stir but was a factor in raising morale when it was desperately needed.

The islanders sat up and took notice when we embarked upon a policy of renovation and improvement for the dark, dank, untended public conveniences of which some dozen or so were scattered around St Helena. The main difficulty in this was that the first and only secondary school was being built and all carpenters, bricklayer, plumbers and electricians were required on site. This was the No.1 priority. Since all requests for repairs and maintenance for buildings had to be processed and undertaken by the Public Works Department, the best that I could do was to reach agreement that stores, i.e. cement, timber, paints, etc., could be drawn from there in a refurbishment scheme for the conveniences. Using the skills of existing staff and starting with a near derelict and disgusting convenience, one by the steps on the wharf, the first refurbishment was undertaken. Used by all the local workers, fishermen and seafarers – for we had many Round the World Yachts calling in – I chose the colours blue and white for the 'loos', and that alone was enough to cause a few second glances. Daily cleaning and supervision of the facilities rapidly produced a new attitude to the use of them. Graffiti and vandalism became a thing of the past.

We discovered an old bath house under the cliffs which had become a junk store for all kinds of rubbish and had been locked up for many years. It had last harboured a few chickens, the fleas of which were starving when we emptied it. The place was disgusting and it so happened that the 'girls' were on duty that day. They calmed down after the job was done and I gave them the rest of the day off and paid for them to have their hair done. Once clear I installed a shower unit and some deep sinks for laundry purposes. There had been no facilities for the 'yachtees' except for a wash-basin in the grim confines of the filthy conveniences at the wharf. Anchored in the Bay as they were this would have been their first sight and experience of St Helena.

Although I had no means of heating the water, the crews were delighted to find even this small laundry and shower unit after weeks at sea with no charge being made for the service. A distinct improvement.

I wish I could say the same for the attitudes of those persistent expat hecklers mentioned previously. In fairness I should perhaps say that I was considerably older then they were, was trained in local authority enforcement and had neither the sympathy nor the wish to understand the modern fiction of 'a caring society' with its implication that no one did so twenty years previously. I still think it's pretentious humbug but it is taught and believed as a doctrine by the socially minded of the students, particularly the school teachers. They interpreted it from the standpoint that I cared not for the well-being of the inhabitants as they groped their way towards a better future and understanding of the outside world. Perhaps their views were tempered by the fact that the British Government had to submit a tri-annual report to the Anti-Colonisation Committee of the United Nations detailing the progress that was being made for the Island to become independent.

The view taken by the 'Opposition' was that the Islanders would improve their lives over a period of time which was for them to decide, as they were the owners and inhabitants of the Island. Expatriates should not interfere. It was pointed out on many occasions that the Public Health Ordinance of 1849 governed the committing of public health nuisances, including the contamination of fresh water supplies and the keeping of animals.

Clearing the stinking goat pounds and pig pens out of Jamestown was a long process. That it finally succeeded was due to a combination of determination, calling on the law where necessary, the support of the weekly *Government Gazette* and a spot on the local St Helena Radio when I required it thanks to the Programme Editor, Tony Leo. Perhaps 'Lady Luck' also came into it.

From high up in the valley ran the original fresh water stream, which was extremely valuable, although of intermittent quantity but permanent flow. When a small reservoir was built upstream, it largely rendered it of small account as all the premises in town then had a piped supply.

On its banks and at the backs of the houses the pigs and goats flourished. The stench of each pen and sty was awful. None of them had proper drainage and the earth underfoot was soaked in urine and trampled in faeces. Quite often the animals were slaughtered on the banks of the 'Run' as the stream was called and the contents of the stomachs and intestines were extruded into the water to follow the blood, urine and faeces down to the final discharge point in the Bay.

The 'Run' was a protected freshwater stream specifically mentioned in the provisions of the Public Health Ordinance of 1849. What was being done was totally illegal. The practice had to be stopped as Priority No. 1, with the animal pounds a close run second. This was where Lady Luck entered the picture. Many of the mothers and wives of the miscreants were as sick of the stinking pounds as I was but in true Island fashion they stuck by their men and said nothing, until that is one elderly mother took my side in a big row with her son, Charlie.

He was one of the worst and she gave him a hard time, getting off her chest all the resentment she had felt over so many years. Charlie backed off. His mother being a church-going senior citizen much respected in the area told the tale to her friends and acquaintances as Charlie began to dismantle his animal shelters. Others followed as the women staged a 'Lysistrata' type confrontation. One other was a Sergeant of Police, Rex Williams, who was

adamant that he would see me in hell before he would comply. I
told him that before that happened I would see him in Court and
many were the Islanders who had scores to settle so I would not
be short of witnesses. He saw the light quite rapidly after that.

I was interviewed on the local radio at the height of the
disagreements and Tony Leo and I agreed to leave it over for a
week to see if I could answer the queries and complaints which he
felt sure would be forthcoming. We met at the Radio Station a
week later when much to our amused relief there had been no
response whatsoever. We then knew that we were carrying the
majority of the population with us.

In retrospect I knew that the 'Hearts and Minds' contest was
finally won when I took the Baptist Minister to Court. His name
escapes me but he was an arrogant type of Afrikaner with the brains
to match. He had been on the Island for some little while with his
'Baby Doll' wife, scarcely twenty, one would think. She, as I recall,
pranced around the manse in bare feet but had some music ability
as she played the pedal operated harmonium for church services.
In short they were an oddly matched couple but who seemed to
be well thought of by the church members.

A complaint was made to the Department by a neighbour when
the front door of the house had been accidentally left open with
the most appalling smell being emitted. We were at first refused
admission but a Search Warrant issued by the Attorney General
soon cleared that hurdle. Once inside the most dreadful scene of
animal carnage was revealed. The Reverend was keeping everything from goats to rabbits to ducks to chickens and these had
attracted hordes of mice and rats throughout the ground floor of
the house and the loose rubble walls of the courtyard and
foundations.

When necessary a goat was slaughtered for family consumption
in the kitchen. This was never cleaned properly and dried and
congested blood was found under the oil-cloth covering the table
top which itself had soaked up much of the excess. The sacks and
pallets of animal foods stacked in and around the kitchen and larder
were over-run with heavy infestations of rodents and were seized
and condemned on the spot. But however bad the scenes in the
kitchen, nothing could have prepared me (worldly-wise as I was in

these matters) and my hard-bitten crew for what greeted us when the door was opened into the back courtyard.

Overcrowded rabbit cages were stacked one above the other along one wall with most of the animals dead or dying from enteritis. Streams of infected liquids from the stomachs and intestines ran from the anal passages of the infected animals down into the cages below and dripped onto the paving slabs. Chickens and ducks fared little better. Both were enclosed in the same pen with a miniscule pond containing the most foul and faecally-contaminated water. Perches were available upon which the half-starved chickens could clamber, there to deposit their droppings upon the even more unfortunate ducks below.

As the Charge Hand, Brian Francis, succinctly put it 'These aren't animal pounds, this is an animal concentration camp'. All the animals were seized and put down and we undertook the clearing and cleansing of the yard. A concentrated rodent control scheme was put into operation, complicated because of the dry stone and rubble construction of the foundations and walls of the old building.

It was fortunate that I had been suitably shocked several months before to discover that clinical waste from the hospital, including amputations etc., was being incinerated in free-standing 40-gallon waste oil drums at the back of the main hospital building. I found the money to import a purpose made oil-fired, fan-assisted animal carcass incinerator which I installed nearby. The accountants had been annoyed about the 'fiddling' of the estimates, the money having been found under 'Pest Control' in the approved estimates which I managed to transfer to 'Animal Carcass Disposals'. Freely interpreted I reckoned it would include feral cats and rats and the bodies of the poor creatures from the Baptist manse. If the Clinical Waste went into the same incinerator then so be it. Fortunately the Government Secretary took the same view and the accountants were over-ruled in their admonitions.

The Minister was charged with as many offences as we could substantiate under the laws relating to animal cruelty and nuisances and pleaded 'Guilty' immediately on his first appearance. He asked for time to pay the fine and was banned from keeping animals. None of it was of consequence because he left on the next voyage south to the Cape, ostensibly on leave. During his absence an audit of the Church finances revealed that a considerable amount of money was missing. Since he had been appointed to his living by the Baptist Church in South Africa the Reverend's activities came under scrutiny there. A report was sent to the authorities about the goings-on in St Helena and after that I heard no more, but the wealth of favourable publicity for the Department was a great bonus.

Refuse collection and disposal

There were two ready-for-scrapping refuse collection vehicles in daily use, a side-loader and a rear-end compressor, both of which were constantly in and out of the repair yard. Neither of them (unfortunately) was ever put on the list for the annual Board of Survey, i.e. scrapping. We had no passenger carrying vehicles of our own except one ancient Land Rover used daily by the Pest Control Section. They were fully occupied battling the various rodents, insects and feral cats which roamed the Island. Of the insects, the main pest was a large variety of cockroach which swarmed at various times and created much distress, until I found in the course of a food hygiene inspection that the backyard at Benjamin's Bake House and Shop had some broken drains. Once opened the cause of the major downtown infestations became obvious. The drains were encrusted with dried bits of dough, a staple of the insect's diet, which had been built up over many years. From then on insecticidal spraying was undertaken every time manholes were opened, whether for sewer baiting for rats or for blockages.

By the time I left after three and a half years' service new vehicles had either arrived or were in the pipeline, which was a great boost to the Department. Strangely enough the old compressor had a nickname which no doubt had not been coined by the manufacturer, Shelvoke and Drewery in England, but whence its origin I do not know. The name was 'Chew-Chew', denoting the way in which the refuse was chewed up prior to being compressed in the body of the vehicle. Once a companion vehicle had been delivered I announced a competition over the Radio in which I invited the schoolchildren to submit names for the incomer. The office postbags bulged with the responses, the efforts expended to obtain the first prize of £5 being not only commendable but highly diverting and in some cases ingenious. There was a ring-fenced condition in that the submitted names had to have a relevance or at least a tenuous link to the existing 'Chew-Chew'. Inevitably many replies duplicated each other but three entries stood out. Of these one really was outstanding. The name suggested was 'Chuck 'n Chew', the rhythm of throwing in the refuse to be chewed up being perfectly implied. A ride downtown from the school in the new vehicle plus a £5 note made one child's day.

I managed to purloin an old lorry from the scrap yard and by nefarious means and the help of the workforce got it going sufficiently well to be used for the collection of the heavy scrap metal and old vehicles and rusted oil drums scattered over the land. No charge was made for the service of collection and disposal, which was a key factor in its success. For general purposes there was an old tip up on the plateau but which had no covering material for the rubbish, which was simply dumped and set on fire and which then smouldered for weeks at a time. A casual discussion with the Fisheries Officer suggested a solution to our disposal problem of the heavy-duty scrap metal.

With the help of the Fisheries Department a sandy outcrop was located about half-a-mile from the harbour, some 50 metres or so down which was thought would make an ideal breeding area for the fish. The only thing lacking was cover in which the young fish could grow safely to maturity. From our point of view dropping the skeletons of old vehicles and the rusted and unwanted remains of heavy scrap metal onto the ledge was an ideal solution. Months later a Fisheries Team of divers reported upon the success of the enterprise. Depositing of any kinds of refuse, particularly of the faecal variety, is strongly forbidden under European Law, which I freely confess to transgressing in this instance. Artificial reefs, such as we made, can be of immense benefit as cover and an eventual food source from the marine growths.

Pigs and the killing thereof

Pigs were kept in pounds, smallholdings and back yards throughout the Island except for Jamestown which had been largely cleared of animal stock. The upper reaches of St Helena as I have said before are reached by steep, narrow roads with many hairpin bends and passing places which cavort up and down the hills in a multiplicity of turns. If the villages and hamlets cannot be reached by road, then tracks wander off into the hinterland and these very often peter out and only a rough footpath will remain. Frequently these fringe the heights so that the final stage of the journey is reminiscent of crossing Helvelyn Ridge in the Lake District. As the hills are very often shrouded in mist the timing of the visits to the lonely and remoter properties is of great importance. I mention all this because the rearing and killing of the pigs so as to claim the subsidy given by the Agricultural Department was important to the small-holders, having due regard to the thin soils and intermittent rainfall with which they were familiar. It follows that the Meat Inspection service we provided was difficult to implement in these hilly regions especially when many were killed at Easter or Christmas.

The first of these periods that I remember, my Assistant Ray Hudson and I saw a total of 74 over the two days prior to Christmas day. Each place visited had a kind of 'Hill Billy Party' in swing on the veranda with Country and Western Music roaring out from the ghetto blasters. The Americans in Saudi Arabia, mainly from the east coast, refer to this as 'Shit Kickin' Music' and I could well understand why! It was difficult to refuse the hospitality of these 'partygoers' but because of the workload and the roads to be travelled it had to be done. I found that it was usually acceptable to come away with a can of beer to be opened later.

There were two converted stables or byres which served as rudimentary slaughterhouses at the farms at Longwood and Bamboo Hedge on the road to Sandy Bay. They normally took care of the large animals on one or two days in the week but in downtown Jamestown at the back of the market and built as part of it was the worst example of these. In the United Kingdom slaughterhouses of this kind became illegal in the late Fifties and had been either closed or demolished and replaced by modern abattoirs. The Jamestown one was operated by a shifty-eyed, bandy-legged jockey of a man. Egregious in the extreme and scruffy as he was, there was yet something engaging about Randy's

crafty grin and sly looks. We had many a 'discussion' about the
state of the place and his style of killing and dressing the carcasses
but it was mainly to no avail. There was even an old pole-axe
hanging on the wall which I suspected had been in use until quite
recently. It was a relief to see the plans for the demolition and
redevelopment of the market area, which some two years later
came to fruition. It had always been an embarrassment to inspect
the beasts in what amounted to a combination byre, a killing and
dressing hall, a cooling room and a butcher's shop all in one part
of the market hall in the heart of Jamestown.

One of the best times in the week was Saturday morning if I
had meat inspection to carry out up in the hills. Then it was
possible for Pam to come with me, away from the confines of the
town, and to enjoy the ride and some of the most spectacular
scenery in the world. She would be welcomed by the wives and sit
in the parlour or on the veranda and enjoy a cup of tea whilst the
work was done. When both flowers and vegetables were scarce it
was always useful to have these social contacts.

Always to be remembered and as an example of the kindnesses
forthcoming were the trips down to Ben Mason's. This was the
name of the small-holding and not the name of the owners at the
time. They were Jessica March and her brother who tilled the steep
and terraced hillside below their small house set into a steep incline.
The house was reached by a one in four dirt track a quarter of a
mile from the main road. The track was rough at the best of times
and in the wet was positively lethal, snaking as it did around the
hairpin bend in the middle. What with the towering hill on one
side and a precipitous, unguarded fall to the valley on the other it
was not a trip for the faint-hearted. It was certainly not one for my
nimble and sturdy Flat Panda, but the March household possessed
a battered SWB Land Rover of uncertain vintage but which I
guessed to be from the Fifties. With Jessica at the wheel, low gear
ratio on, four-wheel drive engaged and engine roaring the skidding
wheels made the trip in even the worst of the weather.

One usually walked or scrambled down the hillside and once at
the house there was always a warm beer set aside for me, a soft
drink for Pam and a slice of currant cake for both of us. The view
from the veranda was fabulous, down to the sea far below. There

was no electricity line to the house and paraffin fridges, with which we were familiar from our Africa days, were in use together with lamps and candles at night, and yet Jessica was the Island's most famed lace maker and worked at this craft mainly in the evenings. She it was who had been chosen to make a set of lace dinner mats as a gift from the Islanders on the occasion of Prince Andrew's wedding to Sarah Ferguson.

Social life

We lived for a brief time near to Napoleon's old home at Longwood but when we were offered a house almost next door to the church in Jamestown we were delighted to move. The house was the middle one of three and had been in existence at the time prior to 'Boney's' arrival in 1815. Our neighbours were Gerry (Bogey) Henry, the Police Chief and Geoffrey Benjamin, the head of the Laboratory at the Hospital. Both were congenial neighbours but we knew Gerry and his wife Winnie the better. Possibly because they both played golf at which game they were not only keen but also good. The golf course was up at Longwood and was over a hundred years old. It had been somewhat emasculated from its original length because the British Government pinched some of the land to build on as part of the diplomatic wireless service war against the illegal Rhodesian Government. We rapidly gained a wide circle of friends and acquaintances and because our downtown house was so 'handy' it was a favourite watering-hole at many times.

The higher level of social activity was, to a great extent, set by His Excellency, the Governor and his Lady. The incumbent when I arrived was Dick Baker and his wife, Connie. He it was, who as Government Secretary, carried the white flag (lace curtain) of surrender wrapped around a brolly to the Argentine forces at Fort Stanley in the Falkland Islands. He was a lovely man and his wife was a true blue member of the old school of colonial wives – loyal, forebearing, industrious, charming and possessor no doubt of that inner core of steely will that one reads of from as far back as the Indian Mutiny. The supporting cast was headed by the Government Secretary, Eddie Brooks and his wife, Jennie. The Bakers and the Brooks were long serving members of the Colonial Service, having been posted together to the islands in the South Pacific and West Indies.

There was one retired Ex-Governor on St Helena, namely Geoffrey Guy, who with his wife 'Johnnie' and the others mentioned, were the last of the old school of colonial servants. We count ourselves privileged to have known them, for their successors were not of the same quality.

Whilst it may seem old fashioned as a practice the invitations to dinner parties or lunch or evening drinks always came via a Card which not only specified the venue and event but the time and the dress code expected by the host. This (outmoded) system cleared many a hurdle for the guests and is not to be sneered at. It was not only the invitations to Plantation House – everyone who hosted a function at their homes would follow the same procedure. We did more than our fair share of hosting such events and it was here that Pam's expertise in the kitchen came to fruition. Her self-taught culinary skills largely brought about by her industry and skill with the *Robert Carrier Cookbook* during our two years in Kawambwa Township in Zambia (already mentioned) paid handsome dividends.

Apart from the usual invitations there were one or two special events which occurred every year. They were headed by the Queen's Birthday Garden Party at Plantation House to which all of the Island's hierarchy were invited. A great event with the band in attendance and notable for a display of lovely hats by the ladies. On a less celebratory note was the invitation by the Island's Resident French Consul to a drinks gathering to 'celebrate' the birth of Napoleon. The Consul was a Monsieur Martineau, who dwelt at Napoleon's final residence of Longwood House. There he seemed to have established a monopoly of Napoleonic memorabilia and literary works and it was said had become a millionaire in the process.

When Napoleon's remains were exhumed and transported to Paris for his final interment at Invalides some thirty years after his death, it was agreed that his dwellings at the 'Pavilion in the Briars' and at 'Longwood House' as well as his grave would be ceded to France, and French Territory they have remained. Ceremonial parades are held whenever warships of the French Navy pay courtesy calls to St Helena.

In his writings and pleadings following his exile Napoleon blamed everyone for his downfall including all his Marshals, but particularly directed his spite and malice against the Duke of Wellington. He totally and wrongly blamed him for the decision to incarcerate him in the South Atlantic. He had either forgotten, or perhaps (unlikely) was never told, that the Russians and Austrians sought him as a war criminal for immediate execution. Since he had thrown himself upon the mercy of the British Government, it was faced with a difficult problem and distant banning from Europe seems to have been considered the best option. The Duke was said to have been in favour of such a resolution. He was reported to have said that Napoleon's escape from Elba and his following escapades, culminating in the climactic battle of Waterloo, left Europe with another 20,000 destitute widows.

The man chosen as the Governor of St Helena, Sir Hudson Lowe, had strict instructions to make sure that 'General' Bonaparte never again threatened the world. It was a form of address that was considered a gratuitous insult, as he still considered himself to be an 'Emperor'. It seems to have been the start of a serious but petty dispute between arrogance on the one side and dour duty on the other. The isolation apart, Napoleon and his staff and entourage were treated well and enjoyed ample provisions, unlike many of the other people on the Island. Every last cleft in the sea cliffs was sealed and guarded, every possible landing place was placed under military guard, but within the land the captives could journey wherever they wished subject to normal regulations and escorts. Many are the cannons and control points still to be seen, the one astounding feature being the size of the guns dragged up to commanding positions on the hills. The old saying of 'Men of steel and ships of wood' seems particularly apt.

On the last day of his life, six years after his arrival, Napoleon rode over the valley to the Mount Pleasant Estate for lunch. The view from the terrace at the rear is stupendous. It follows the narrow, very steep and twisting road past Bamboo Hedge Farm and the wee Chapel to Sandy Bay. It passes the huge outcrops of rocks known as Lot and Lot's Wife, as the hills on either side close in towards the coastal fringe.

He was taken ill that night and when he died his own doctor carried out a post-mortem. The cause of death he declared was a perforated stomach ulcer, demonstrating such by placing his finger in the abdominal tear. Nevertheless many people still believe that the British poisoned him with arsenic, a proposition discredited many years ago.

The leaving

We had invitations for some twenty-five 'Farewell' events in the three weeks prior to our departure. This sort of schedule requires both stamina and timing but invitations to lunch, drinks and dinner by three different hosts at three different locations on the same day took some figuring.

The day we left with the ship being prepared for sailing from the Bay at 1 p.m. we reversed the steps that we had taken some three and a half years earlier. We started from the house and it was the most emotional walk ever undertaken by the two of us. The tone had been set a few nights' previously when our close friends and neighbours presented us with a copy of the *Island Gazette* with a 'Spoof' front page headed TONGES GO HOME with an 'Exposé' Article below.

As when we arrived, the roadside was lined by Islanders, but this time everyone knew us, and many were the people who came from the crowds to hug us and wish us well. It was with heavy hearts that we passed from the Steps to the RMS *St Helena* and were settled into our cabin for the voyage to Ascension Island. There we would catch a RAF flight to Brize Norton and England.

There was however one more task to perform before we finally severed our physical ties with the Island. It came as we had dried our tears and joined the other voyagers in the lounge bar for a drink prior to sailing. As the visitors were requested to go ashore an announcement by Geoff Shallcross, the Chief Purser, came over the tannoy: 'Would Mrs Tonge please come to the Office?' She went unbeknown to what was afoot and I next saw her crying her eyes out as she came back into the lounge some twenty minutes or so later. After calming her down I discovered that she had been escorted to the Bridge, there to be faced by Capt. Smith who required her to blow the ship's siren upon leaving the anchorage. This she had done and as she well knew its booming resonance around the Bay and the cliffs signalled the final act of that part of our lives spent in the South Atlantic. She was given a Certificate signed by the Captain signifying her membership of 'The Whistle Blowers' Union', which I think she still possesses.

CHAPTER 6

The Orkney Islands 1990–2002

BY THIS TIME IN MY LIFE I was 57 and it was 1990 and I should have got the 'Travel and Contracts' Bug out of my system. It was not to be and even at this stage I had an interview for a job in Lesotho which I failed to get. Somehow I could not become interested in a District EHQ post even in such lovely places as Kings Lynn or the Cotswolds, which the family thought I should accept if offered. Perverse creature I may be but even I knew the effects of hunger and what a shrinking bank balance could do, and when I was offered an interview in the Orkney Islands I thought I had best look into it. After all, I reasoned, we had not seen anything of the north so perhaps I was being offered a life-line with the best of both worlds, i.e. a permanent and pensionable post and a chance to travel within the British Isles.

Little did I know that acceptance would bring with it both joys and sorrows of a different kind unknown to us anywhere else. The real 'sorrows' actually came at the end of our 12 years in the Islands when I was diagnosed just prior to retirement as suffering from 'Parkinson's Palsy', to give it its correct name. A second hammer blow came when entirely through my own stupidity and given the stress of moving house back into England, I turned an easily controlled angina problem into a highly unstable and intermittent one, ultimately requiring a double heart by-pass which was only partly successful. In a chronological sense these events marked the end of my professional life with a vengeance, but at the age of 72 I am still functioning, although as the old gag goes 'When doing the Hokey-Cokey I find myself putting it in when I should be shaking it all about' much to the consternation of the family.

There are some 70 islands in Orkney of which about 20 are occupied. The largest is Orkney Mainland which contains the main ports of Stromness and Kirkwall, the latter, which faces the northern isles, is the administrative centre. The Mainland encompasses the great Fleet Anchorage of Scapa Flow, sadly now no

194

longer used by the Royal Navy, but a Mecca for diving enthusiasts. Stromness marks the entrance from the Atlantic, but there is also a southern exit past the oil processing island of Flotta and then into the Pentlands Firth, a ferocious a piece of water at its gale-backed and tidal worst as exists in the world. Five old German battleships lie scuttled after the Great War in Scapa Flow.

The tragic end to the *Royal Oak* when she was torpedoed at anchorage by U-47 in October, 1939, left her lying on her side at the bottom. Classified as a 'War Grave' and marked as such, she is a permanent reminder of the futility of war and the tragic end to the lives of 900 members of her crew who died that night.

The Islands have been home to crofters and fishermen and seafarers for many centuries but the 5,000 year old Neolithic settlement at Skara Brae was unknown until a violent storm in 1871 uncovered it. Now recognised as the finest of its kind in Europe it is a major tourist attraction. Together with the stones at the Ring of Brodgar and the burial mound at Maeshowe, the three form the corner stones of an insight into the lives of the inhabitants so many years ago. The Islands can be reached by various means of transport but all routes have to cross the Pentlands Firth, that ferocious strip of water mentioned earlier. Some twenty miles lie between Scotland and the Islands. Starting from Stromness the ferries skirt the land past the significant rock pillar known as the 'Old Man of Hoy' to their destination at Scrabster, the port near to the main town of Thurso in Caithness. It is a short hop by air from Wick on the Scottish mainland to Kirkwall, but even then the storms and gales and sea mists (Haar) from the north, south, west and east can ground all traffic and cause the cancellation of flights as well as the ferry crossings.

Travel and ferries

Generally people do not realise how far it is over land and sea to travel the length of the British Isles (some 800 miles), and particularly that part which is Scotland. I always figured that when driving to Orkney from Shrewsbury I was half way home when I got to Stirling (some 300 miles on the way). The ferry port at the far end of the M6, M74, M8 and A9 was Scrabster. The journey there took one past the lovely cities of Perth and Inverness, which we were delighted to enjoy whenever there was time. Edinburgh, Glasgow and Aberdeen were somewhat off the line of march northwards but eventually we became familiar with them too, spending one lovely weekend at the Caledonian Hotel in Princes Street for Christmas shopping. The weekend was only spoiled when in driving north on the Sunday morning I was booked for speeding.

This event occurred as I came off the dual carriageway at the head of the Drumochter Pass with no other traffic in sight for miles, apart that is from a lone car parked in a lay-by as I whistled past at 89 mph. Just what an unmarked police car was doing there at noon on a Sunday morning prior to Christmas when all decent Scots were in church still bothers me. I should not really grumble for I was once clocked at 104.7 mph on the M62 and got away with it by displaying a Saudi Driving Licence and promptly returning there at the end of my leave. Win some, lose some.

In the course of the 12 years we spent there all of the family came up on more than one occasion. Simon always undertook to drive it from Paignton in Devon. The others came by train and ferry in the early days but they also tackled the air route. All at various times fell foul of the weather. The sea mist (Haar) was totally unpredictable and planes could suddenly be grounded, leaving the passengers at the mercy of buses and ferries and hotels in their endeavours to complete the journey.

It was not only the visitors who suffered the weather and sea conditions. I would have to cite the experience of the Director of Environmental Health who flew by 'Brit-Norman Islander' from Kirkwall to the island of Westray, a flight of some 30 minutes duration. Once there the Haar came in and all traffic was grounded. Even the small Inter-Island Ferries were affected, so bad were the conditions. He managed to book into the local hotel and there he stayed for the next two days.

Orkney Mainland had been 'extended' during the war by the construction of the 'Churchill Barriers', linking the other Islands of Burray and South Ronaldsay. The Islands to the north – Westray, North Ronaldsay, Eday, Sanday and others could only be reached by air or the local ferry services. A steady stream of central and local government officers going about their various duties trotted in and out by these means.

The first year of settling in to a new post, house and social scene is always the worst time. We had been offered the 12-month tenancy of a terraced council house set in a small square reached on foot from the road about 100 yards away. All the houses overlooked each other and there was a claustrophobic element about the place. Pam felt it more than I did since she was alone for much of the day and in true island fashion she was not invited round for coffee at any time by the other housewives there. Come to think of it there was rarely a welcome on the mat from the Orcadians, extremely reserved as they were. Such Scots as we were friendly with were usually 'Incomers' like ourselves. We came to know that there was more than the friendly rivalry we had heretofore experienced in the world with the Welsh, Irish and Scots. Although the Orcadians often voiced to the world that they were such and not Scottish, they nevertheless thought in the same terms as the Highlanders centred around Inverness and the sad and lonely moor at Culloden. For them the Highland Clearances both in 1745 and the nineteenth century happened yesterday and revulsion of the English lingered on. The Islands had belonged to the Norwegians for seven hundred years prior to their incorporation for political purposes into Britain. To this day Norwegian National Day is celebrated every year in Orkney.

It took us 15 months to get our housing needs and finances together and we then moved to a magnificent six-bedroomed house on the hillside overlooking Kirkwall Bay with a view stretching to the north isles. It had been a damn close run thing as we had made up our minds to leave unless we could resolve our domestic arrangements. The house had been built with a B & B objective and was generally well equipped for this purpose. There was ample hot water to serve two bathrooms, the kitchen and the vanity units in each bedroom. With ample parking, garage and workshop containing the third WC, Pam embarked upon her career as a Seaside Landlady, at which she found herself adept and skilful.

The most serious crisis occurred at the end of our first season when the catch on the oven door broke and could neither be repaired nor replaced. A new oven was the answer. 'Ah,' said Pam, a gleam in her eye, 'If we have a new oven then it will be situated elsewhere. It will go there' said she pointing to a different wall. 'That means moving the refrigerator,' I said, 'and if we do that then where will it go, and for that matter it will involve a complete re-wiring and changing all the fittings. Do you realise how much this will cost?' 'Yes,' she said, and I knew the battle was lost. In came the designers, out came the cheque book and revised mortgage and three months and 10,000 quid lighter we had a beautiful new kitchen. Whilst it was cosy it was rather more an efficient work-place than the family gathering room of popular image. Built-in cupboards, deep freezer, refrigerator and dish-washer eye-balled the cooker and double-sink which in turn overlooked the garden and bay below. The centre-piece was undoubtedly the 'Island', a beautifully designed and constructed unit occupying centre stage of the new kitchen.

It is only right that I mention here the lovely West Highland Terrier that we obtained in Kirkwall. 'Daisy' became a feature of the house and family life both there and in England when we retired. It was a very sad day when we had to let her go because she was so ill. After 12 years of total love and affection that she gave us it was a blow from which even now we can remember the pain.

Conferences

Entirely on official business but taking advantage of the opportunities to tack on holidays at the end of meetings or conferences whenever possible, we visited many previously unthought-of venues in the British Isles and abroad. Included amongst these would be Wexford in Ireland, Amsterdam in Holland, Bergen in Norway and the conference centres of Harrogate and Bournemouth. Meetings were regularly held in the great cities of Scotland and even as far afield as Oban on the West Coast, although we never managed to get to the Western Isles.

I received a request from the Administrator on Ascension Island, Tony Green whom I knew from St Helena days, to visit and carry out a Health and Safety Audit needed because of the abandonment of its base there by the American Space Agency and the downsizing of the RAF facilities, leaving a possible hazardous waste problem. The task was undertaken by a member of staff who also later that year gave a paper to a Tourism Conference in Barcelona on the Orkney Shellfish Industry and its large exports to the Iberian Peninsula. Little do the tourists know that the lobsters and crabs and whelks and winkles they eat when on holiday there come mainly from the far north.

With all our travels I am sure that the most memorable conference we attended was the annual one of the Association of Port Health Authorities in the City of London, the main venue the Guildhall. Lunch there and whilst cruising on the river were memorable events, as was both a reception and dinner held on the overhead walkway of Tower Bridge, but the highlight has to have been dinner at the Mansion House hosted by the City. Truly magnificent.

For the guests, i.e. Pam, visits were laid on to the Bank of England Museum, the Cabinet War Rooms under Whitehall and a tour of both Houses of Parliament, whilst we poor delegates sweated over such topics as the effect of 'Pets' Passports' on the control of imported animal diseases, particularly rabies. Overall the River Thames was a centre piece, as it always is, of London, and displayed itself magnificently. Going from Tower Pier to the Thames Barriers and back as we did and further upstream as far as the Albert Bridge when twilight and dusk was bringing the riverside lights to life is memorable. The history and legends of London, the City and the River are so interwoven that one can only urge future family members and visitors to visit and explore this unique heritage. My wife and I would agree that in all our travels this experience is certainly one of, if not, the finest of all.

Duties and responsibilities

In the early years the Department mainly concerned itself with farming and food, prior to the advent of the Food Safety and Environment Agencies and their effect upon the local authority with the transfer of powers and duties. This also coincided with the BSE scare and the resultant incineration policies of the British Government which emasculated the beef industry.

The Orkney herds were not decimated in the same way but its beef exports were severely restricted and throughput at the abattoir suffered. Funds for the construction of slurry tanks and silage pits became scarce so that no new ones were approved and authorised. Thus two major planks of the work undertaken by the Department were removed.

There was still plenty of work, the variety of which was at times extraordinary. From the hotels to tourists to dog fouling to committees to oil spills to shellfish harvesting to health education to housing and problem families to food processing and certifications for export . . . The list seems endless in retrospect. Cheese and cheese making, particularly of the goat variety, could cause problems, but the impact of a new brewery in a converted chapel did not and is now a well established asset to Island life, as of course is the 'Highland Park' distillery.

The Agencies mentioned sparked a re-vamping of the role of the Environmental Services. The Director resigned, the Principal EHO was transferred at his request to the Environment Agency, and the ultimate result was that the Council saw fit to ask me to head the new body as the Chief Environmental Health Officer.

A case of history repeating itself since I had already carried out similar work in both Africa and the Middle East, and for the next nine or ten years I did the same in Orkney. In relating two wildly divergent happenings I will attempt to give a microscopic picture of the problems, both large and small, the latter amusingly so, with which to end this part of life in the Islands.

One of the endless problems with which one had to contend was that of the public conveniences. There were some 50 of these scattered about the Islands, some substantial and some just a single WC on the quayside of a small island. The Mainland ones caused us the most trouble. Not only was vandalism and misuse common, the opening and closing hours were forever being nagged at by the Councillors. The less they were open then the less they cost in staff and cleaning and repairs. Such was the dominant thought process. The pleadings that I made on so many occasions in Committee that 'public convenience' meant exactly that: a 'convenience' for the 'public' . . . but all to no avail. Open at 8.30 a.m. and close at 6 p.m. throughout the year, this when at the height of the summer there was sunshine and daylight for 24 hours, many tourists were well in evidence at midnight and the pubs did not close until 1 a.m. Moreover the conveniences were closed all day on Sundays in the winter. It was a criminal offence to urinate in a pubic place, which included all the back alleys, car parks and stone walls, but this was ignored by the Council and out of necessity by desperate people, but not by the Police.

There were desperate scenes when the passengers from a liner in the bay came ashore to enjoy a service in the Cathedral. The service ended at 12 noon, the nearby public conveniences did not open until 12.30 p.m. The sightseeing around the ancient grave-stones was memorable, such an interest had never been exhibited before!

From my point of view the funniest event occurred when a written request from my office to the maintenance section to 'Repair a leaking U-bend in the Shore Street conveniences' was transcribed somewhere along the computer trail, involving a pernicious spell-check no doubt, into 'Repair a leaking U-Boat '. Spell-Checks are so common that this is the sort of result to be expected but perhaps not in such a dramatic form. I was attending the Annual Conference of the British Toilet Association, which carries out a relentless war against the closures of these units through out the British Isles. It also surveys all the entrants for the quite famous 'Loo of the Year' Award, which is much sought after. I was able to bend the ear of the Secretary, Richard Chisnall, at the dinner, a most convivial affair, and told him of the incident in Orkney which he then incorporated into his speech to the delegates. A very funny variation on the 'It may be shit to you but it's my bread and butter' theme.

Whales

A fairly common occurrence in the Islands was the stranding of whales on the beaches, particularly after strong gales trapped them against the land. Unless the rotting carcases were a public health nuisance being near to dwellings then the policy was to leave them *in situ* to rot away in their own good time, since there was no use for them in the modern age. Otherwise the local authority had the duty of disposal, which in most cases meant burning or burial. A decisive factor to be taken into account would be the length of the whale. A cetacean, to give it its correct name, over 25 feet in length is regarded as a 'Crown Property' and as such is the responsibility of the Receiver of Wreck (now incorporated I believe into the Marine Safety Agency). In reality in such a case the local authority acts as an agent for the disposal of the carcass.

It may be of interest to know that the importance of the length, according to legend, is that the King was entitled to the olfactory glands, from which perfume could be made, whilst the Queen cornered the market with the whalebone corsets for her ladies. The smaller varieties were for the 'peasants', so it was said.

The final bill for disposal would be accepted by the Receiver and the local authority would be reimbursed. One or two whales would be the usual yearly total. The problems became much more acute and serious when there was a mass stranding and financial budgets were strained to the limit.

This happened when eleven mature Sperm Whales stranded on the beach on the northern island of Sanday one weekend in December, 1994. There they died and the local authority was handed the task of disposing of them. Many solutions had been proposed and many had been tried over the years but in the modern age when the bodies were of no use for food or fuel or to be rendered into oil or the like then only burning or burial were realistic. Some months earlier a rotting carcass had been towed off a beach in Papa Stronsay. A week later it had drifted ashore on North Ronaldsay where the Special Breeds Sheep feed on seaweed only. Two months later the remains of the same whale had been washed ashore at Otterswick on Sanday. Unlike the mass stranding this one was well away from habitation but the local people complained to their local MP about the smell. Fortunately the site had already been visited by staff from the office, the conclusion being that the tons of rotting seaweed on the beach stank far more than the whale. I replied to Jim Wallace the MP at the House of Commons with these facts and heard no more.

The reader will have seen how sensitive a simple 'whale' issue can be and like the involvement of the House of Commons so the media en masse will descend scenting (if you will excuse the pun) a good story. The eleven whales, being mammals, decomposed into a stinking 600-ton problem within days, which then demands an urgent and rapid solution. Once the press gets its fingers into this 'human interest' story, then their 'need to know' hormones are stirred on 'behalf of their readers' and it is then only a single step to seeking the requisite 'villain'. What better whipping boy can there be than a local authority and its officers.

Alerted by the local 'Stringers', the press and media hordes descended. All of them required the facts and preferably photographs but in the winter months access to and from Sanday can be limited. Such correct information as we were able to give out was limited on a daily basis – after all the whales had given up the ghost days before and there were no international volunteers arriving to join the struggle to re-float the animals. Small facts had to be embellished to ensure a good angle or give a distorted perspective, such as interviews with disgruntled Council Tax payers, anything to sell newspapers. The worst possible slant was put upon the work being undertaken by the local authority, a somewhat easier target than the Receiver back in Southampton. One had to be very circumspect in sticking to the facts, hence my wife learning about them when she saw me being interviewed on Scottish Television, whilst lying in her hospital bed in Aberdeen. The reason escapes me.

It is quite obvious that the only feasible disposal would be by burial. There was only one possible route off the beach and up to the land. It was little more than a footpath, which first of all had to be widened and roughly graded for the powerful towing vehicles. Legally the ownership of the farmland included the beach. The farmer very much desired that the stinking and decomposing carcasses be removed, but further difficulties were encountered in that the proposed site transgressed a Viking Burial Ground. Further negotiations took place and another but less convenient site was found in the scrub and marginal agricultural land off the beach. Fees were agreed, contractors appointed and authorisation for the burials went ahead. There was one final hurdle to be overcome and that was the agreement hammered out to fence the land securely. At last it was all done and dusted and the burials were carried out successfully. The cost was in excess of £20,000.

Perhaps it has been noted that one further method of whale disposal has not been mentioned. I refer to explosives, which have been used with varying degrees of success, but never, I believe, in Orkney. At the time of the mass stranding in Sanday, a Demolition and Explosives company from Aberdeen was prepared to volunteer its services (at a cost), but the offer was declined. At about the same time an article was sent to us by one of the media. It details the disposal of a stranded and deceased whale on a beach in America. It is taken from a video account and relates the problems and savage consequences of underestimating the power of explosives and coupling it with an extremely poor Health and Safety review and risk assessment.

The tape is from a local TV news programme in Oregon which sent a reporter out to cover the removal of a 45-foot, 8-ton dead whale that washed up on a beach. The responsibility for getting rid of the carcass was placed upon the Oregon State Highways Division, apparently on the theory that highways and whales are very similar in the sense of being large objects. The highway engineers hit upon the plan of blowing up the whale with dynamite. The thinking was that the whale would be blown into small pieces which would be eaten by the sea gulls. That would be that. A textbook operation. They moved the spectators back up the beach, put a half-ton of dynamite next to the whale and set it off. The reporter then goes on to say that what followed was the most wonderful event in the history of the universe. The whole whale carcass disappeared in a huge blast of smoke and flame. The happy voices of the spectators can be heard shouting 'Yayy' and 'Whee'. Then suddenly the crowd's tone changes. There is a new sound like 'Splud'. There is a woman's voice shouting 'Here come pieces of . . . MY GOD'. Something smears the camera lens.

Later the reporter explains: The humour of the entire situation suddenly gave way to a run for survival as huge chunks of whale blubber fell everywhere. One piece caved in the roof of a car parked a quarter of a mile away. Remaining on the beach were several rotting whale sectors the size of condominiums. There was no sign of the seagulls, which had probably permanently relocated to Brazil.

Farewell to Orkney

At long last it was time to retire. I was 68 plus and younger blood was required. I neither understood nor even cared about the new doctrines and management techniques as decreed by the New Labour Government. 'All socially aware and caring' local authorities were besought to aspire to this heavenly utopia, a recipe in my view for passing the buck at innumerable committees and Council meetings. The lack of decision making and the bearing of individual responsibility is an open scandal, but then so is the destruction of the solid worth contained in local government as I knew it.

The round of farewell dinners and lunches was a familiar one, as were the good wishes of our friends and colleagues. Only the faces changed over the years, but not the endearing qualities that were common to all and made them such firm friends in the first place. For us a way-out sense of humour was a magnet never better exemplified than in the person of Tony Marsh. His exploits with the alcohol contents of a red wine bottle and his subsequent outrageous and hilarious behaviour were incredible events witnessed time without number by his lovely, gentle and self-effacing 'Divine Spirit' of a wife, Lois, this being his favourite name for her.

Tony, in spite of his reputation for imbibing too well, never let it get in the way of his work and he was both an efficient and hard-working member of the staff who is now in his rightful position as the Head of the Department, having been overlooked unfairly once before by the Council.

Tony and Lois headed the final group when we first of all dined at the Queen's Hotel and then after a last drink at the bar, replete and complete with car, bag, baggage and the dog Daisy, boarded the *Sunniva*, the night ferry to Aberdeen, as they and Ian and Kathleen, Bill and Rae, Val and Steve and the rest waved their farewells from the quayside. That old 'Heavy Heart' syndrome rose again in both of us, the only difference from twelve years previously in St Helena being that no whistle-blowing was required of Pam by the Captain.

Off then to pastures new. The house had taken a bit of selling and did not realise as much as it was worth in our view, but we did not realise the impact this would have as we travelled south to Shropshire, our retirement destination. We had targeted the area from Shrewsbury to the south but rapidly realised that our financial resources were not sufficient to counter the incredibly steep rise in property prices since we had assessed the situation some three years earlier.

We therefore rented a house for three months and implemented Plan B, which was to search to the north, centred upon Ellesmere and the lakes. How fortunate we were when we found and bought a house in the lovely village of Cockshutt some 17 miles from the county town. For the past three and a half years we have been extremely happy here with wonderful friends and neighbours to help and sustain us.

A highlight of our existence here in North Shropshire has to have been Pam's 70th birthday celebration, which took well over a year to plan and execute unbeknown to her. The event was planned with meticulous care so that she knew nothing of it even when the guests came from far afield in the British Isles and Africa. Starting from the local hostelry, the Leaking Tap, a bus load of us travelled to the Racecourse at Bangor-on-Dee some 20 miles away, there to enjoy a splendid day out. Many had never been racing before and both they and the children had a great time. We returned to the Tap where a wonderful buffet had been arranged and where the cake-cutting and celebrations continued until the witching-hour. The following day was open house at our home in The Briars. Again a scorching hot day with a barbecue at lunch-time operated by Mansel and Lisa our next door neighbours. What genuine people they are and what good friends.

As I write this so we are anticipating being on the move yet again. In spite of all the treatments and surgical procedures since retirement, a combination of the unsteadiness of the Parkinsonism and its wobbly effects is fought over by a daily diet of 25 assorted tablets. This coupled with a fluctuating blood pressure has decreed that I lead life on a level surface around the home. The fear is that I might fall down the stairs and break my neck or at least severely injure myself. Privately I hate the thought of leaving this lovely house but see no other option than to seek the shelter of a two-bedroom bungalow from either the North Shropshire Council or the Shropshire Rural Housing Association, both of which have suitable ones in the village, but which understandably is the most favourite and sought after village location by all applicants.

A year after that was written we had sold the house to our daughter and moved into a lovely bungalow. Life could not be sweeter, with family and friends crowded upon us. Having had to give up my favourite golfing pastime, I have now sold the car and surrendered my driving licence. To ease the pain I bought the computer just for fun and the odd bit of writing. Embarking upon this tome has certainly drawn down my intellectual capacity, but, most important, however long and hard it has been, the memories have won in the end.

Index